AMERICAN CIVILIZATION

An Introduction to Research and Bibliography

Edited by LIONEL D. WYLD

AMERICAN CIVILIZATION

An Introduction to Research and Bibliography

Edited by LIONEL D. WYLD

everett/edwards, inc.

post office box 1060 / deland, florida 32720

SIGNIFICANT · EDUCATIONAL · MATERIALS

FIRST EDITION

Library of Congress Cataloging in Publication Data

Wyld, Lionel D.
    American civilization: an introduction to
    research and bibliography.

    Includes bibliographies and index.
    1. American studies — Addresses, essays, lectures.

I. Title.
E175.8.W9   917.3'03   75-89568
ISBN 0-912112-03-4

"...[T]here is now enough experience with courses, curricula, scholarship in the area of American civilization so that we know, at least, what we are trying to do. We realize our successes and our failures; we are aware of our strong and weak points. We have not, and no one feels this, found the answer. But we have by now at least achieved a sure sense of direction in our search for it."

—Robert H. Walker
American Studies in the United States, 1958

"American civilization is studied most effectively by a college or university which is studying at the same time local institutions within the United States and foreign civilizations beyond our national boundaries. Likewise an American curriculum is most effective when it combines national materials with materials which are both more and less than national."

—Tremaine McDowell
American Studies, 1948

TABLE OF CONTENTS

About the Editor

LIONEL D. WYLD has taught at the University of
Notre Dame, the University of Buffalo, and Rensselaer
Polytechnic Institute. He has been Visiting Professor
and Acting Director of American Studies at Maxwell
Graduate School, Syracuse University. With a history
colleague, Professor William Pease, he designed and
taught "The Growth of American Culture" during the
first year of the Rensselaer Senior-Sequences Program,
and he introduced the first graduate proseminar in
the American field at Buffalo.

Educated at Hamilton College, he has his A.B. in English
literature and political science, and an A.M. and Ph.D.
in American Civilization at the University of Pennsylvania.

Mr. Wyld has written and lectured widely on his principal
extra-curricular interest, the Erie Canal, and he is a
member of the Board of Directors of the Canal Society
of New York State. The author of *Low Bridge! Folklore
and the Erie Canal,* he also edited the Erie Canal
sesquicentennial volume, *40' x 28' x 4': The Erie Canal —
150 Years,* now a collector's item among canal buffs.
He served as President of the New York Folklore Society
from 1964 to 1967, served for many years on the guest
staff of the pioneer Technical Writers Institute at
Troy, and he has participated in technical society
programs and chaired several panels dealing with American
Studies, English, and the interplay of technology,
culture, and the humanities.

About This Book

American Studies programs have been with us for more than three decades now, but the textual materials continue as widely scattered and as disparate as when the programs were first introduced at Harvard, at Yale, and at Pennsylvania. Of course, disparateness is part of the strength and vitality of American Studies in one sense, for it is essentially a kind of operations research — a pooling of knowledge and tools and methodologies from many traditional disciplines. Each chapter in this book, representing a contributary discipline in what has come to be known as "American Studies," was prepared by a specialist in the subject area. The volume thus offers the instructor and the student a usable introduction to inter-disciplinary studies: a pro-seminar, as it were, between two covers.

As Professor Piccard points out in Chapter II, "if one of the hazards of a university program is an ethnocentric parochialism, one of the challenges it offers is its universal methodological scope." American Studies brings us knowledge and awareness of diverse areas and even of diversity itself; but, importantly, it rests on the premise that such knowledge and awareness give the student a sense of fundamental inter-dependence and interrelatedness among all branches of endeavor and among all constituent elements of what we broadly construe as a culture or a civilization. Professor Brunger's discussion of the influence of Van Ranke and the German seminar system, and his statements concerning the development of formal graduate training for historians have as much to do with the field of education as with history; one finds both Brunger and Professor Gollin citing works such as *The American Mind* and *Of Plymouth Plantation;* Professors Raemsch and Clarke find useful and usable material for their own respective disciplines of anthropology and folklore in many of the same sources, notably indigenous Indian life and lore; Piccard finds help toward understanding our political science in a novel or other art form as well as in the chambers of the State House and Capitol; Professor Hayner sees the story of philosophy in America paralleling to a large extent that of the development of American civilization as a whole; Professor Kettlewell, in pointing out that American architecture may well have been the most important in the world, emphasizes the need for greater cultural and artistic awareness on the part of educators from elementary school on; and Mr. Harvey, in the final chapter to this volume, comments appropriately on the music of America as reflected in the development of a people and a civilization.

Only by an examination of varied disciplines can an approach be made toward answering the question, What is American civilization? This book is a step in the process. By no means complete nor comprehensive, it does nonetheless offer a basic framework. The student should never cease to inquire, to ponder, to ask more questions, to seek further answers; and, of course, to search out other disciplines and their methodologies, in areas not included in this volume because, quite simply, there had to be space restrictions and time limitations imposed.

Of the several books now available on American Studies, this is the first to present material written entirely and specifically for the purpose at hand. Each section or chapter is uniquely the contributor's own. Beyond providing certain guidelines and generally standardizing bibliographic entries, the Editor has resisted purposefully the tendency (at times strong) to impose his viewpoint upon content, style, or direction of critical comment. Each contributor was allowed free rein in presenting his topic-field. (This would, after all, be the case in the interdisciplinary seminar employing guest lecturers in various fields.) It is the Editor's conviction that diversity, after all, is essential to American Studies; and the Editor has tried to provide a useful and authoritative handbook of papers which will serve to introduce validly this challenging and increasingly significant academic pursuit, the study of American civilization.

—Lionel D. Wyld

Rolling Acres
Cumberland, Rhode Island
August, 1974

Acknowledgment Note

This general note of appreciation is addressed to all those persons whose willingness to provide critical comment, clerical help, or moral support made the frustrations of editing considerably more bearable. In particular, among those colleagues who served as critics for parts of the manuscript and offered valuable and usable suggestions for refinement of contributors' drafts, special thanks are extended to Professors Douglas Washburn of Rensselaer Polytechnic Institute and Emile Gelé of Cazenovia College; Mr. Ralph Hopkins of R. H. Hopkins Co., Inc., Syracuse; and the Rev. Dr. Norman V. Haight of DeWitt Community Church and Syracuse University. The editor's principal aide in preparing the final typescript was Joanne M. Keene. Finally, Dick and Jane Langford, who believed in the project when it was just a gleam in the editor's eye and kept it on the lists at a time when many publishers were restricting new ventures, are due the appreciation of editor and contributor alike.

CHAPTER ONE

American Studies: General Introduction

The Study of American Civilization

Lionel D. Wyld

Speaking strictly from bias, I can think of no "discipline" more relevant to today's educational scene than American Studies. The very nature of the interdisciplinary studies approach makes it meaningful in terms of the involvement so much talked about on today's campuses.

In the beginning, literature and history were — and still are in many institutions — the two "core" disciplines around which American Studies developed. Today, American Studies represents, as has often been suggested, a kind of loose federation of contributory disciplines, ranging beyond literature and history and including (at various times and institutions) sociology, anthropology, folklore, art, economics, philosophy, theatre, and music. There is evidence that a new discipline is, in fact, emerging from it all — and there are both departments of American Studies as well as programs. But whether one wishes to see American Studies as a discipline or a cooperation among disciplines, the purpose and concerns remain essentially the same: to study the various aspects of what one must refer to as "an American culture" and to derive from the cooperation of the contributing disciplines and the interaction of colleagues from associated fields a broader and one hopes more meaningful knowledge about both the culture and any component of it. The "American Studies" approach, therefore, ought to provide a more valuable perspective for the study of American literature, or American history, or any other of the traditional fields; certainly, it is a much more interesting and viably rewarding approach than heretofore obtained for both student and teacher.

The idea of gathering together a group of informed and inquiring minds to consider a common problem — whether it be *The Scarlet Letter* or the impact of Progressivism — should not seem strange but natural in our educational programs. To further paraphrase Robert E. Spiller, American Studies suggests an approach planned in the spirit of inquiry rather than authority, to consider values rather than mere facts, but sacrificing neither one to the other, and stimulate us to question anew rather than just to consider the results of past thinking.[1]

The Program in American Civilization at Pennsylvania, where Professor Spiller played so important a role, was among the pioneers; established as a graduate option in 1938-39 and an undergraduate major in 1942, Pennsylvania's program may be considered, for historical purposes of orientation, as fairly typical of the movement. "A by-product of discontent with the rigid departmentalization of the liberal arts curriculum of the 1930's," he wrote, "it started by asking rather than by answering a question. That question was: 'How can we once more learn to see our civilization as a whole and study the inter-relationship of all of its parts as every great civilization of the past has been studied and understood? '"[2] Pennsylvania's program began, appropriately enough, within two departments, history and English literature, the way led by two distinguished scholars — John Bach McMaster and Arthur Hobson Quinn — "without apparent collusion," as Professor Spiller records it. "Here," he said, "was a common concern for the understanding of a single civilization — our own — on the part of scholars in different disciplines, approaching the material from different angles and using different methods of analysis while seeking a common goal."[3]

Similar thinking went on at Princeton University. On the basis of committee recommendations, President Harold W. Dobbs and the faculty there approved a Program of Study in American Civilization in February 1942. Like the Pennsylvania program, Princeton's drew upon existing departments and developed along the lines of interdepartmental cooperation. The Princeton and Pennsylvania programs were reflecting in part the impact of the Harvard report on *General Education in a Free Society* (1945), in part the frustrations of the Depression Era (as suggested by Professor George Rogers Taylor of Amherst), and in part by the then-immediate challenge of totalitarianism abroad as the United States became engulfed in World War II.

As John William Ward reported upon the Princeton program, "The theory implicit in any coherent program of study of American civilization is that reality lies in the whole and not in the parts, that the part has meaning only in relation to the whole," and he emphasized that "the Program in American Civilization is not another department, it is a perspective on materials which the student must get in depth in various departmental courses."[4] Both of these observations have significance for the American Studies movement; for during the next two decades the direction and validity of American Studies would be the subject of frequent debate in academic circles.

That American Studies has always operated on the premise of the whole as something more than the sum of its parts seems axiomatic today. Almost from the beginning, curricular innovations have allowed for interdisciplinary seminars and pro-seminars, designed purposely to cut across traditional departmental lines, and, on occasion, to involve two or more faculty from otherwise separate areas of study.

Since American Studies programs have developed along both interdepartmental and inter-institutional lines, perhaps one other example of an early program may be in order. The faculty at the University of Delaware began its specific interest in cutting across traditional lines in 1951; and with the

fortuitous opening of the Henry Francis du Pont collection of
the nearby Winterthur Museum that year, a graduate program
in American Studies was inaugurated which combined seminar
work at the University with laboratory work at the museum.
The Winterthur Program in Early American Culture, officially
begun with a Rockefeller Foundation grant in 1952, has
become a model for such inter-institutional endeavors and the
Program itself together with the University-affiliated Weymss
Foundation, has served both as a rallying point for American
Studies scholars and a sounding board for methodological
discussions. Within a decade, Delaware undergraduates also
could undertake a program in American Studies, the stated
aim being "to enlarge and enrich the students' understanding
of his own country in its entirety." The Delaware student,
noted the program director, Charles H. Bohner, "is encouraged
to ask questions not ordinarily raised within the structure of
the traditional departments and to see his society as a whole
greater than the sum of its parts."[5]
    One notes a common language in many of the pioneering
efforts, which invariably speak of American Studies as
significantly assessing American civilization to achieve an
awareness on the part of the student that culture is not
compartmentalized. In addition, one reads often, in the early
prospectuses, that the aim is to raise more questions than are
answered or, as the Rutgers University catalog put it, "not to
solve but to deepen understanding of" complex issues and
problems of American culture. In any perusal of offerings at
various Eastern institutions, then and now, one immediately
senses that the underlying philosophy of American Studies is
not one of course-taking and problem-solving, and that
American civilization is a point of departure for study and
discussion, not a tag to denote an underlying assumption.
Although there is evidence that some universities and colleges
are changing to an emphasis that "American is a civilization"
(rather than examining the question, "Is America a civilization? "), most still recognize the essentially interdisciplinary —
or, perhaps more appropriately today, multidisciplinary —

nature of such studies and programs.

Interestingly enough, considerable attention on American Studies has developed as far down as the high school level.[6] The American Studies approach seems especially suited, too, for the junior college program and the proliferating community colleges. In commenting upon this trend within the two-year college, one writer observed that American Studies courses and programs "have made significant contributions to the curricular patterns" in the junior colleges where they exist.[7]

For a number of years academicians argued the merits of American Studies' emergence as a discipline in its own right; and Henry Nash Smith, in an oft-cited essay of 1957, asked pointedly, "Can 'American Studies' Develop a Method? " From the time of Tremaine McDowell's early *American Studies* (1948) to the present day, the question of status and approach has been vigorously debated.[8] McDowell and Spiller alike saw the interdisciplinary character of American Studies as basic and essential; though they and others felt that should American Studies reach a point of departmentalization and methodological maturity its vigor could diminish, by 1958 Spiller saw American Studies as "tending to take an increasingly unified form" as the relationships of the core subjects to a common center became more clear. In the spring of 1970 David W. Marcell, who heads the program at Skidmore College, provided a perceptive review of the American Studies movement in an article somewhat narrowly titled "Recent Trends in American Studies in the United States," and Professor Spiller reviewed prevailing American studies approaches in a 1973 article on "Unity and Diversity in the Study of American Culture."[9] One can assume that American Studies is yet in a fluid state, which is really another way of saying that the vitality remains. If the "answers" become pat, the methodology uniform, and the curricula static, then American Studies will perhaps have indeed achieved a disciplinary status beyond debate, but at the same time will have ironically found its *raison d'etre* gone.

Interest in American Studies led inevitably to a correlative
professional organization, the American Studies Association,
and an "official" scholarly journal. *American Quarterly* began
at the University of Minnesota in 1949 but moved quickly to
Pennsylvania, from whence it has issued forth ever since.
William Van O'Connor was editor at Minnesota; Robert E.
Spiller became editor at Pennsylvania, followed by Anthony
N. B. Garvan, Robert W. Walker, Hennig Cohen, Murray G.
Murphey, and Bruce Kuklick. The ASA has been active since
the early 1950s. For many years national and regional
meetings were held in conjunction with other, older organizations, like the Modern Language Association, the American
Historical Association, and the American Folklore Society. In
the fall of 1967 the first national biennial meeting of the ASA
was held in Kansas City, with subsequent sessions in Toledo
(1969), Denver (1971), and San Francisco (1973).

Regional chapters or affiliates bring together scholars and
other interested parties for annual or semi-annual regional
meetings. At present eighteen such groups are thriving:
Chesapeake Chapter of ASA, ASA of Kentucky and Tennes-
see, ASA of the Lower Mississippi, ASA of Metropolitan New
York, ASA of Michigan, Midcontinent ASA, ASA of the
Middle Atlantic States, American Studies Group of Minnesota
and the Dakotas, New England Association for American
Studies, ASA of New York State, ASA of Northern California,
Ohio-Indiana Chapter of ASA, ASA of Pacific Northwest,
Rocky Mountain ASA, Southeastern ASA, Southern California
Chapter of ASA, ASA of Texas, and ASA of Wisconsin and
Northern Illinois.

The widespread interest in American Studies was not
restricted solely to continental United States. Partly as a result
of Fulbright awards, which saw a steady flow of American
scholars into numerous teaching posts in foreign countries, and
partly as a result of the inevitable foreign interest in the
United States following World War II, various American
Studies activities developed abroad, notably in Canada, Japan,
India, Germany, England, New Zealand and Australia, and

Scandinavia. The European Association of American Studies held its constitutive meeting in April 1954 and began a Newsletter "to serve as a link between members of the EAAS, and to facilitate their professional and personal contact, and generally to promote cooperation and coordination of efforts within the field of American Studies in Europe." Influential in this undertaking was Sigmund Skard, Professor of American Literature and Director of Amerikansk Institutt of the University of Oslo, who served as first editor.[10] The *Deutsche Gesellschaft für Amerikastudien* was founded in 1953; and various groups, some formalized and some less structured but no less significant, developed. A useful survey was provided in 1958 by Professor Skard in his *American Studies in Europe: Their History and Present Organization.* In Asia, the obviously close ties between Japan and the United States since the War resulted in a number of scholars and students, many in American Studies, being exchanged between the two countries in the intervening years. The *Canadian Review of American Studies* began publication in 1970, and the *Journal of American Studies* (an outgrowth of activity by the British Association for American Studies) has achieved widespread recognition since its Vol. I, No. 1 was issued in April, 1967. *American Studies: An International Newsletter (AS:AIN),* published by the Committee on International Exchange of Persons of the Conference Board of Associated Research Councils and distributed as a supplement to *American Quarterly,* frequently contains articles and notes on American studies programs and other activities abroad.[11]

Despite the tremendous interest on the part of students in the United States, of university and college faculty, of academicians abroad, and of the publishing world (that has provided an avalanche of textual materials, often reprinted traditional works catchingly labelled "American Studies"), there has been precious little original material available beyond that in the journals. The serious American Studies student ought to read, of course, McDowell's *American Studies,* previously cited, if only for now—historic purposes; and ought to be familiar with the books that have been published to date, such as Joseph T. Kwiat and Mary C. Turpie, eds., *Studies in American Culture: Dominant Ideas and Images* (1960); John A. Hague, ed., *American Character and Culture* (1964); Robert Meredith, ed., *American Studies: Essays on Theory and Method* (1964); and Ray B. Browne and others, eds., *New Voices in American Studies* (1966). While most of these reprint material which originally appeared in various journals or compile papers originally presented at scholarly gatherings, the editors have generally made useful remarks by way of introduction, and the advantage of having the papers gathered together for easy access is not to be discounted. Many of the authors and their views are integrally connected with the American Studies movement and ought to be known by the student regardless of his own particular interests in the field. *An Introduction to American Civilization* by Richard M. Fox (1967) was written essentially for teaching American civilization classes for foreign nationals; chapters range from "America's Political System" to "The American Character." An indispensable bibliographic source, published in 1972, is *Articles in American Studies 1965-1968*, edited by Hennig Cohen.

In addition to the printed word, an American Studies student might profitably seek out other sources of information and knowledge — museums, historic restorations, art galleries, etc. Viewing a painting or an artifact in a museum or visiting an area where mills once flourished or "urban blight" has taken over may provide the inquiring and perceptive person with ample incentive to pursue further the cultural ramifications for which the single event is only seemingly an isolated one.

Certainly, American Studies is already reaching maturity and, in such a situation, may well be in need as much of re-assessment as of growing-pains analysis (the case thus far). As Professor Marcell sums it up, "That American Studies remains in a state of ferment and transition cannot be doubted. But the ferment has attained a kind of constancy;

indeed, its regularity may have become what amounts to a defining characteristic of the field." It is the total "American civilization" that defines and unifies the subject, he observes, concluding that, should American Studies "truly become a discipline, it will necessarily be unlike anything that ordinarily goes by that name. Its contours will be vague, its subject matter multitudinous, its method pluralistic, individualistic, and often unscientific. More than other disciplines, American Studies will be conditioned by the interest, capabilities, and limitations of the institutions and individuals who create it."[12]

One can, after all, only have conceptual knowledge of the historic past, trust his instincts and experience in the present, and hope his inferences for the future are appropriate. American Studies began somewhat under pressure of political actuality in the not-so-good good old days of the American 30's; as a field of study, it developed rapidly as a postwar phenomenon — a phenomenon for which the felt-need was self-evident. Its future lies in the unknown complex of education that itself faces almost daily revolutionary pressures. If any knowledge is viable, certainly investigation of what constitutes a civilization has never been denied; and, one sincerely hopes, despite differences and disparateness, the investigation of what constitutes American civilization will continue to prosper on American campuses, as well as on those in the worldwide scene.

NOTES

1. Robert E. Spiller, "Preface" to Dixon Wecter and Others, *Changing Patterns in American Civilization* (Philadelphia, 1949). Spiller was speaking specifically about Pennsylvania's Benjamin Franklin Lecture series, but his comments have application to American Studies in general, as indicated by both the title theme for the Lectures and his own extensive writing on the field.

2. Robert E. Spiller, "American Studies at Pennsylvania," *The Pennsylvania Gazette*, 56:5 (January 1958), 10.

3. Ibid., p. 11.

4. For these and other relevant comments, see the pamphlet by John William Ward, *The Special Program in American Civilization at Princeton* (Princeton, 1957).

5. Charles Bohner, *American Studies at Delaware* (undated brochure).

6. See. e.g., *American Studies and the High School* (undated Wemyss Foundation pamphlet), which deals with the programs at McLean High School (Va.) and Newfane High School (N.Y.). Others, such as the Cumberland High School (R.I.), which has a two-year required sequence in American Civilization, might be cited.

7. See Bruce A. Lohof, "American Studies Makes Its Way Into the Junior College," *Junior College Journal*, 39:6 (March 1969), 48-51.

8. See, e.g., Tremaine McDowell, *American Studies* (Minneapolis, 1949); Leonard Koester, "Where is the American Department? " *Journal of Higher Education*, XI (March 1940), 135-137; Richard H. Shryock, "The Nature and Implications of Programs in American Civilization," *American Heritage*, III (April 1945), 36-43; Arthur E. Bestor, Jr., "The Study of American Civilization: Jingoism or Scholarship? " *William and Mary Quarterly*, 3rd ser., IX (January 1952), 3-9; Carl Bode, "The American Studies Movement and the Professor of English," *College English*, XVI (November 1954), 125-127; Richard M. Huber, "A Theory of American Studies," *Social Education*, XVIII (October 1954), 267-271; Roy Harvey Pearce, "American Studies as a Discipline," *College English*, XVIII (January 1957), 179-186; and Robert E. Spiller, "American Studies: Past,

Present, and Future," in Joseph J. Kwiat and Mary C. Turpie, eds., *Studies in American Culture* (Minneapolis, 1960), pp. 207-220.

Beginning in 1958, a summer issue of *American Quarterly* has included a listing of "Writings on the Theory and Teaching of American Studies."

9. *American Studies: An International Newsletter*, VIII (Spring 1970), 5-12 and *American Quarterly*, XXX (December 1973), 611-618, respectively.

10. Leading representative of the foreign Americanist, Skard served as visiting professor at Pennsylvania in 1957; his lectures formed the basis of his *The American Myth and the European Mind: American Studies in Europe 1776-1960* (Philadelphia, 1961). For European readers, he edited (with A.N.J. den Hollander) the comprehensive *American Civilization: An Introduction* (London and Harlow, 1968).

11. Various articles in *American Studies: An International Newsletter* have dealt with specific countries; for example: Australia and New Zealand (Winter, 1970), Canada (Autumn, 1971), Britain (Winter, 1971), Italy (Spring, 1972), Soviet Union (Autumn, 1972), Japan (Winter, 1972), India and Yugoslavia (Spring, 1973), and France (Spring, 1974). For an earlier view of American Studies activity in Japan, see Arthur Thompson, "The Development of American Studies in Japan," *American Studies*, V (July 1960), 1-8. A.N.J. den Hollander, "Headaches, Harvests and Hopes: Fulbright Americanists in Europe," *Ibid.*, 10-18, provides an insight into the concern of Europeans with American subjects. A specific note on Continental interest may be found, e.g., in Jean Louis Auclair and M. E. Grenander, "American Studies in France," *College Englisl* 27 (March 1966), 494-496. A general review is "A decade of American Studies," *ACLS Newsletter*, XXI (June 1970), 1-6.

12. Marcell, *op. cit.*, pp. 11-12.

BIBLIOGRAPHY

Bibliographic Essay

One of the greatest problems in providing a bibliographic note for American Studies is the infinite diversity of interest, of aim, of concern, and of background of those who may be pursuing degrees or academic interest in the field. In the present volume, the disciplines represented have ample specialized bibliographies provided by the various contributors; yet, the Editor feels obliged to point out that many resource materials do not fall conveniently — or even peripherally — into disciplinary camps. Everyone acquainted with the field ought, of course, to be familiar with such works as Parrington's or Curti's, Commager's *The American Mind* (1950) and Goldman's *Rendezvous With Destiny* (1952), the basic *Literary History of the United States,* or the multi-volume "History of American Life Series." But many works defy arbitrary and precise categories: works such as *American English in its Cultural Setting,* by Donald J. Lloyd and Harry R. Warfel (Knopf, 1956); *American Cities in the Growth of the Nation,* by Constance McLaughlin Green (Harper & Row, 1965); *American Vaudeville as Ritual,* by Albert F. McLean, Jr. (Univ. of Kentucky Press, 1965); *Voices in the Valley: Mythmaking and Folk Belief in the Shaping of the Middle West,* by Frank R. Kramer (Univ. of Wisconsin Press, 1964); *Ideas, Ideals, and American Diplomacy,* by Arthur A. Ekirch, Jr. (Appleton-Century-Crofts, 1966); *The Artist in American Society,* by Neil Harris (Vanderbilt Univ. Press, 1966); *Erie Water West,* by Ronald E. Shaw (Univ. of Kentucky Press, 1966); *Irish/Charles G. Halpine in Civil War America,* by William Hanchett (Syracuse Univ. Press, 1970); *American Takes the Stage: Romanticism in American Drama and Theater 1750-1900,* by Richard Moody (Indiana Univ. Press,

1955); or *America in the Fifties and Sixties,* by Julian Marias
(Pennsylvania State Univ. Press, 1972), to name but a few
wide-ranging titles that come easily to mind from among
books published in the last two decades.

For the student of American civilization, *American
Quarterly (AQ)* is a must; and he should, of course, seek out
the various allied and peripheral journals related to specific
areas of interest among the contributory disciplines. (See B.
Mergen's article, listed in the *Selected Bibliography* below.) In
addition, a number of the affiliated regional American studies
groups issue newsletters that contain items of interest and
value; the New York American Studies *Newsletter,* for
example, has been issued two or three times a year since its
inception in 1957 and is available upon request. Issues of *AQ*
usually contain a listing of the regional affiliates, and a letter
to any of the current Secretary-Treasurers will provide the
interested reader with information about a group's activities
and the availability of any publications. Updated information
regarding regional meetings and subjects of papers presented
can be found in the "American Calendar" section of each issue
of *AQ.*

A number of publishers have for some time been issuing
various works in American Studies. While not all of them
include volumes exclusively of interest to the field (the term
"American Studies," as suggested in the foregoing General
Introduction, is a semantically murky one, so far as publishing
is concerned), many university presses and commercial
publishing houses have series of considerable relevance and
interest. Several volumes of the Daedalus Library — published
by Houghton Mifflin Company and the American Academy of
Arts and Sciences — are relevant. They include *The Professions
in America,* edited by Kenneth S. Lynn; *The Woman in
America,* edited by Robert Jay Lifton; *The Negro American,*
edited by Talcott Parsons and Kenneth B. Clark. Of peripheral
interest are *Utopias and Utopian Thought,* edited by Frank S.
Manuel; *Science and Culture,* edited by Gerald Holton; and
The Contemporary University: U.S.A., edited by Robert S.

Morison. Johnson Reprint Corporation has a proliferating "Series in American Studies," under the general editorship of Joseph T. Kwiat of the University of Minnesota. Oxford University Press has "The Urban Life in America Series" (general editor: Richard C. Wade), with titles including *Pullman: An Experiment in Industrial Order and Community Planning, 1880-1930*, by Stanley Buder; and *Spearheads for Reform: The Social Settlements and the Progressive Movement, 1890-1914*, by Allen F. Davis. George Braziller has published "The American Epochs," a 6-volume series of source documents in American history from Colonial times to 1915. Braziller is also the publisher of "The American Culture" (series editor: Neil Harris), related to the arts, changing patterns of work and leisure, and the changing physical environment. The University of Chicago Press has its "American Civilization Series" with some highly useful titles, and Yale University Press has an on-going series called "Publications in American Studies."

An earlier series of considerable general cultural interest is the "Rivers of America Books" (Rinehart), and a more recent offering is the "American Forts Series" (for example: *Thundergate: The Forts of Niagara*, by Robert West Howard; *Vincennes: Portal to the West*, by August Derleth), published by Prentice-Hall. Bowling Green University Popular Press has offered a number of provocative titles in the emerging emphasis on popular culture and its relation to American Studies evolvement. An appropriate example is *Challenges in American Culture*, ed. Ray B. Browne, et al. (1970). Certain volumes in the "Crosscurrents" series of Southern Illinois University Press, e.g., *The College Novel in America*, by John O. Lyons, and *The Grotesque: An American Genre* by William Van O'Connor, are worth consulting. The "York State Books" series of Syracuse University Press is an outstanding example of materials being made available in relation to a regional segment of American civilization. The series includes contemporary interpretation and scholarship, as well as reprinted works of significant historic and literary interest.

One should not overlook such materials as those published for Colonial Williamsburg's Institute of Early American History and Culture by the University of North Carolina Press; such titles as *The Pursuit of Science in Revolutionary America,* by Brooke Hindle, provide considerable insight into more specialized areas not too frequently ventured into by the American studies programs. *Books About Early America,* a bibliography in pamphlet form listing over 400 titles, is available from the Institute at nominal cost. The field of technology, increasingly important today, is well covered by the annual bibliographies in *Technology and Culture,* the journal of the Society for the History of Technology. If one were to consider works dealing with such other areas as contemporary education, sponsored research as it affects culture, the numerous architecture-worth-saving movements, local history, and popular culture, the list of titles would be extensive. The suggestions could be expanded, but one should browse in various library sources and search out the materials of particular interest.

Selected References

The following list comprises a basic bibliography of American Studies materials, chiefly in the areas of methodology, developments in the field, and reference source-books.

American Character and Culture. Ed John A. Hague. DeLand, Fla.: Everett/Edwards, 1964. (Charles E. Merrill Lecture Series in American Studies lectures, Stetson University, with four additional essays.)

The American Culture. Approaches to the Study of the United States. Ed. Hennig Cohen. Boston: Houghton Mifflin, 1968. (Articles from *American Quarterly.*)

The American Experience. Approaches to the Study of the United States. Ed. Hennig Cohen. Boston: Houghton Mifflin, 1968. (Articles from *American Quarterly.*)

American Perspectives. Ed. Robert E. Spiller and Eric Larrabee. Cambridge: Harvard Univ. Press, 1961.

American Studies. Essays on Theory and Method. Ed. Robert Merideth. Columbus, O.: Charles E. Merrill, 1968.

American Studies in Transition. Ed. Marshall W. Fishwick. Philadelphia: Univ. of Pennsylvania Press, 1964.

Articles in American Studies 1954-1968. Ed. with a Preface by Hennig Cohen. Ann Arbor: Pierian Press, 1972. (A cumulation of the annual bibliographies from *American Quarterly.*)

Frontiers of American Culture. Ed. Ray B. Browne, Richard H. Crowder, Virgil L. Lokke, and William T. Stafford. Lafayette, Ind.: Purdue University Studies, 1968. (Papers from the Second Conference on American Culture, Purdue University.)

A Guide to the Study of the United States of America. Washington, D.C.: Library of Congress, 1960.

McDowell, Tremaine. *American Studies.* Minneapolis: Univ. of Minnesota Press, 1948.

Mergen, Bernard. "Surveying Journals of American Studies: A Guide for Students and Teachers." *American Studies: An International Newsletter,* XII (Spring 1974), 28-37. (Informative compilation by subject area, with addresses, prices, and some critical comment.)

New Voices in American Studies. Ed. Ray B. Browne, Donald M. Winkelman, and Allan Hayman. West Lafayette, Ind.: Purdue University Studies, 1966. (Papers read at the Mid-American Conference on Literature, History, Popular Culture and Folklore, Purdue University, spring 1965.)

Skard, Sigmund. *American Studies in Europe: Their History and Present Organization.* 2 vols. Philadelphia: Univ. of Pennsylvania Press, 1958.

Studies in American Culture. Dominant Ideas and Images. Ed. Joseph J. Kwiat and Mary C. Turpie. Minneapolis: Univ. of Minnesota Press, 1960.

Tate, Cecil F. *The Search for a Method in American Studies.* Minneapolis: Univ. of Minnesota Press, 1973.

Walker, Robert H. *American Studies in the United States. A Survey of College Programs.* Baton Rouge, La.: Louisiana State Univ. Press, 1958.

Weber, Robert, ed. *America in Change. Reflections on the 60's and 70's.* Notre Dame, Ind., and London: Univ. of Notre Dame Press, 1972. (Revisions of papers presented at a conference on American culture.)

Wecter, Dixon, et al. *Changing Patterns in American Civilization.* Philadelphia: Univ. of Pennsylvania Press, 1949. Also: Perpetual Edition; New York: A. S. Barnes, 1962. (Benjamin Franklin Lectures, University of Pennsylvania, 1948).

CHAPTER TWO

American Studies:
The Discipline of Political Science and Government

Research on the Politics of American Civilization

Paul Piccard

Politics is Pervasive

Plato reminds us that we live in caves, mistaking the flickering shadows projected on the walls for a reality that lies beyond our perception. One trouble with the caves inhabited by political scientists, politicians, and front-page journalists is their exaggeration of politics and public events. In seeking knowledge of American civilization we can nevertheless learn much by understanding the views and methods of political science and by being realistically modest about the accuracy of our own perceptions.

Much of what a student of government looks at appears to have a political dimension. The front-page stories illustrate this easily: wars and rumors of wars, taxes, impeachment, old laws broken and new ones proposed, judicial verdicts, public school problems, race relations, urban issues, drugs, and environmental pollution. Automobile accidents, airplane crashes, fires, floods, and the weather are partly political, since government agencies have responsibilities for reducing, rectifying, or reporting such events. Even the inside pages cast political shadows on the walls of a political scientist's cave: competing professional football leagues take their battles to court, the

19

government shoves a champion prize fighter off his throne, the marriages of the society section are regulated by law, the entertainment section poses questions of constitutional rights against censorship, and government involvement in the behavior reported as financial news seems deep indeed.

Beyond the news, public policy pervades private affairs too. Family structure and responsibilities, occupation of dwellings, contracts, legal tender, the notion of private property, smoking (what at what age), drinking (what and when), and sex (with whom, where, and how) are all matters of law. Once a person enters the cave of political science, history becomes political history (presidents, princes, and battles rather than artisans, neighbors, and daily routine); economics becomes political economy (laws and national systems rather than individual decisions); anthropology is cultural, not physical; sociology and psychology are group oriented; geography deals with man's relationship to the environment rather than physical nature itself; and education is by the public, for the public. The interface between science and government becomes more interesting than pure science alone. Religion as a scholarly discipline, philosophy, literature, and poetry speak to political scientists about the condition of life: what we can dream, what we must suffer, whether we are damned to a life of avarice and torment, or whether we can learn to live together and love.

Music as part of the cave we live in is likewise tainted by public policy. It makes propaganda and exacerbates not only the generation gap but also national differences. The national anthem of the United States is a martial air unlike "America the Beautiful." Politics makes some Rebel-yelling white Southerners think that the juxtaposition of "Dixie" and "The Battle Hymn of the Republic" creates a fair balance (southern nationalism and white supremacy on one side, the American creed and national unity on the other). The protest songs of the cities and the counter-protest response of the countryside are highly politicized. Woodstock might have been music, peace, and love, but it was also politics. To understand America is to hear it as well as to see it. Politics sometimes makes a different kind of noise than do jazz, folk, soul, country, Broadway, pop, rock, and imported music, but America's music sometimes plays a political tune.

Well-informed political scientists will be less interested in this chapter of our book than in any of the others. Here is set forth what they already know; from the others they may extract new details from the shadows of American politics. The first thing this chapter has said, then, is that politics, especially to political scientists, seems to be a pervasive part of American civilization. It can be seen or heard in almost everything American. To study America is to study its politics.

These introductory observations about the pervasiveness of politics make a second point implicitly: *politics* as a word is judgmentally neutral. Virtuous men would pursue politics for worthy objectives; wicked men, for corrupt purposes. Real men play a mixed political game, sometimes sacrificially and other times possessively. To study the political behavior of Americans is to try to understand the mixture of motives and results; it is not to dwell exclusively on either those who give or those who take. Seeing politics on the front pages, in the sports sections, and in our homes and hearing it in our music demonstrates only that public concerns and preferences are ubiquitous. It tells us nothing of good and evil.

Anyone who is hung up on the conventional derogatory connotations of the words *politician* and *politics* will understand political scientists better by translating the pejorative terms into *statesman* and *statesmanship.* Then the political scientists' tendencies to project politics into so many images on the walls of their caves will not be mistakenly assumed to be cynical or judgmental.

American Democracy

Many political-science graduate students get into trouble on comprehensive oral examinations because they cannot answer what the faculty regard as freshman-level questions about their own government. The function of a brief treatment of American democracy, such as follows, is not to provide the answers to those questions but more simply to

sketch out the boundaries within which questions may be
raised and research conducted. Political scientists want to
know who governs America and how. The "How? " asks *by
what process* and *with what results?* In a later section of this
chapter we can examine some of the scholarly methods
employed in seeking the answers; in this and the next section
we look at the American political scene as it appears in broad
outline on the walls of one man's cave. We shall consider
government and democracy first and then go on to other
American political institutions.

Whatever is true of all governments is true of American
government; whatever characterizes democracy in general
applies to democracy in America. One hazard in "American
studies" is parochialism, but that danger may be minimized by
keeping observations about America within the context of a
larger world and striving to develop from a better understanding of American civilization some further truths about all
mankind. American government, then, like all governments, is
best understood as a process and a relationship; democracy is a
special variation with some distinguishing procedures and
relationships. The governmental process is essentially a matter
of transforming personal preferences into public policies. It
involves notions of influence, power, authority, legitimacy,
legality, coercion, officialdom, and decision. Some commentators used to rely heavily on *sovereignty* but the word is so
ambiguous when undefined and so irrelevant when tightly
defined that we can get along better without it when talking
about attributes of the state. Good political questions are
Harold Lasswell's, "Who gets what, when, how? "[1], James
Prothro's, "Who gets helped, who gets hurt? "[2], and Robert
Dahl's "Who Governs? "[3]. In other words, which preferences
of which people become public or official policy at whose
expense? Any research which helps to answer these questions
makes good political science.

In any of their forms, these basic questions of politics
assume a division of the population into governors and
governed. The division may be sharp and relatively static as in
traditional societies or it may be fuzzy and vacilitating, but it

is there; and it is this relationship between the ins and the outs that distinguishes different processes of government from each other. A democratic process is marked by a responsible, temporary relationship in which the governors are somehow beholden to the governed and the governed have a genuine opportunity for redirecting or replacing the governors.

Democracy can be given tighter, artificial definitions so that no regime can meet the stipulations. Political scientists used to use *democracy* to mean actual, indirect democracy and they would say *pure democracy* when referring to that fictitious ideal. Recently some people have spoken of *participatory democracy*, but the meaning of that term is usually left to the whim of the person who uses it, often with a beautiful disregard for the tough problem of reconciling basic conflicts. Democracy is only a special kind of government, it is not anarchy or utopia. Like all governments, it provides answers to the questions of whose preferences prevail in the face of disagreement. It does not guarantee that deeply felt desires will be satisfied or that sincere efforts will be rewarded; it does require sensitivity and a bona fide opportunity for success through persuasion. It demands both temperance in victory and grace in defeat. As few as two or three percent of a population are capable of overthrowing a tyranny; the minority who suffer democracy to survive may be even smaller. No constitution can spell out the working details of these requirements and no definition of *democracy* can be descriptive or realistic if it sets up an impossible ideal.

American democracy is something between the utopian ideal of pure or participatory democracy on the one hand and on the other a recklessly loose definition which accepts after the fact whatever is perpetrated on an acquiescent population. This latter concept starts with the conclusion: America is a democracy, therefore whatever process operates is democratic. Nonsense. Whenever America's governors act irresponsibly, when their authority becomes entrenched, when the genuineness of the opportunities for popular redirection and replacement is whittled away, when the apparent choices between personalities do not present real options between alternate policies, then the United States falls short of the tenets of its own democratic system.

The American dilemma[4] is the gap between creed and performance. This is a normal, human shortcoming and Americans indulge themselves in a special kind of conceit when they act shocked at discovering human limitations in themselves. They either ignore or are tolerant of the gap between autocratic creed and regime. They appreciate the inability of ancient despots, medieval princes, and twentieth-century dictators to achieve in practice what they preached in philosophy. But Americans like to act surprised and even disillusioned when they observe that their great philosophic goals have not been reached in the magic moment of their own short lives. The only way humans can bring aspiration and achievement into alignment is to accept prevailing practices instead of holding out for improvement. Americans have not reconciled themselves to such a dismal success; they prefer a worthy failure and continue to seek a better society than is possible.

The American creed is widely understood and accepted in general terms: all men are created equal; they are entitled to life, liberty, and the pursuit of happiness; the proper function of law and order is the protection and promotion of individual rights and freedoms; governments that betray these principles are not worth preserving; good government is limited, constitutional government; the national defense, domestic tranquility, prosperity, a more perfect union, and liberty and justice for all are to be prized and pursued.

Perhaps at no time in the development of American civilization has the gap between creed and performance been greater than at the outset. Both the Declaration of Independence and the Preamble to the Constitution were the products of a slave society engaged in the bloody process of stealing the land from its natives. This observation is made not to downgrade the founding fathers but to get contemporary shortcomings into better perspective. The country has done some bad things (by anybody's definition) since its founding, but one of the good things (according to the view presented here) it has done is to educate many people to the old injustices. Some Americans still believe in individual or racial superiority rather than equality; some think they are entitled to happiness on their own terms, not its pursuit along with their neighbors; some regard law and order as a way to promote privilege and protect the status quo; some would preserve the establishment at almost any cost; and some seem to believe that defense, tranquility, and justice are only possible with a virtually unfettered military and police power. These latter people represent the gap, not the creed. If the country is to be damned because these people are so influential, so is it to be praised because it has brought up so many others to believe in and work for the creed.

Every treatment of American democracy is plagued by ambiguity and uniqueness. Nobody, anyplace, ever spelled it all out in such definite language that the rest of us could accept it and pass it on to each new generation. The approach here has assumed some common understanding of majority rule and minority rights. It has also supposed that some Americans have tried without success to define democracy and describe the American brand of it in terms of freedoms and standard of living. If such an approach can be redirected into research on process and relationship, a better understanding of who governs — and how — will be possible.

American Political Institutions

The preceding section has attempted to illuminate some of the problems of American democracy as the starting point for research on who governs and how. This section considers other aspects of American politics with emphasis on those features which distinguish this democracy from others. The American combination of political institutions is unique; democracy is possible under other arrangements.

The United States is a democracy — not a perfect one, certainly not the only one, but contrasted with many tyrannies men have inflicted on each other it is impressive. It is also (and in some cases only incidentally) republican, federal, presidential, two-party, and mixed-enterprise. The first three of these are constitutional in a formal, legal sense; the last two are less definite but more fundamental. All together they provide for constitutional (i.e., limited) government. Let us look first at the informal ones before returning to the official ones.

Choice is an absolute requirement for democracy. If we have only the appearance of choice (as both left-wing and right-wing believers in a conspiracy theory of government claim and as Skinner argues so persuasively)[5] , then we have only the appearance of democracy. Political parties give meaning to elections. They present the candidates and marshall the voters. Some nations utilize a wide variety of parties to reflect each of several different ideological positions. Americans rely primarily upon only two. The difference is more a matter of timing than principle. Eventually the vast variety of private opinion and preference is reduced to parliamentary or congressional votes of yea or nay. In a multi-party system the officials come together as party members and reach their compromises. In a two-party system, much of the compromising is done before the election. Another feature of some party systems is cohesion and discipline within the parties. Membership is formal and meaningful. This is possible in both two- and multi-party systems but Americans do not prefer it. Their parties are loose, discipline almost nonexistent, and membership largely a matter of self-identification.

The American party system is much harder to portray than the above suggests. Nationally, America seems to have a two-party system but the national parties are impossible to identify. Sometimes the national party is a convention that lasts for about one week once every four years. Sometimes it is a congressional caucus or a national committee or a leadership conference. Scholars acknowledge the role of the states in the party system but then the picture gets even more messy. In what sense is the Democratic Party of Michigan, say, like the

Democratic Party of a Southern state? How many states have a two-party system? [6] And how many counties, cities, towns, townships, special districts, and villages (many of which are plagued with "nonpartisan" elections) have any party system at all? The party system is critical to democracy, and America's is most visible at the national level; but the traditional understanding of its characteristics and consequences does not tell us who governs the country. We could use a lot of descriptive research to prepare the way for better analytical research. After that, Americans might sharpen their judgments and attempt some new prescriptions.

Closely aligned with the study of political parties is the attempt to do research on public opinion, pressure groups, electoral behavior, and social and political psychology. These kinds of pressure, lobbying, electioneering, and tactical questions are easily lumped together as "political behavior." We probably will not understand who governs or how until we know a lot more about all of these matters. Many of the pieces to these puzzles are local and can be managed during short-term research projects. Much is already known.

The American political economy is mixed; it defies all the economic "ism's" such as socialism, communism, capitalism, and fascism. The fiction that the United States has a capitalistic, free enterprise, or free market system is transparently political in the narrow partisan sense of *politics* and it can be easily refuted. Research in American history, economics, or political science demonstrates the mixed nature of the economy. Government's role in the economy is fundamental: titles, deeds, charters, licenses, money, tariffs, subsidies, the farm program, the social security system, pure food and drug regulations, and consular services, for examples. The government owns and operates some economic enterprises (socialism) and polices others (fascism), but if it keeps its hands off still others (laissez-faire) in the direct sense, it is nevertheless indirectly involved in all of them.

Political scientists have been interested in economic policy for a long time but much remains to be learned both about how it was and how it is. Government's role in the economy is interesting in itself; the political influence of American economic interests is the other side of the same coin. That makes a fascinating study not only for economic policy but also for political party activity and other aspects of American public policy. Who could understand America's wars without some appreciation for the role of economic considerations? What else did President Eisenhower (a Republican Army general) have in mind when he warned his countrymen about the military-industrial complex? [7]

As in other affairs, when it comes to the economy, the United States is neither Cuba nor Spain, neither Sweden nor West Germany. One of the reasons its economic system is different is that its democracy and party system are different, as we have seen. The formal, legal structure of the government, to which we now return, likewise differs.

The United States is officially federal, presidential, and republican. We cannot understand political parties exclusively at the national level; neither can we grasp fully any other activity (not even national defense) without regard for the states and their municipal corporations. Morton Grodzins got this message across to political scientists in a most convincing way.[8] He persuaded many students of government, if not as many historians, that in the United States each level of government is and has been involved in the work of the other two.

Most of the rhetoric about states rights and national interests simply cannot support critical analysis. Everyone picks and chooses when to support one level of government or another.

A simple, reasonable test demonstrates this conclusively and affords good opportunities for research on the questions of which level is preferred for what functions, and why. Ask people either by survey questions or by examination of their public record, which level or levels of government, if any, they prefer to have deal with a variety of subjects. Let the list of subjects range from matters of apparent international concern to more local interests and on to purely personal affairs. About four items (e.g., national defense, highways, sewers, and prayers) would serve to evoke different answers from almost anyone but for some people a longer list might be required before they would give a second and third response. Anyone giving different answers demonstrates conclusively that the preference for one level of government or another, or the desire to avoid government involvement, depends not exclusively on some general principle of federalism but rather on some combination of factors including specific elements in the immediately perceived problem. Something about the difference between controlling nuclear weapons, say, and premarital sexual relations changes most people's answers about government involvement. No theory of federalism controls such preferences even though it may have some influence. Just as with the economy and the political party system, Americans approach federalism pragmatically – they want to see what works for them, not what fits some neat, coherent philosophy or doctrine. That much about American federalism seems quite clear but a lot of research remains to be done to determine just how each level is involved in the work of the others, as well as why people prefer one level to another in particular circumstances.

The United States is officially presidential as distinguished from parliamentary. The president is elected separately and has his own constituency. The label *presidential* is used to refer to the three-way separation of formal authority: legislative, executive, and judicial. Government functions might be organized, classified, and divided differently but this presidential system dates from the nation's eighteenth century origins. The trouble with understanding this aspect of the system is that American school children are taught too effectively to recite empty formulas about separation of powers and checks and balances, such as: Congress makes the laws, the President carries out the laws, and the Supreme Court interprets the laws. Sound familiar? It may be easy to memorize but it does not help us to understand what is going

on. Its acceptance would hinder rather than facilitate produc-
tive research.

In a sense, Congress does make the laws, but the President
is the chief lawmaker from a number of different points of
view, including the Constitution. To say that the President
carries out the laws with a bureaucracy as large as the one he
presides over is to make a little joke, even without examining
the political tug of war between various pressure groups and
the formal government structure.

As for interpretation of the law, to say that the justices do
that is no more helpful than observing that they pull their
trousers on one leg at a time. The statement is true but it is
neither distinctive nor characteristic. Everyone who works
with the law, especially a law enforcement officer, interprets
the law. The typical responsibilities of the courts, moreover,
involve adjudicating disputes between parties where interpretation of the law is not an overt issue. Interpretation looms
larger in the appellate courts, particularly the Supreme Court,
but the landmark judicial decisions on which the Court's
popular reputation is based are rare indeed. On a more routine
basis both the Congress and the President are likewise engaged
in interpreting the law and nobody gets "the last word." The
Supreme Court once declared the income tax unconstitutional.
That is no help on April 15 each year. The Court once
outlawed national child labor legislation, but within less than a
generation it swallowed child labor laws although the Constitution had not been amended on this point during the interim.
We have not heard the last interpretation of the law yet and
the ones we hear in the meantime will emanate from each of
the three branches of government.

Whether Grodzins was right about American federalism or
not,[9] certainly all three branches of American national
government, under the system of checks and balances, exercise
some of the authority of the other two. The President's
legislative powers are greater than those of any member of
Congress; his judicial powers are extensive and in criminal
cases he can set aside any conviction in a federal court. But he

cannot act alone even in executive affairs, for the Congress supervises his administration as well as finances it, and the Supreme Court sometimes reviews his acts. The Congress and the courts, likewise, share each other's jobs. If neither gets the last word on what the law will be, each has a chance to say what part of the law is going to be for the present.

Again, this confusion of jurisdiction is a matter of practical politics, not doctrine. The description of the confusion is more realistic than would be a neater picture painted by repeating old slogans and pretending a sharpness which is not there. But just how does the President play legislator? How does the Congress exercise judicial authority? How do these criss-crossing jurisdictions relate to democracy, political parties, federalism, and the other aspects of American politics? These questions remain subject to research and will presumably never be answered finally because the answers will probably continue to change as the incumbents and the times change.

The United States is a republic. This label is saved for last because it is least. The word used to be only a quaint reminder that we had no crowned head; that is about the only workable definition to give it. Some John Birch Society publicity, however, has tried to make an issue of it by distinguishing between *republic* as indirect democracy, and *democracy* as direct democracy. If that is all that is meant, the problem is only verbal, a mere matter of definition, and we could all rewrite our dictionaries to adopt this usage. The "New Left" people might share a preference for such a new vocabulary. Apparently, though, the distinction has some hidden emotional content that makes it worth arguing about in some circles. This is not one of those circles. The United States is a democratic republic (unlike the United Kingdom); it is also a republican democracy (unlike the citizen segment of ancient Athens or other purported examples of participatory democracy). This point is probably not a very fruitful one for further research although some of its overtones might be a legitimate part of the study of opinion and political psychology.

Political Science Methodology

Since the problem of defining *science* is extraordinarily complicated, the possibility of agreeing on the meaning of *political science* is very remote. James L. McCamy thinks it would be helpful to use *science* to refer to research in any field, including not only the social sciences but also the humanities.[10] At this most general level the word probably refers to objectivity, integrity, relative precision, and accepted standards of logic and evidence. That leaves room for a great variety of scientific methods. Along with astronomy, such a broad concept of science denies the necessity of laboratory experiments and replication; with Fleming's accidental discovery of pencillin, it avoids requiring predictability; with the assumptions of medical research about the value of good health, it precludes the fatuous notion of a "value-free" science. The reference above to "accepted standards" of logic and evidence suggests properly that science is partly a matter of community — of communication, of being in communion.

Scientists are people who think of themselves as scientists and who are thought of as scientists by others with the same self-image. Crackpots can be right and scientists can be wrong but the former do not belong to the community of the latter. Some natural scientists and their fans think it inappropriate to extend the term *science* to the social sciences. Many scholars, however, regardless of their field are content to go about their research and let others do the same without worrying about the label. Some social scientists, even so, are deeply concerned with methodology. They resent any implication that their own work is not "scientific" and they resist the pretensions of "unscientific" interlopers within the social sciences. In its extreme form this last position involves intolerance of variety in research methods and interests, a retreat from the content of the subject-matter, and a commitment not to science but to scientism. (Scientism is a religious belief which forgets Plato's and more modern scientific warnings about the problems of perception in an empirical world-cave, exaggerates the abilities of scientists, and demands from the laity unquestioning homage to the new high priests.)

People who seek a better understanding of American civilization can avoid much of the debate about scientific method. Whether studying the political aspect of America is more or less scientific than studying the country's literature, history, geology, or meteorology is largely irrelevant. Research in all fields is designed to sharpen the accuracy of the perceived images. Political science, by whatever name, can contribute to this sharpening process.

Historically, political science seems to have passed through some identifiable phases. In the early years of the American Political Science Association, coinciding practically with the early twentieth century. the discipline concentrated on legal form, structure, organization, laws, older political philosophy, and the like. The next phase was one of growing interest in political parties, pressure groups, public opinion, the legislative and judicial processes, public administration, and so on. These were additional, not substitute interests.[11] After World War Ii, the profession entered its nonsensical controversy over method, the so-called behavioral revolution. Little but rhetoric has been added to that debate since Prothro's essay[12] although some personality clashes and jurisdictional disputes are still mistakenly portrayed as conflicts between traditionalists and behavioralists. Prothro made the point that all political scientists study political behavior, that all use quantitative concepts whether in the sloppy way this chapter has (many, most, some, often, etc.) or in the more precise ways of statistics, and that all prefer sound generalizations (i.e., good theory) to mysticism. What is left to argue about?

The behavioral approach was added to the older interests of political science and although the emphasis within the discipline may have shifted as a consequence, some political scientists still recognize as shared concerns that subject-matter pursued by their turn-of-the-century predecessors. As the quantitative analysis associated with the behavioral method is being digested, a sensitivity to its limitations is developing among "new left" as well as "traditional" scholars.[13] American political science is adding still another phase to its development: a post-behavioral concern with policy as such. Some political scientists are now interested in and able to contribute to a policy science.[14]

All of these phases of political science are represented in the question, who governs and how? The "How? " raises question of law, form, organization, procedure, influence, politicking, and allocation of rewards and punishment. All of the study of the politics of American civilization then, may be seen as dealing with some aspect or combination of pattern, process, product, and principle. Students of the American scene are pursuing research on these matters. The grandest attempt is to draw them all together for the purpose of establishing general principles; the meanest is to get lost in the extraordinarily accurate measurement of the most insignificant detail.

Some "case studies" fall into this last category as we find out more than we want to know about a small, historical conflict in a unique and remote setting. But insight, realism, and data for broader generalizations come out of such specific studies. Also in the "meanest" category are elaborate statistical analyses of off-the-cuff questionnaire responses of atypical, isolated university student populations. But this kind of research can be specified and its results conveyed while the grand theorists may be chasing ultimate truths in an iffy world where nobody else can follow. In the narrow case, other political scientists could replicate the work but none would want to; regarding grand theory, we are all curious, but we seem damned to gain insights individually, not as a profession or society.

For a student bound by time and financial limitations, what routes into this variety of research methods are open? The library; local, small-scale, home-made surveys; the library; interviews; the library; the mass media; and the library. With somewhat more time, correspondence for questionnaires or individual responses is possible. The library may seem an unlikely place of emphasis since politics is raging in a world outside the building (if no longer off the campus) but too much ground has already been covered to ignore the reports available. Students of astronomy are given Copernicus for a running start; they are not expected to figure out the solar system on the basis of their own observations. Although no political scientist has yet done for the political system what Copernicus did for the solar system, many have made contributions worth absorbing.

The literature can be approached through texts, professional journals, government documents, journalism, or subject-matter questions that cut across the other four. The questions are much to be preferred on three grounds: they reflect life, which is a series of specific problems; they make use of the researcher's curiosity, which motivates a lot of adult learning; and they avoid the great bulk of materials available but not immediately relevant.

To say that questions arise from curiosity may not be quite enough. The process can be disciplined and formalized to some extent. Some research designs call for the formulation of the question as an hypothesis, the restatement of it in negative terms as a more easily tested null hypothesis, the gathering of evidence leading, one hopes, to the rejection of the null hypothesis, and the establishment of the hypothesis. A lot of political science is so primitive that it offers conclusions in the form of hypotheses to be tested by future research. For example, someone thinks he finds out exactly how one city is governed so he offers his conclusion tentatively, subject to research in other cities.

One problem inherent in this so-called scientific, inductive method is that it presumes a starting point of specifics from which generalizations may be drawn. Scientific knowledge grows inductively, to be sure, but the process is necessarily circular as each individual scientist proceeds sometimes inductively and at other times deductively. The "starting point" is lost in each scientist's infancy. Specific details cannot be collected except on the basis of some prior generalization. The world is too full of too many facts for anyone to start

collecting them randomly and then looking to see what
generalizations they support. But "prior generalizations"
cannot be drawn out of thin air; they are always based on
some earlier collection of specifics or particulars. The process,
in both its inductive and deductive phases, is greatly influenced by the culture which defines both *what questions are
worth asking* and *which evidence is relevant*. We cannot escape
Plato's cave.

One way to pursue hypotheses or subject-matter questions
is to break them down into aspects that can be identified in
indexes to books, general reference works, the New York
Times, professional journals such as *The American Political
Science Review*, or government documents. The many publications by the national government are especially helpful and
well indexed.[15] *Congressional Quarterly*[16] makes the national
documents easier to use. Some United Nations publications
also provide a research base for some topics in American
studies. Aside from contemporary news, the methods and
sources used by historians are available to political scientists
and library-bound researchers will not be able to utilize much
more than that.

American government and politics is such a traditional
field of study that many text books are available. They suffer
from the ambitions of a very few authors (sometimes only one
or two) who try to cover all of American politics. No small
team of political scientists has enough specialized expertise to
cover that much. Text books, however, offer a coherent,
integrated outline of the subject.

Students, fortunately, need not choose between these
approaches; they can study the texts and the specialists. The
leading text books on the American government college
market all include not only a great deal of information, they
also make profuse references to the authorities. See, for
examples, the texts listed in this chapter's bibliography: Burns
and Peltason, Dolgreare and Edelman, Dye and Zeigler, Irish
and Prothro, Monsma, and Nimmo and Ungs. A quick way to
build a bibliography, then, is to start with the most general

text and go from it to the works it cites. One shortcoming in this approach is that the text is dated and refers to even older work.

Interdisciplinary Topics

If one of the hazards of American studies as a university program is an ethnocentric parochialism, one of the challenges it offers is its universal methodological scope. Political scientists live, perceive, and write in a political cave. Their tendency to see politics in almost everything means that almost anything can be better understood with the help of political science. Well trained scholars in other disciplines likewise concentrate on one point of view and gain special insights with their particular expertise. Students of American civilization may be somewhat culture-bound but at least they can be eclectic in drawing on the best that is available in a wide variety of traditional approaches. This is important because the United States is not just what any one of the old academic departments understands. Real life does not come in three-credit-hour packages of brand X, Y, or Z. In American studies we can cut across the artificial compartmentalization of the university's organization chart.

Some of the ways to integrate approaches to American civilization are fairly obvious. *The Last Hurrah* by Edwin O'Conner is literature; it is also historical, political, and sociological. O'Conner had real insight into the transition from immigrant-family life styles and politics to the assimilated younger generation in the post-New Deal world. Scholars in English, History, Political Science, and Sociology Departments all have contributions to make in digesting that one work of fiction. Robert Penn Warren provided the same range of opportunities for bringing together various specialties in *All the King's Men*. Some political novels are futuristic and if they leave the historian somewhat out of it, they bring in some medical and physical sciences. *Brave New World,* by British author Aldous Huxley, anticipated many of the issues of drugs, government, and science which seem to be looming ever

closer before us; just as Edward Bellamy's *Looking Backward*
(1887) presaged a host of economic, political, and social
reforms witnessed in the twentieth century.

What are the real problems of life today? Many of them
are personal — matters of sex, identity, vocation, direction,
etc. A complete examination of any of these raises public
policy issues, e.g., the nature of sex education in the public
schools, the prohibitions in laws relating to sexual relations
and aberrations, the availability of birth prevention information and devices, taxation of families (exemptions or penal-
ties?), marriage and divorce laws, child support requirements,
police protection against child-abuse, conjugal rights (if any)
of prisoners and military personnel, abortion policies, sexual
transformation rights and consequences, and censorship of
pornography. Political scientists do not know very much about
most of these topics but nobody can have a full understanding
of them without touching on the political aspects involved in
each.

Other real problems in life today are interpersonal. Of
these, many are community-wide or even national in scope.
The population problem runs the whole gamut from private to
international relations. Four major national problems (with
personal and international dimensions) are war, race relations,
urban dysfunctions, and pollution. Like academic departments, these four problems are not cleanly distinguishable. A
GI casket with one black body inside it on the way home from
Vietnam summed them all up and cried out to all available wisdom for explanation. Politics alone did not send the soldier first
to a ghetto, or force him out of it into the draft pool unprepar-
ed for a desk job. But we shall never understand why he was
killed, or with what consequences for society, if we ignore the
impact of public policy on every step of the way from his
parents' birth to his widow's pension. If more of his fellowmen
both at home and abroad had pursued politics as the art of
reconciliation instead of as a moral crusade, he might not have
gone forth to kill and to have been killed. The contrast
between politics as the art of reconciliation and as a

puritanical moral crusade was drawn by Alan Simpson.[17]

Race relations and politics in America are inextricably interlocked, but a full understanding of the various manifestations of the problem requires contributions from anthropology, economics, geography, history, psychology, and sociology at least. Poets and novelists have tried to deal with it; ethics and religion impinge on it. Comprehensive scholarship on black America and on race relations in America will draw on all of these traditional disciplines.

Now that most Americans are living in metropolitan areas they have become sensitive to some of the problems of congestion. Political scientists see issues of government pervading the whole urban scene but cities are only partly governmental. City planners draw on architecture, economics, geography, history, law, sociology, and other systematized bodies of knowledge in their attempt to alleviate urban problems in the future. Just as planners are interdisciplinary, so must be the other people doing research on America's cities. Knowledge of the cities, moreover, is critical to an appreciation of the strengths and weaknesses of American civilization. The label *civilization* is basically a reference to cities.[18]

Pollution may be primarily a matter of technology and economics but Adam Smith's invisible hand[19] is apparently too slow about guiding us towards the joining of our private and common interests for us to rely on it without invoking government policy. The shape of the policy will be influenced by what the natural scientists and engineers tell us is possible, by what the philosophers tell us about responsibility, by what the geographers contribute to our understanding of human life within its physical environment, and so forth.

So it goes: America is worth studying out of curiosity and as a prerequisite for alleviating its problems. Every facet of the country cuts across academic disciplines so that American studies are often partly but never wholly matters of political science. Integrating the widest possible range of scholarly contributions is required for understanding the United States and its people. Out of a better understanding may come better prescriptions. Agreement on what is or might be "better" results from education. The study of American civilization, including American politics and political science, is an important part of that education.

NOTES

1. Harold D. Lasswell, *Politics: Who Gets What, When, How* (e.g., New York: Meridian Books, 1958).

2. This phrasing of the question is from Professor Prothro's class lectures at Florida State University and the University of North Carolina; the sense of it appears in Marian D. Irish and James W. Prothro, *The Politics of American Democracy* (4th ed.; Englewood Cliffs, N.J.: Prentice-Hall, 1968), p. 723.

3. Robert A. Dahl, *Who Governs? Democracy and Power in an American City* (New Haven: Yale University Press, 1961).

4. Gunnar Myrdal, *An American Dilemma* (e.g., The Complete Twentieth Anniversary Edition, 2 vols.; New York: McGraw-Hill Book Co., 1964).

5. B. F. Skinner, *Science and Human Behavior* (e.g., New York: The Free Press, 1965).

6. Austin Ranney and Willmoore Kendall, "The American Party Systems," *The American Political Science Review*, 48 (June, 1954), 477. Hugh A. Bone, *American Politics and the Party System* (4th ed.; New York: McGraw-Hill Book Co., 1971), ch. 4, "Other Party Systems."

7. "Farewell Address" of January 17, 1961, in, e.g., *Vital Speeches of the Day*, 27 (February 1, 1961), 229.

8. "Centralization and Decentralization in the American Federal System," in Robert A. Goldwin (ed.), *A Nation of States: Essays on the American Federal System* (Chicago: Rand McNally, 1963), p. 1. Or see alternatively his "The Federal System," in *Goals for Americans: Programs for Action in the Sixties* (A Spectrum Book; administered by the American Assembly, Columbia University; Englewood Cliffs, N.J.: Prentice-Hall, 1960), p. 265.

9. *Ibid.*

10. *Science and Public Administration* (University, Ala.: University of Alabama Press, 1960), p. 207.

11. Francis J. Sorauf, *Political Science: An Informal Overview* (Columbus, Ohio: Charles E. Merrill Books, 1965), p. 10.

12. James W. Prothro, "The Nonsense Fight over Scientific Method: A Plea for Peace," *The Journal of Politics,* 18 (August, 1956), 565.

13. V. G. Kalenskii, *Politicheskaia Nauka v SShA* (i.e., *Political Science in the USA;* Moscow: Yuridichoskaia Literature, 1969). Cited from the review by Donald R. Kelley, *The Journal of Politics,* 32 (May, 1970), 450. Some domestic "new left" criticism agrees with Kalenskii.

14. On the origins of *policy sciences,* see Daniel Lerner and Harold D. Lasswell (eds.), *The Policy Sciences: Recent Developments in Scope and Method* (Stanford: Stanford Univ. Press, 1951). For more current material see various articles and especially the bibliography in Gene M. Lyons (special ed.), "Social Science and the Federal Government," *The Annals of the American Academy of Political and Social Science,* 394 (March, 1971), 1ff.

15. *Monthly Catalog of United States Government Publications* (Washington: Government Printing Office, monthly and annually).

16. See this and other publications of Congressional Quarterly Service, 1735 K Street, N.W., Washington, D.C. 20006, and the competing Congressional Information Service, 500 Montgomery Building, Washington, D.C. 20014.

17. *Puritanism in Old and New England* (Chicago: University of Chicago Press, 1955), p. 114.

18. Kenneth E. Boulding, *The Meaning of the Twentieth Century: The Great Transition* (e.g., Harper Colophon Books; New York: Harper & Row, 1965), p. 3.

19. *An Inquiry into the Nature and Causes of the Wealth of Nations* (e.g., 2 vols.; University Paperbacks; London: Methuen, 1961), I, 477.

BIBLIOGRAPHY

American Political Science Review. Washington, D.C.: American Political Science Association. (Quarterly)

Annals of the American Academy of Political and Social Science. Philadelphia: The American Academy of Political and Social Science. (Quarterly)

Bone, Hugh A. *American Politics and the Party System.* 4th ed. New York: McGraw-Hill, 1971.

Burns, James M., and Jack W. Peltason. *Government by the People.* 8th ed. Englewood Cliffs, N.J.: Prentice-Hall, 1972.

Carr, Robert K., et al. *Essentials of American Democracy.* 7th ed. Hinsdale, Ill.: Dryden Press, 1974.

Dahl, Robert A. *Who Governs? Democracy and Power in an American City.* New Haven: Yale Univ. Press, 1961.

Dolbeare, Kenneth W. and Murray J. Edelman. *American Politics: Policies, Power, and Change.* 2nd ed. Lexington, Mass.: Heath, 1974.

Dye, Thomas R., and L. Harmon Zeigler. *The Irony of Democracy: An Uncommon Introduction to American Politics.* 2nd ed. Belmont, Cal.: Wadsworth, 1972.

Goldwin, Robert A., ed. *A Nation of States: Essays on the American Federal System.* Chicago: Rand McNally, 1963.

----- ed. *How Democratic is America? Responses to the New Left Challenge.* Chicago: Rand McNally, 1972.

Irish, Marian D., and James W. Prothro. *The Politics of American Democracy.* 5th ed. Englewood Cliffs, N.J.: Prentice-Hall, 1971.

Jones, Charles O. *An Introduction to the Study of Public Policy.* Belmont, Cal.: Wadsworth, 1970.

Kramnick, Issac, acad. ed. *American Government '73 '74 Text.* Guilford, Conn.: Duskin, 1973.

Lipsky, Michael, *et al.* (advisors). *American Government Today.* Del Mar, Cal.: CRM Books, 1974.

McClosky, Herbert. *Political Inquiry: The Nature and Uses of Survey Research.* New York: Macmillan, 1969.

Merritt, Richard L., and Gloria J. Pyszka. *The Student Political Scientist's Handbook.* New York: Harper & Row, 1970.

Monsma, Stephen V. *American Politics: A Systems Approach.* 2nd ed. New York: Holt, Rinehart and Winston, 1973.

Myrdahl, Gunnar. *An American Dilemma.* The Complete Twentieth Anniversary Edition; New York: McGraw-Hill, 1964. (2 vols.)

Nimmo, Dan, and Thomas D. Ungs. *American Political Patterns: Conflict and Consensus.* 3rd ed. Boston: Little, Brown, 1973.

Rosenbaum, William A., John W. Spanier, and William Burris. *Analysing American Politics: A New Perspective.* Belmont, Cal.: Wadsworth, 1971.

Schattschneider, E.E. *Two Hundred Million Americans in Search of a Government.* New York: Holt, Rinehart and Winston, 1969.

Sorauf, Francis J. *Political Science: An Informal Overview.* Columbus, O.: Charles E. Merrill, 1965.

Vines, Kenneth N., Alan Newman, and John Patterson. *Research in American Politics: Introductory Exercises in the Use of Political Data.* New York: Holt, Rinehart and Winston, 1971.

Wirt, Frederick M., Roy D. Morey, and Louis F. Brakeman. *Introductory Problems in Political Research.* Englewood Cliffs, N.J.: Prentice-Hall, 1970.

CHAPTER THREE

American Studies: The Discipline of History

American History

Eric Brunger

Thirty years ago, a committee on historiography, established by the Social Science Research Council and chaired by Charles Beard, examined the nature of history. One of the first points they noted was that the term was used in three ways:

1. *History-as-actuality*, the events themselves,
2. *History-as-record*, the remains, or artifacts testifying to the events,
3. *Written history*, an account of what happened, history books.

It was this latter meaning of the word that most people referred to when using the term "history," and it is important that such an account of the past was filtered through the mind of the historian, a point we shall refer to later.

Essentially, history deals with three interacting factors — man, space, and time. Each of these has its own complexity, and its own special science or sciences. Man may be studied physiologically or sociologically; space may be studied geographically or environmentally; but the third of these factors, time, is the particular emphasis of historians. Briefly, they view man in space through time, but to contemporary historians, the result is not simply a chronicle of events, nor does the historian consider himself merely a chronicler, or recorder. There is more of the historian in history than people generally realize. An historian is the product of his time and training. Throughout his writing of history he is affected by these factors. He is always making judgements — what to leave

45

out or put in, what is of more or less importance, what witness (source) is more reliable than another, who of his characters is grinding what axe. His answers to these judgement questions will affect his "telling of the tale" and, thus, his readers' view of history.

One might say that there are two kinds of history, *why* history and *how* history. *How* history is generally simpler than *why* history. It is descriptive in nature, seeks to establish facts, tries to discover what happened. If there is an error in it, other than purposeful error, it is the result of faulty methodology, of failure to ascertain certain facts, or to use certain sources. It is essentially an error in the *process* of establishing the facts. *Why* history, on the other hand, is interpretative, the examination of the events, their interrelationships, factors motivating personal behavior, and the like. It is preceded by *how* history — what happened must be established first — then we can get to why it happened. But there is a further distinction to be noted: *how* history is finite; *why* history is infinite. Once the facts are established, the task of the *how* historian is done. The facts themselves do not change unless new material is discovered, in which case the task was not finished in the first instance, and it is possible that many things thought to be fully established by historians are actually not.

Why history, on the other hand, because it is interpretative in nature, is never finished. Not only do we have different interpretations of the historical forces involved, but different times produce different views. The relevance of certain events depends in part upon the time in which they are studied. At one time, and by certain historians, the interpretations of the Renaissance were largely confined to its importance in the history of art, at another time to its development of modern finance, or the politics of the city-state. Interpretations of World Wars I or II, for example, will differ if they are written immediately after or much later than the events themselves. What is of great interest to men of one period may not be of such interest to men of another.

Carl Becker, one of the great American historians of the twentieth century, was referring to *why* history when he wrote "Everyman his own historian." Each man, each society, each age, each place may view the events of the past quite differently, yet validly, and the same man, time, place, age, may take different views from one time to another. So, history is not simply "the facts in the case;" it is also the interpretation of the facts and the use that is made of them.

The broad field of history has been so used through all of human development. Historians of antiquity used history to develop citizenship, and pride in country; Christianity used history to support its thesis of the struggle between God and Satan; Renaissance historians wrote to glorify their patrons or their city-state; some nineteenth-century historians were philosophers who sought for broad patterns to explain causal forces. Yet all of these are uses of history, history as the handmaiden of patriotism, theology, science, economics, or absolutism. The attempt to write history for the sake of history, what we refer to as "objective" history, began about 1830 in the seminars of the German historian Leopold Von Ranke. The objective of history according to him was to establish the facts as accurately and thoroughly as one could. He emphasized the search for sources and his views dominated historical scholarship through the last half of the nineteenth century, and even has its supporters today. In terms of methodology, he is still a model for historians. The difference between his view and that of current historians is essentially whether the establishment of facts is enough, whether that is all there is to history. Given the limitations of man, some historians question whether objective history is possible; it is probably clear to the reader that it is only the beginning.

The historian is thus faced with a kind of relativism stemming from this descriptive and interpretative nature. Consequently, it is not surprising that different historians using the same sources would come up with the same basic facts; but they would more than likely differ in their interpretation of these facts, of the varying weight they would place on different sources, or on the different factors that are involved.

There are other complexities in history. To polarize points of view in terms of causation, are the forces which move men material or spiritual in nature? Was Augustine or Marx correct in the analysis of the great driving force behind human growth? Is history the working out of God's will, or is it the result of the modes of producing and distributing goods and services? Another problem, that of methodology: is history science or art? Is it the searching out of facts, the scientific method; or is it the use of language, the art of letters, which places it in the broad stream of human experience? Is William Bradford or Henry Adams the better historian? Bradford in *Of Plimouth Plantation* writes as something more than a simple chronicler as he accepts God as the motivating force in human events. But accepting this causation frees him from further causal analysis, and he is able to go on recording the history of his people at Plymouth. Adams, on the other hand, is searching for the very thing that Bradford has accepted. One man writes history having accepted a theory of causation, the other in order to find a theory of causation. So what, then, is the essence of history?

Historians usually accept the dual nature of science (research) and art (narration), but there still remains great debate about the spiritual or material interpretation. One can see this in the attempts to distill the essence of the American experience. Is the United States, essentially a great technological success, a materialist society? Or is it a freedom-loving, democratic nation, a spiritual culture? Is it, indeed, a culture at all? This might seem like a foolish question, but it is essentially the question that Max Lerner was examining in his *America As A Civilization* (1957). To what extent is American culture derivative, and to what extent is it unique, and what, after all, is the final balance? American Studies is in large part the search for an answer to this question. As a field of inquiry, it is based upon the belief that it is through the insights provided by varied disciplines from art through the social sciences that an answer can be found. At the same time, it represents an awareness that it is the larger and deeper unity of all these fields of inquiry which will provide the answer, if indeed, such a spiritual mystery can be resolved. It is the purpose of this essay to provide the reader with a guide to the contribution that can be made by the discipline of history, and to that task we now turn.

Encyclopedias, Dictionaries, Reference Tools, and Guides.

As the larger part of this essay will focus upon American history, perhaps the writer will be excused for reminding the reader not to overlook the general reference tools of the library beginning with something so elementary as the card catalog, or the usually more current shelf list. Students should be wary of getting right at the "hard stuff" of specialized monographs, though some historians advise going directly to the source materials themselves. It is important that major encyclopedias like the *Brittanica* procure some of the foremost scholars to write their articles, and that the limitations of space often produce some of the most succinct writing. There are the more specialized encyclopedias such as that of the *Social Sciences* (15 vols., 1930-34) and some of these specialized works contain information of an historical nature that is not found elsewhere, as for example, does Liberty Hyde Bailey's *Cyclopedia of American Agriculture* (4 vols., 1907-09).

The *Cumulative Book Index* when used in conjunction with the *Book Review Digest* can save considerable time and energy. The capsule reviews in the latter should be not an end but a beginning only, as the key function for the student is to use them to locate the original review which must then be read in its entirety, so the student may judge for himself whether the work being reviewed needs to be examined more thoroughly. Another time-saver is the *Union List of Serials and Periodicals*, listing, as it does, the newspapers and magazines published in the United States, along with the publication dates and the run of the periodicals. The coding system which locates the holdings of the major libraries in the United States is of special value to a student who is located at a base library where the periodical collection is limited.

new edition

In the more specialized field of American history itself, bibliographical research begins with the *Harvard Guide to the Study of American History* (1960), now available in paperback (Atheneum). Though the bulk of this work consists of bibliographical listings by chronological periods of primary sources and monographic-periodical works, it also contains good brief essays on the nature of history, research and writing, the materials of history, aids in research, and historical sources. It is not complete, of course, as it lists the key works only and is naturally limited by the date of its publication. A different approach, closer to what one would describe as "American Studies," is the *Guide to the Study of the History of the United States of America* (1960). Published by the Government Printing Office, with a supplement in the offing, this is reasonably priced and, along with the Atheneum paperback, will provide the student with an excellent basic bibliographic library.

James Truslow Adams' *Dictionary of American History* (5 vols., 1940) and Richard B. Morris' *Encyclopedia of American History* (1953) are handy beginning tools for subjects in the field, the first being arranged alphabetically, and the second, chronologically. Since the geographical setting is important in understanding historical developments, the student should be familiar with the comprehensive Charles O. Paullin's *Atlas of the Historical Geography of the United States* (1932), which is available in major libraries. For his own library, he can obtain the less comprehensive, but still valuable atlas by C. L. and E. H. Lord, *Atlas of the United States* (1944).

Brief capsule accounts of the lives of major and some minor figures in American history can be found in the *Dictionary of American Biography*, edited by Allen Johnson and Dumas Malone (22 vols. and supplements, 1928-44). For his own library the student might consider the one-volume, abridged version, *Concise Dictionary of American Biography*, published by Scribners. If this is too expensive, the Morris *Encyclopedia* mentioned above is a one-volume work with a section devoted to capsule biography. The student is probably familiar with such current sources as *Who's Who*, the various volumes of *Dictionary of American Scholars*, and similar reference sources for persons of note.

Monographs: Interpreting History.

As has been noted in the first few pages of the essay, interpretation is a vital part of historical writing and the student should be familiar with such works. Two informative monographs here are Michael Kraus' *A History of American History* (1937) and Harvey Wish's *The American Historian* (1962). There are useful monographs on most of the major American historians, and the reader should not overlook the various professional journals in this regard. There is the excellent article by Professor John Higham, "The Rise of American Intellectual History," *American Historical Review*, LVI (1951), as an example. Not infrequently articles of this sort appear in other publications such as Howard K. Beale's "Causes of the Civil War" in the Social Science Research Council *Bulletin* No. 54 (1946), or the excellent essay on the radical historians of today that appeared in the *New York Times Magazine Section*, Summer 1970. In the writer's view one of the most valuable periodicals for insights into the current issues in American historiography is the *New York Review of Books*, a twice-monthly publication which permits extensive exploration of issues raised by the publication of a new work. The later exchanges by the author, reviewer, and others in the "Letters" column will keep students informed on what issues are currently being hotly debated in American history.

There are available summaries of current interpretations. The *Thirty-first Yearbook of the National Council for the Social Studies: Interpreting and Teaching American History* (1961) contains bibliographical essays on the major periods. The American Historical Association, through its Service Center for

Teachers of History, prepared a pamphlet series, now published by Macmillan, which brings the latest interpretations in
convenient summary. The re-evaluation process is continuous,
and John Higham has edited a collection of such essays in *The
Reconstruction of American History* (1962), available in
paperback. One of the most entertaining and readable accounts is John Garraty's *Interpreting American History,
Conversations with Historians* (1969); this is in the form of a
dialogue with selected major historians, each an authority in a
special field, in which Professor Garraty made use of the
modern technological device of the tape recorder. Finally,
some manual on history writing is useful, and Henry Steele
Commager's *Nature and Study of History* (1965) is one of
several good works providing a lucid examination of techniques and problems by one of America's leading intellectual
historians.

Professional Journals.

Since any such works as those cited are limited by the date
of their publication, the student should become familiar with
the various professional journals which contain articles and
book reviews. The oldest of these is the *American Historical
Review* (1895-   ) which contains articles on the broad
spectrum of history. An interesting study of historiographical
trends can be made by an analysis of the annual presidential
addresses located therein. The key national journal devoted
solely to United States history is the *Journal of American
History*, formerly the *Mississippi Valley Historical Review*
(1914-   ). It is of significance to our study of American
history in relation to American Studies to note that the name
of the journal devoted to United States history originally bore
the name of the great central confluence of this country, and
that the association which began its publication received its
initial impetus from history scholars from that section of the
country. Of course there were, and are, other journals which
devote themselves largely to the United States. There are many
regional and state journals such as the *Pacific Historical*

Review, the Pennsylvania Magazine of History and Biography, the New England Quarterly, New York History, the William and Mary Quarterly, and the Journal of Southern History. There are journals organized along other lines, such as the Journal of Negro History, and the new Journal of Popular Culture. Many state and city societies have long published valuable collections of source materials. Ethnic groups, religious groups, business and labor interests, geneological societies, and almost any kind of genus and species of human interest has published materials for the study on American culture. Finally, one must not overlook the greater availability of such collections through the development of microfilm and microcard publication programs.

Periods of American History

American historical writing, like history itself, does not break down into neatly defined and precise periods. Characteristics of one era blend into the next. Those of an earlier period may appear in a later era, surface briefly, and disappear; or they may appear before their time, remain dormant to reappear later when the intellectual climate is more receptive. But there are identifiable emphases around which periods can be constructed. Clusters of ideas and assumptions and of methods of historians mark a distinction between what went before and what came after.

Bearing these qualifications in mind, we might group the writings of American historians into four general periods. The first, from about 1600 to 1800, covers the colonial era. At the beginning of this period, history is written in terms of men and events guided by forces beyond their control. It is essentially a chronicle. By the end of the period, history was seen by its authors as the emergence of a new chance for mankind, guided by the sturdy example of the Americans. From the end of the Civil War to 1914 is the third period, when the early romantic emphasis carried over from the second period gave way increasingly to the scientific emphasis coming largely from the influence of the natural sciences. Overlapping the third period, beginning about the turn of the century and continuing to the present, we see the emergence of the "New History" with its emphasis upon social evils, drawing its impetus heavily from the concurrent stress upon economic causation, and ending with the radical visionaries of our own day, the historians of the "New Left."

Colonial Era.

A concern with history came early in the American experience. During the colonial period it was the most important subject, second only to religion. William Bradford's *Of Plimouth Plantation* recorded the experience of his small group of permanent pioneer settlers, combining, in a sense, religion with history. Writing under the assumption that his were the "Chosen People," he recorded their experience in England, Holland, and Plymouth. The idea of America as a land of moral and material rebirth is a dominant theme in his account, a rather constant value in American history. He is also the first to show a characteristic common to most of the writers of history in America from his day until the middle of the nineteenth century: historian by avocation. Bradford, like Thomas Hutchinson, William Smith of New York, George Bancroft and the rest were all busy with other duties. Bradford, Hutchinson, and Bancroft were all public officials. Even Adrian Vander Donck of the Dutch New Netherlands was a patron very busy with the day-to-day duties of the colony that would later become New York.

The general approach of these colonial writers was annalistic; they dealt largely with events, recording them as they occurred and offering little in the way of historical causation theory. Where this existed it was the acceptance of the working out of God's purpose, or the natural consequence of the inequality of talent, wealth, and power. The first would be exemplified by Bradford's works, the second by Thomas Hutchinson. There was no real attempt at historical analysis, though this did not mean there was no statement of causes and consequences. The attempt at historical explanation was not the search for an historical theorem, or system, it was rather an answer to the question of how events happened, facts to explain facts. What happened first explained what happened next, a simple kind of arithmetical analysis which explained events in terms of prior events. Even in Bradford, where the actors were playing out roles in God's drama, the reasons why the Pilgrims left Holland was explained simply in terms of what was happening to them there. Bradford and Hutchinson, and, to a lesser extent, Colden, are really writing about their own times, how they saw them, even though they may do some looking backward to others, e.g., Hutchinson used Bradford. Of course there were differences. If Bradford was interested in the fate of his sturdy band of saints, Hutchinson, writing in the next century, was much concerned with the growing problems of the British empire. Serving as a colonial administrator of that system, native-born son of the colonies, his interest focused upon the political and economic problems of what later came to fruition as the American Revolution. Further, he was under the influence of the growing set of assumptions that is labelled the Age of Reason. Isaac Newton's theory of the mechanical functioning of the universe had a decided impact upon all thought, and the natural law of science became the jumping off point for an analysis of society, law, economics, politics — all of those institutions in the world of man.

1800 — Civil War.

Writers in the early national period, like George Bancroft, were still descriptive in their emphasis, and Bancroft, like Bradford, accepted the plan and purpose of history as divine. To him the destiny of the American people was being guided by a benevolent Providence; this was the meaning of the American experience. His history was not analytical, nor was most American history during this period, nor for some time later, with one exception.

This exception was Richard Hildreth. His attempt to get at

some meaning other than theological was a pioneer effort.
Hildreth raised the question of the common man and his place
in the American experience. He asked about the "Age of the
People" and gave several examples of evidence that it was
beginning. He was concerned about wealth and its impact
upon society, even recognizing the relationship between crime
and the lack of economic security. He raised questions about
what later came to be called the labor theory of value, was
concerned about a larger GNP, though he didn't call it that, in
order to raise the conditions of the poor, saw large national
standing armies as "a sort of substitute for the (English) poor
law." The relationship of ends and means in the matter of
improving the lot of the people is very interesting. Hildreth did
not put wealth first. What was needed, he said, was "(to
impart)...to them a vastly greater portion than they have ever
yet possessed of those primary elements of power, sagacity,
force of will, and knowledge, to be backed by the secondary
elements of wealth and combination." It is interesting to note
the common background of these men, and of several we shall
mention later. All except for Adrian VanderDonck and
Cadwallader Colden, were from New England. Several of the
major historians of the nineteenth century, such as Francis
Parkman, William Prescott, and Henry Adams, shared this New
England heritage. These men held other things in common as
well: they were men of independent means and, as a
consequence, independent judgement as well. Their emphasis
was upon political and military history, an area of American
life in which their ancestors had played a role. The nature of
government and the political man had been a chief concern of
the eighteenth century and their nation was a new one that
had established itself by means of war. All of these elements
had their effect. Historians like Bancroft and Parkman shared
an interest in style as well and considered themselves men of
letters. They appreciated the finely turned phrase and the
idealistic sentiments of liberty and progress.

However, we must not carry these common characteristics
too far; they were individuals after all, and their lives differed.

Bancroft, for example, disturbed his patrician friends by taking an interest in the laboring man, becoming active in politics, even running for elective office. He served in patronage posts, Customs Collector for Boston, and in the cabinet of James K. Polk. His claim to fame rests, however, on his *History of the United States from the Discovery of the American Continent* (12 vols., 1834-82) in which he portrayed his United States as a product of Anglo-Saxon ideals developed in the freedom of the New World setting. Bancroft's writing was consistent with the American beliefs in progress and the common man. His Puritan ancestors had adopted the Hebraic concept of God's "Chosen People," and Bancroft extended this to his Americans.

Of particular importance among the Romantic school was Francis Parkman. Like Bancroft, he saw American history as the victory of Protestant democracy over Catholic authoritarianism. His nine-volume *France and England in North America* (1865-92) is still read today despite his obvious bias. In addition to a depth of research and careful attention to detail, he developed a feel for the setting in which the events he described took place. Indeed, though not robust in health, he traveled many miles on horse and on foot to know the area of which he wrote. It is his style that deserves the special attention of today's historian; he developed the narrative technique to the full, and few historians have matched him since.

Perhaps, in passing, we should mention another type of writer, Washington Irving. While not selective or searching as an investigator (he borrowed liberally from the imagination of Mason Weems), he too had a fine style and his *Life of Washington* (5 vols., 1855-60) established the image of that national hero for readers throughout the nineteenth century.

All of the foregoing were in the aristocratic tradition except for Hildreth, and perhaps, Bancroft. While strongly nationalist in sentiment, they took a dim view of the common man, or more accurately the growing urban masses, and were staunchly Protestant in faith and patrician in outlook.

Beginning with George Bancroft, who studied at the University of Goettingen, many American historians took their training in Germany where they came under the influence of Leopold VonRanke. He introduced such techniques as the diligent search for sources, the tools of internal and external criticism, and the rules of evidence. He urged his students to tell it as it happened as accurately as the sources would allow. VonRanke's ideas brought about changes in the writing of American history. For one thing, specialization began to develop, and his historical seminar technique was introduced into American universities. Further, American history, formerly political and military in emphasis, took on new dimensions. John Bach McMaster became interested in social history and was the first to use newspaper sources extensively. His *History of the United States from the Revolution to the Civil War* (8 vols., 1883-1913) was a history of the American people as well as their leaders, though he did include the political-military account as well. Bancroft's milti-volumed work took American history to the Constitution; McMaster brought it to the Civil War. The works of these and other historians of the post-Revolutionary period emphasized the emergent national consciousness of the new country. There was a tendency toward "hero" history, a good illustration of the relationship between the concerns of men and their consequential historical emphasis.

Civil War to 1914.

A shift in historical approach took place later in the nineteenth century, and as the Romantic school began to peter out, it was replaced with the "scientific" school. Perhaps a man like Henry Adams serves as the bridge, for his *History of the United States during Jefferson's and Madison's Administrations* (9 vols., 1889-91) combined the new scientific characteristics with the romantic objectives. Adams employed extensive foreign and domestic archives in assembling his data, and, in so doing, illustrated one element in this new approach, the search for sources. At the same time, he was quite interested in literary style and followed in the tradition of patrician nationalism.

This decade of the eighties was, in fact, of rather signal importance in American historiography. Henry Baxter Adams of John Hopkins University introduced the seminar technique which is still the fundamental training pattern for scholars in the field. In 1884 the American Historical Association was founded, and three years later, Frederick Jackson Turner and Reuben Thwaites helped found the State Historical Society of Wisconsin which began the collection, cataloging, and publishing of source materials so vital for the study of the West. In 1888 Turner entered the doctoral program at John Hopkins University, continuing his already established interest in the West and the frontier. The course of American historiography was firmly fixed by this time; training would be regularized toward the Ph.D., and though significant work would be done by writers without that distinction, the field itself would be dominated in publishing and teaching by the products of formal graduate school training.

Further, the decade of the eighties marked the peak of the influence of Social Darwinism and its evolutionary thesis had a decided impact upon historical scholarship. The decade itself was one of crisis. The growing split between labor and management erupted in the Haymarket Square incident of 1885 and culminated in the violence of the first years of the nineties. The flood of immigrants from southern and eastern Europe reached large proportions, to continue unabated until World War I. There were more and more new elements being added to the American experiment that historians would have to consider. Attempts at social reform motivated by humanitarian impulses became increasingly significant in American life, culminating in the complex of ideals and objectives called Progressivism. Out of these problems and new facets emerged the "New History" seeking to use the past as a guide to needed social reform. Prominent among these forces was the emphasis upon the theory of economic causation developed by historians and the newly developing behavorial sciences. Two of

the most influential of these latter were Frederick Jackson
Turner and Charles Beard. Both were midwesterners by birth
who came east for their graduate study, Turner to Johns
Hopkins and Beard to Columbia. Both focused upon economic
forces as the key determinant in the course of American
history.

Turner's key contribution came in his essay on "The
Significance of the Frontier in American History" delivered at
the American Historical Association meeting at Chicago in
1893. In his subsequent writing, including *The Rise of the
New West* (1906), he expanded upon the central theme of this
paper. He regarded the frontier as the unique factor explaining
much of America's development. The ideas of section, the
safety valve for eastern urban-industrial unrest, and the
frontier as the seed bed for the continued rebirth of
democracy with its egalitarian character in the border between
civilization and the wilderness had considerable influence on
the direction of American history writing for the next fifty
years. Though Turner in his later work qualified his earlier
enthusiasms, scholars during the next decades turned to the
frontier as a source for understanding American development.
Men such as Fred Shannon of Illinois showed the safety valve
theory to be unsound, and he along with Paul Wallace Gates
demonstrated the ineffectiveness of the Homestead Act as an
agrarian democratization measure. The debate still continues
and some recent work indicates that Turner might have been
overdrawn in his thesis rather than completely wrong. The
concept of the frontier was larger than economics or politics,
as Henry Nash Smith has shown in his *The Virgin Land*
(1950), and Arthur Moore in *The Frontier Mind* (1957). It is
the idea, or vision, behind the frontier concept that keeps it
alive as a viable contribution to understanding the American
people.

The second of these influential historians, Charles Beard,
had an even greater impact than Turner, in part at least,
because his *Rise of American Civilization* was among the most
widely used textbooks for more than a quarter of a century.

Beard's use of economic interests as an analytical tool began with his *Economic Interpretation of the Constitution* (1913) where he sought to demonstrate that the framers of America's fundamental document of governance were motivated by self-interest rather than by the grand spirit of selfless patriotism. Beard's analysis of domestic developments in terms of economic interest led him even further, to considerable social criticism, which, in turn, reflected a characteristic of the "New History" of James Harvey Robinson who taught at Columbia while Beard was a student there. He was not satisfied that historians were all as objective as they thought themselves to be, and he stressed the social conditioning that all men undergo and the resultant influence, often unrealized, and undetected, in their judgements as historians.

Since 1914

Samuel Eliot Morison, on the other hand, stressed again the goals of objectivity and the common sense nature of the historical tools of investigation. In *Puritan Pronaos* (1936), Morison, along with writers such as Perry Miller (*The New England Mind*, 2 vols., 1939 and 1953), reappraised the Puritan background emphasizing its positive contributions in democratic institutions, popular education, religious thought, and literature. This refurbishing of the Puritan Fathers is a good illustration of the central theme of Morison's "Faith of a Historian." Regardless of the emphasis one might place upon such concepts as the frontier, or Puritanism, or economic motivation, these must be dealt with by American historians. Puritanism has such a pervading influence in American life that one might say all Americans are Protestants. And the very nature of America as a wilderness setting requires continued re-evaluation of the frontier concept. As for economic determinism, from the Social Gospel to the Third World Front, a readjustment of American wealth has been a central concern.

This recognition that the establishment of fact, or descriptive history, is not enough to provide an understanding of a

culture is the motivating force behind what is now called
intellectual history. The seminal writer in this field was
Vernon L. Parrington with his *Main Currents in American
Thought* (1927). A self-confessed liberal interpretation of
American development, his work is grounded in the ideas of
the eighteenth century, the concept of progress, egalitarianism,
and the perfectibility of man, which had the status of Faith in
that time. Parrington's approach was more sophisticated, of
course, and was essentially an analysis of the conflict between
the rural-agrarian construct of the United States and the
emergent urban-industrial capitalism of the years after the
Civil War. He was heavily influenced by Beard's economic
interpretation and his analysis of American thinkers and
writers was cast in the direction of their political and social
content. Later scholars have been critical of his sweeping
generalizations, particularily his assessment of certain writers
and his antagonism to conservatism generally. However, his
work is still widely read; indeed, it may still be the starting
point for the study of ideas in the United States.

Carl Becker continued the analysis of conceptual history,
particularly in his *Heavenly City of the Eighteenth Century
Philosophers* (1932), a positive evaluation of the rights of man
theory and the genius of the American political system as the
protective methodology of government. Later work has
redressed the balance of judgment on these *philosphes,* one of
the best studies being that by Peter Gay on Rousseau. Like
Beard, Becker placed an emphasis upon relativism in historical
judgement, as can be seen by his presidential address before
the American Historical Association in 1931, "Everyman His
Own Historian."

Two widely used texts in this field are Merle Curti's
Growth of American Thought (1943) and Ralph Gabriel's
Course of American Democratic Thought (1940). Curti's work
is in the relativist tradition and liberal in interpretation, while
Gabriel, accepting the concept of social conditioning in
history, comes down against ethical relativism. Shortly after
the appearance of these texts, the field of American intel-

lectual history took off with the publication of several monographs. One of these, Arthur Ekirch's *Idea of Progress in America 1815-1860* (1944), surveys a basic concept in the American fabric within several contexts. The views of early nineteenth century economists is well treated by Joseph Dorfman in his *Economic Mind In American Civilization* (3 vols., 1946-49). Another early nineteenth century set of ideas is examined by Charles C. Wright in his *Beginnings of Unitarianism in America* (1955). Wright examines the concepts of revelation and rational thought as ways to truth in the first half of the nineteenth century. Daniel Boorstin looks at the American Philosophical Society in his *Lost World of Thomas Jefferson* (1948).

The influence of certain patterns of ideas in the last of the nineteenth and early twentieth century are covered by such writers as Richard Hofstadter in *Social Darwinism in American Thought 1860-1915* (1944); Morton White, *Revolt Against Formalism* (1947), which analyzes the ideas of John Dewey, Thorstein Veblen, and Charles Beard; and Henry S. Commager, whose *American Mind* (1958) provided a good survey of the major trends in American thought during the twentieth century. A similar quality survey by Herbert W. Schneider treats *Religion in Twentieth Century America* (1952).

Out of the attempts to understand the United States by this analysis of ideas and movements comes the school of thought referred to as the "consensus" historians. Including such prominent historical scholars as John Higham, David Potter, Louis Hartz, and Daniel Boorstin, this school seeks to emphasize the similarities rather than the differences in the American experience. While not ignoring the conflict in American life, they insist that it has generally moved forward within the liberal context of the assumptions of John Locke as to the nature of government and the rights of man.

The latest school of thought to develop in American history is referred to as that of the New Left. These scholars, including such men as Staughton Lynd (*Class Conflict, Slavery, and the United States Constitution* [1968]), and

Eugene Genovese (*The Political Economy of Slavery* [1964]),
employ a Marxist rationale in their examination of American
development. The problems which most interest them historically are those which are reflected in the contemporary
scene. Thus they seek a re-examination of slavery and the
place of the Negro in American life. In another context they
seek a re-examination of American foreign policy, of which
they are generally critical. As intellectual historians risk the
danger of presentism in their search for unifying symbols in
the American past, so too, do historians of the New Left risk
the scientific fallacy of making the facts fit the thesis. When
Leopold VonRanke urged his students to be assiduous in their
search for sources in order to recount what happened as
accurately and fully as they could, he meant, of course, all the
facts. American historians today may be in danger of losing
sight of this sage advice. Perhaps the goal of an objective
history is an impossible one, but if the reader is aware of the
role of interpretations in its writing, he will not then be misled
and can, as indeed he must, make the judgment himself.

BIBLIOGRAPHY

American Indians

Andrist, Ralph K. *The Long Death. The Last Days of the Plains Indians.* New York, 1964.

Beal, Merrill. *"I Will Fight No More Forever": Chief Joseph and the Nez Perce War.* Seattle, Wash., 1963.

Brandon, William. *The Last Americans.* New York, 1974.

Brophy, William A. and Aberle, Sophie D. *The Indian: America's Unfinished Business.* Norman, Okla., 1966.

Cash, Joseph H. and Hoover, Herbert T., eds. *To Be an Indian an Oral History.* New York, 1971.

DeLoria, Jr., Vine. *Custer Died for Your Sins.* New York, 1969.

Fenton, William, ed. *Parker on the Iroquois.* Syracuse, 1968.

Hagan, William T. *American Indians.* Chicago, 1961.

Josephy, Alvin. *The Indian Heritage of America.* New York, 1968.

-----. *The Patriot Chiefs; A Chronicle of American Indian Leadership.* New York, 1961.

Olsen, James C. *Red Cloud and the Sioux Problem.* Lincoln, Neb., 1965.

Prucha, Francis P. *American Indian Policy in the Formative Years.* Lincoln, Neb., 1962.

Sheehan, Bernard W. *Seeds of Extinction. Jeffersonian Philanthropy and the American Indian.* New York, 1973.

Steiner, Stanley, *The New Indians.* New York, 1967.

Storm, Hyemeyohosts. *Seven Arrows.* New York, 1972.

Underhill, Ruth. *Red Man's America; A History of the Indians in the United States.* Chicago, 1953.

Waddell, Jack O., and Watson, O. Michael, eds. *The American Indian in Urban Society.* Boston, 1971.

Washburn, Wilcomb E. *The Indian and the White Man.* New York, 1964.

Wilson, Edmund. *Apologies to the Iroquois.* New York, 1960.

Colonial America

Bailyn, Bernard. *The Ideological Origin of the American Revolution.* Cambridge, 1967.

-----. *The New England Merchants in the Seventeenth Century.* Cambridge, 1955.

Boorstin, Daniel J. *The Americans: The Colonial Experience.* New York, 1958

Bridenbaugh, Carl. *Cities in the Wilderness, The First Century of Urban Life in America 1625-1742.* New York, 1955.

-----. *Cities in Revolt 1743-1776.* New York, 1955.

-----. *Rebels and Gentlemen: Philadelphia in the Age of Franklin.* New York, 1962.

-----. *The Colonial Craftsman.* New York, 1958.

-----. *Vexed and Troubled Englishmen, 1590-1642.* New York, 1968.

Brown, Robert E. *Middle Class Democracy and the Revolution in Massachusetts, 1691-1780.* Ithaca, N.Y., 1955.

Bushman, Richard. *From Puritan to Yankee Character and the Social Order in Connecticut 1690-1765.* Cambridge, 1967.

Gipson, Lawrence H. *The British Empire Before the American Revolution.* 15 vols. Caldwell, Idaho, and New York, 1936-1970.

-----. *The Coming of the Revolution.* New York, 1954.

Heimert, Alan. *Religion and the American Mind from the Great Awakening to the Revolution.* Cambridge, 1966.

Leder, Larence H. *Liberty and Authority: Early American Political Ideology, 1689-1763.* Chicago, 1968.

Merritt, Richard L. *Symbols of American Community, 1735-1775.* New Haven, 1966.

Morgan, Edmund S. *The Puritan Dilemna: The Story of John Winthrop.* Boston, 1944.

-----. *The Puritan Family.* Boston, 1944.

Nelson, William H. *The American Tory.* Oxford, 1961.

Powell, Sumner C. *Puritan Village: The Formation of a New England Town.* Middletown, 1963.

Rossiter, Clinton. *Seedtime of the Republic; The Origin of the American Tradition of Political Liberty.* New York, 1953.

Rothermund, Dietmar. *The Layman's Progress.* Philadelphia, 1961.

Schlesinger, Arthur M. *Birth of A Nation; A Portrait of the American People on the Eve of Independence.* New York, 1968.

-----. *Colonial Merchants and the American Revolution 1763-1776.* New York, 1939.

Walzer, Michael. *The Revolution of the Saints: A Study in the Origin of Radical Politics.* Cambridge, 1965.

Early Nationhood

Boorstin, Daniel J. *The Americans: The National Experience.* New York, 1965.

-----. *The Genius of American Politics.* Chicago, 1953.

Bernhard, Winifred E.A. *Fisher Ames: Federalist and Statesman.* Chapel Hill, 1965.

Brant, Irving. *James Madison.* 6 vols. Indianapolis, Ind., 1948-1961.

Bruchey, Stuart. *The Roots of American Economic Growth.* New York, 1965.

Cunliffe, Marcus. *The Nation Takes Shape 1789-1837.* Chicago, 1959.

Freeman, Douglas Southall. *George Washington.* 7 vols. New York, 1948-1957.

Dorfman, Joseph. *The Economic Mind in American Civilization.* 5 vols. New York, 1946-1959.

Hammond, Bray. *Banks and Politics in America from the Revolution to the Civil War*. Princeton, 1957.

Hartz, Louis. *The Liberal Tradition in America*. New York, 1955.

Koch, Adrienne. *Madison's "Advice to My Country."* Princeton, 1966.

Labaree, Benjamin W. *Patriots and Partisans: The Merchants of Newburyport, 1764-1815*. Cambridge, 1962.

Levy, Leonard. *Legacy of Suppression: Freedom of Speech and Press in Early American History*. Cambridge, 1960.

McCormack, Richard. *The Second American Party System: Party Formation in the Jacksonian Era*. Chapel Hill, 1966.

Miller, Douglas T. *Jacksonian Aristocracy: Class and Democracy in New York 1830-1860*. New York, 1967.

Mitchell, Broadus. *Alexander Hamilton: The National Adventure, 1788-1804*. New York, 1962.

-----. *Alexander Hamilton: Youth to Maturity, 1755-1788*. New York, 1957.

Nettels, Curtis P. *The Emergence of a National Economy, 1775-1815*. New York, 1962.

Nichols, Roy F. *The Invention of the American Political Parties*. New York, 1967.

North, Douglas. *The Economic Growth of the United States, 1790-1860*. Englewood Cliffs, 1961.

Nye, Russell B. *The Cultural Life of the New Nation*. New York, 1960.

Parrington, Vernon L. *Main Currents in American Thought*. 3 vols. New York, 1927-1930.

Pessen, Edward. *Jacksonian America*. Homewood, 1969.

Peterson, Merrill. *The Jeffersonian Image in the American Mind*. New York, 1960.

Smith, James M. *Freedom's Fetters: The Alien and Sedition Laws and American Civil Liberties*. Ithaca, N.Y., 1956.

White, Leonard. *The Jeffersonians: A Study in Administrative History 1801-1829.* New York, 1951.

Wood, Gordon S. *The Creation of the American Republic 1776-1787.* Chapel Hill, 1969.

South, Slavery, Reconstruction

Cruse, Harold. *The Crisis of the Negro Intellectual.* New York, 1967.

Degler, Carl. *Neither Black Nor White.* New York, 1971.

Donald, David. *The Politics of Reconstruction, 1863-1867.* Baton Rouge, 1965.

Fogel, Robert W., and Stanley L. Engerman. *Time on the Cross: The Economics of American Negro Slavery.* New York, 1974.

Foner, Eric. *Free Soil, Free Labor, Free Man.* New York, 1970.

Frederickson, George. *The Black Image in the American Mind.* New York, 1971.

Fullenwider, S.P. *Mind and Mood of Black America.* Homewood, 1970.

Genovese, Eugene. *The Political Economy of Slavery.* New York, 1961.

-----. *The World the Slaveholders Made.* New York, 1969.

Jordan, Winthrop D. *White Over Black: American Attitudes Toward the Negro.* Chapel Hill, 1968.

Killens, John, ed. *The Trial of Denmark Vessey.* Boston, 1970.

Oates, Stephen. *John Brown.* New York, 1970.

Potter, David. *The South and Sectional Conflict.* Baton Rouge, 1968.

Roucek, Joseph, ed. *The Impact of the Negro on Western Civilization.* New York, 1970.

Stampp, Kenneth M. *The Era of Reconstruction 1865-1877.* New York, 1965.

Thorpe, Earl E. *The Central Theme of Negro History.* Chapel Hill, 1971.

-----. *The Mind of the Negro.* Baton Rouge, 1961.

Trelease, Allen. *White Terror: The Ku Klux Klan.* New York, 1971.

Woodward, C. Vann. *Origins of the New South 1877-1913*. Baton Rouge, 1951.

-----. *The Strange Career of Jim Crow*. 2nd ed. New York, 1966.

The American Frontier

Arrington, Leonard J. *Great Basin Kingdom; An Economic History of the Latter-Day Saints, 1830-1900*. Cambridge, 1958.

Atherton, Lewis. *Main Street of the Middle Border*. Bloomington, Ill., 1954.

Bartlett, Richard A. *Great Surveys of the American West*. Norman, Okla., 1962.

Billington, Ray A. *The Far Western Frontier 1830-1860*. New York, 1956.

-----, ed. *Selected Essays of Frederick Jackson Turner Frontier and Section*. Englewood Cliffs, 1961.

-----, *Westward Expansion; A History of the American Frontier*. 4th ed. New York, 1974.

Buley, R.C. *The Old Northwest*. 2 vols. Bloomington, 1951.

Caruso, John Anthony. *The Mississippi Valley Frontier: The Age of French Exploration and Settlement*. Indianapolis, 1966.

Clark, Thomas C. *A History of Kentucky*. Lexington, 1960.

Curti, Merle. *The Making of an American Community*. Stanford, 1959.

Dykstra, Robert A. *The Cattle Towns*. New York, 1968.

Eaton, William Clement. *A History of the Old South*. New York, 1966.

Fite, Gilbert. *The Farmers' Frontier, 1865-1900*. New York, 1966.

Leach, Douglas Edward. *The Northern Colonial Frontier, 1607-1763*. New York, 1966.

Moore, Arthur K. *The Frontier Mind*. Lexington, 1957.

Paul, Rodman. *Mining Frontiers of the Far West*. New York, 1963.

Sanford, Charles. *The Quest for Paradise.* Urbana, 1961.

Shannon, Frederick A. *The Farmers' Last Frontier.* New York, 1945.

Smith, Henry Nash. *Virgin Land; The American West in Symbol and Myth.* Cambridge, 1950.

Van Every, Dale. *Ark of Empire: The American Frontier, 1784-1803.* New York, 1963.

-----. *A Company of Heroes; The American Frontier, 1775-1783.* New York, 1963.

-----. *The Final Challenge; The American Frontier, 1804-1845.* New York, 1964.

-----. *Forth to the Wilderness; The First American Frontier, 1754-1774.* New York, 1961.

Wade, Richard C. *The Urban Frontier; The Rise of Western Cities.* Cambridge, 1959.

Webb, Walter Prescott. *The Great Plains.* Boston, 1931.

Winther, Oscar O. *The Transportation Frontier: Trans-Mississippi West, 1865-1890.* New York, 1964.

Immigrants in America

Baltzell, E. Digby. *The Protestant Establishment Aristocracy and Caste in America.* New York, 1964.

Berthoff, Rowland. *An Unsettled People: Social Order and Disorder in American History.* New York, 1971.

Handlin, Oscar. *The Uprooted.* Boston, 1951.

Hansen, Marcus. *The Atlantic Migration 1607-1860; a History of the Continuing Settlement of the United States.* Cambridge, 1940.

Higham, John. *Strangers in the Land; Patterns of American Nativism 1860-1925.* Princeton, 1955.

Jones, Maldwyn A. *American Immigration.* Chicago, 1960.

Rolle, Andrew. *The Upraised, Italian Adventurers and Colonists in an Expanding America.* Norman, Okla. 1968.

Ward, David. *Cities and Immigrants.* New York, 1971.

Wittke, Carl. *We Who Built America.* New York, 1939.

Labor

Bernstein, Irving. *The Lean Years.* Boston, 1960.

-----. *The Turbulent Years.* Boston, 1970.

Brody, David. *Labor in Crisis.* Philadelphia, 1965.

-----. *Steelworkers in the Non-Union Era.* Cambridge, 1960.

Bruce, Robert. *1877: Year of Violence.* Indianapolis. 1959.

Conlin, Joseph. *Bread and Roses Too.* Westport, Conn., 1969.

Dubofsky, Melvin. *We Shall Be All.* Chicago, 1969.

Harrington, Michael. *The Other America; Poverty in the United States.* New York, 1962.

Hugins, Walter. *Jacksonian Democracy and the Working Class.* Stanford, 1960.

Leuchtenberg, William E. *Perils of Prosperity.* Chicago, 1958.

Mandel, Bernard. *Samuel Gompers.* Yellow Springs, Ohio, 1963.

Potter, David. *People of Plenty, Economic Abundance and the American Character.* Chicago, 1958.

Some British Views

Allen, H. C. and Hill, C. P., eds. *British Essays in American History.* New York, 1957.

Brock, W. R. *The Character of American History.* New York, 1965.

Thistlewaite, J. *The Great Experiment.* Cambridge, England, 1965.

Unclassified by Subject

Bass, Herbert J., ed. *The State of American History.* Chicago, 1970.

Billias, George, and Grob, Gerald, eds. *American History Retrospect and Prospect.* New York, 1971.

Cole, Wayne S. *An Interpretative History of America's Foreign Relations.* Homewood, Ill., 1968.

Daniels, George H. *Science in American Society; A Social History.* New York, 1970.

Greene, Theodore. *America's Heroes: The Changing Models of Success in American Magazines.* New York, 1970.

Jones, Howard M. *O Strange New World; American Culture: The Formative Years.* New York, 1964.

Hofstadter, Richard. *The American Political Tradition and the Men Who Made It.* New York, 1948.

Lerner, Max. *America as a Civilization; Life and Thought in the United States Today.* New York, 1957.

Marty, Martin E. *Righteous Empire: The Protestant Experience in America.* New York, 1970.

Osgood, R. E. *Ideals and Self-Interest in America's Foreign Relations.* Chicago, 1964.

Plesur, Milton. *America's Outward Thrust.* DeKalb, Ill., 1971.

Smith, Page. *Daughters of the Promised Land: Women in American History.* Boston, 1970.

Williams, W. A. *The Tragedy of American Diplomacy.* New York, 1962.

CHAPTER FOUR

American Studies: The Discipline of Philosophy

Philosophy in America

Paul Collins Hayner

The story of philosophy in America is to a large extent parallel to that of the development of American civilization as a whole. Admittedly generalization about American philosophy is difficult, since it embraces so many differences in method and perspective. Even as American civilization has been largely an extension of European culture, and only recently has developed a more distinctively authentic American flavor, so American philosophy at first was but a reflection of European philosophy, and often was inferior to its European models. Before the Civil War, American philosophy in the technical sense was practically non-existent, as de Tocqueville remarked in 1835. Even after the Civil War, philosophy in America was strongly influenced, and even dominated, by that of Western Europe. However, in recent years it has gradually managed to achieve a degree of autonomy. With the development of pragmatism, especially, a distinctively American product of philosophical thought has achieved recognition. While the influence from England and the European continent continues to be strong, American philosophers are producing work which is increasingly less dependent on inspiration from abroad.

Philosophy Prior to the Civil War

Puritanism.

To the extent that the shores of America became a refuge for Europeans desiring freedom to pursue a form of religion unhampered by political restrictions, philosophy in the colonies at first had a decidedly religious cast. The Puritans in Massachusetts were strongly Calvinist in outlook; and while their doctrine was by no means the same as that of other colonists, theirs was probably the most influential in the New World at that time.

Puritan doctrine was founded upon belief in the absolute sovereignty of God and the total depravity of man. For while man was created good, the Puritans believed, his freedom tempted him into rebellion against his Creator; as a result he has become completely helpless in the bonds of sin. From this condition God chooses some, "the elect," to be saved by His unmerited grace, their redemption being manifested in "good works" such as discipline, honesty, temperance, industry and frugality. Such works are not the means to salvation but its "fruits," these being incapable of realization by the depraved, "natural man." The "elect," however, are joined together in a religious community of Christian believers under the "Covenant of grace." It is this Covenant which forms the basis for the direction of the life of the community, all of whose members subscribe to the basic doctrines of the Christian faith, finding in the Bible, as interpreted by the Puritan divines, the rule of faith and life. It was from this standpoint that later Puritanism hounded heretics and burnt witches, though this latter phase was by no means typical of Puritan life and may better be regarded as a corruption of the authentic Puritan ethic.

Unlike many forms of Christian faith, Puritanism was by no means anti-rational or anti-philosophical. Following the lead of Calvin himself, the Puritans were convinced that their doctrines formed a logical system, and that this system was implicit in Scripture. They believed that while God Himself remains unknown to man, except insofar as He chooses to reveal Himself, His works are evident in nature, and natural science therefore becomes an adjunct to the knowledge of God. Indeed, since creation is constantly sustained by God's will, its workings may be viewed as direct expressions of God's decrees. Natural science is a science of God's will, in one of its manifestations. Nature is not to be studied as an end in itself, to be sure, but as a grand display of His handiwork. Still, what can be known in this sphere is rationally coherent. Revelation is necessary to arrive at a saving knowledge of God, and science is by no means necessary to salvation; but the saving truth of revealed knowledge is consistent with the claims of reason, even though there are gaps in man's comprehension of the details of the Divine plan.

Such was the spirit of seventeenth-century philosophy among the Puritans. None of it, strictly speaking, was original. Rather, it was a framework within which religious devotion and the practical concerns of daily work and living could be carried on.

It was in the eighteenth century in the work of Jonathan Edwards (1703-1758) that the Puritan viewpoint in America received its most important philosophical expression, although his was more a defense of Puritan doctrine in an age when it had come under wide-scale attacks. Specifically, Edwards sought to show that the Calvinist doctrines are capable of philosophic defense. Thus his writing, "The Great Christian Doctrine of Original Sin Defended," was designed to show that the human condition is indeed accurately portrayed and accounted for by a basic tenet of the Christian faith. His *Freedom of the Will* (1754), too, while defending the determinism which was widely accepted on scientific grounds, nevertheless argued that man is morally responsible and that hence the moral demands of the Christian faith are based on philosophically sound principles. An admirer of the works of Newton and Locke, Edwards sought to show that an empiricist theory of knowledge, coupled with a Newtonian conception of the order of natural events, is by no means in conflict with

Christian principles. He attacked the deist claim that natural
reason is sufficient as a foundation for religion, insisting that
revelation must be employed to give man a firm understanding
of himself and his duties. In Edwards' view, natural man may
be corrupt, but the illumination of the "divine and supernatural light" which is given by God to His elect provides not
only a deep conviction of the reality of God but also, like the
apprehension of beauty, give a vital sense of the glory of God
in the heart. Indeed the religious fervor of the "Great
Awakening" which began in his own congregation was
undoubtedly the prime source of Edwards' doctrine of the
divine light, even though he was not himself in sympathy with
the more extreme forms of the revivalism which took place at
that time.

Edwards' idealistic metaphysics can be seen as one
expression of a point of view which was widely accepted in his
time. Samuel Johnson (1696-1772), for example, whose views
were more directly related to those of the British philosopher,
Berkeley, was also persuaded that idealism provided a sound
framework for the reconciliation of scientific and religious
interests. While he was induced by Berkeley to reject what he
considered to be the implicit atheism of Newton, his aim was
still to support the basic claims of traditional Christianity
through philosophical arguments.

Deism.

The philosophies of Johnson and Edwards, however, were
mainly retrospective and were unable to restrain the surge of
views stemming from the Age of Reason which came to
prominence in America from the middle of the eighteenth
century on. Such views manifested strongly in religion and in
social and political theory, eventually replaced the orthodox
Puritan view of man and the world with humanistic deism and
faith in the perfectibility of man and his institutions. Such
ideas, like those of their predecessors, were modeled after
French and British originals. At the same time, however, they
were given expressions which were peculiarly American and

adapted to conditions which were associated with the American Revolution and its aftermath.

Typical of deism were the views of Thomas Paine (1737-1809) who, along with Thomas Jefferson and Ethan Allen, among others, proposed a point of view in religion which was in many ways directly opposed to that of Puritanism. His book, *The Age of Reason* (1794-1796), was in some ways the definitive expression of the American Enlightenment, although many other American deists differed with Paine on various details. Recognizing no other criterion than reason, Paine rejected all reliance on Biblical revelation, miracles and prophecies as superstition. In theology he recognized only two doctrines, the existence of God and a life after death; and the only duties to be derived from faith, he believed, were encompassed in "doing justice, loving mercy, and endeavoring to making our fellow creatures happy." George Washington and Thomas Jefferson were only two of the many political leaders of the eighteenth century who were influenced by such views, heartily endorsing the position that religion is basically a simple, uncomplicated matter, readily within the grasp of any rational creature, devoid of mystery and properly exercised by each individual as he sees fit. Religious freedom, so called, and the principle of separation of church and state, which became basic Constitutional guarantees, derived from the teachings of such deists.

Humanism.

Of equal importance were the Enlightenment views widely held at this time on social and political issues. In place of the Puritan view of human depravity, there grew up the notion that man, as man, is innately good. The views on morality held by the deists were decidedly humanistic. Man could by his own efforts and through the use of reason achieve the good life for himself in this world and within the framework of human institutions. Man's difficulties were viewed as the result of ignorance and of the failure to apply scientific techniques to the improvement of the social environment. At the same

time the social environment was viewed as capable of change
for the better, with a corresponding increase in human
happiness. The world of man, it was thought, was capable of
practically endless improvement.

It was in the field of political philosophy, however, that
probably the most enduring results of Enlightenment philosophy are to be found. Beginning with the writings of such
Europeans as Locke, Montesquieu, and similar writers, American political propagandists wove into the fabric of the
American Revolution principles which are basically Enlightenment in origin and execution. The political liberalism which
inspired Thomas Jefferson, for instance, was based on the
notion of "natural law" and "natural rights." These furnished
the justification for the achievement of political independence
from the British since life, liberty, happiness and property
were viewed as inalienable rights to be secured as the means to
the foundation of social order. While great disagreement was
evident among the proposals for the newly created government
in America, still the basic items were such as to unite in one
political unit a highly miscellaneous group. The later development of American society and its political institutions in the
direction of an amalgamation of peoples with diverse religious,
economic, and social traditions was in no small measure a
result of the philosophy on which the Revolution was fought.
Independence was declared and a Constitution was eventually
adopted.

Conservatism.

Following the Revolution and up until the Civil War,
American Philosophy took a decidedly conservative turn.
Indeed what little philosophizing there was in this period was
directed toward a retreat from the "radicalism" of the
Revolution. Alexander Hamilton worked for a strong Federal
government and John Adams opposed the equalitarianism
which seemed to be implied by revolutionary doctrine. John
C. Calhoun led the Southern attack against the views of
Thomas Jefferson. With the growth of the American frontier

the liberal views of the Jacksonians were able to prevail for a while, though the trend in the more populous centers of the East was in the direction of the development of the institutions of industrialism in the North and slavery in the South. Economic interests came to overshadow the interest in human rights which had been prominent before.

A corresponding change took place in the religious climate. Deism gave way to various forms of emotional revivalism at the same time that various denominations sprang up and were active in establishing schools and colleges. College presidents were invariably clergymen whose philosophy tended toward a defense of authority and the use of arguments to support tradition and inculcate the established lessons of mental, moral and natural philosophy. Philosophy became a bulwark against radical innovations and social and political reform.

One school of philosophy which did develop into a significant school at this time was Scottish "Common Sense" realism. Introduced by John Witherspoon and Samuel Stanhope of Princeton, its chief exponents were James McCosh, Francis Wayland and Noah Porter. This philosophy gave strong support to traditional religion at the same time that it promoted emphasis on scientific studies. According to these realists, man may achieve an immediate grasp of objective facts and of causal principles through direct intuitions of the mind. No less objective in the view of the realists are standards of right and wrong, the truth of God's existence, and the immortality of the soul. The result of such philosophizing was to establish on the one hand a religious orthodoxy along the lines of American denominationalism together with a justification for the various academic subjects of the standard college curriculum, and thus to bring together, into one intellectual package, science, scholarship and religion.

Transcendentalism.

It was, however, with the appearance of Transcendentalism that a much more distinctively American school of philosophy was developed. While its origins were European, its conclusions

were American. Transcendentalism began in and around
Boston, partly as a meeting of minds of those who took a
Unitarian approach to religion. Its chief representatives were
Ralph Waldo Emerson, Henry David Thoreau, William Ellery
Channing, and Theodore Parker, in which group some his-
torians would include Henry James, Sr., and Walt Whitman.

The more immediate impetus to the development of
Transcendentalism was a distaste for the narrow empiricism of
Locke and the rigid formalism of the Enlightenment. Clearly
from this point of view it was in large part a product of the
romantic movement. The romanticism of such German philosophers as Schelling and English poets such as Coleridge had a
direct impact on the thought of the Transcendentalists.

What appealed to Emerson, Parker and the rest was the
romantic claim that human experience and knowledge ultimately rest on a much broader basis than sense experience and
the scientific method. So while not despising empirical science
they proclaimed its limits in terms of the operations of the
Understanding, and upheld Reason as the source of wisdom
and as a kind of revelation accompanied by strong and deep
feeling. Poetry, they believed, provides a more reliable access
to truth than the grubby probabilities of physical science.

No less important, however, was the ethical idealism
Transcendentalism inherited from Calvinism. In this respect,
two opposed trends are noticeable. On the one hand,
Transcendentalism continued the moral seriousness of Calvinism, proclaiming the priority of ethical over material values,
and denouncing the crude manifestations of the commercial
spirit developing in America at this time. Abolition, women's
rights and the temperance movement were largely fostered by
this continuing insistence on the need for the achievement of
high moral standards in personal and social conduct. Transcendentalism kept alive this heritage from Calvinism and transmit-
ted it to the American philosophy of a later age where it forms
a considerable part of the drive of pragmatism. John Dewey's
philosophy is in many ways an expression of the attempt to
make ethical ideals relevant and influential in social and

political life.

On the other hand, Transcendentalism repudiated the pessimism and the sense of sin characteristic of Calvinism. From the Unitarian views of Channing and Parker, the Transcendentalists imbibed the notion that man is essentially good and capable of significant moral improvement by his own efforts. God, they believed, is not only good and just, but also loving. Rather than angry or vindictive, as Calvinism believed, God is a benevolent Being who has given to man not only the key to self-improvement, but also the freedom to achieve, by rational effort, the Kingdom of Heaven on earth.

In metaphysics, all the Transcendentalists were idealists. Emerson's essay *Nature* is typical of the views of this group. Using Reason rather than Understanding, it is possible to penetrate the True Reality lying beyond the world of sense, the world of transient phenomena. This, the "Transcendent," the real world, beyond the reach of empirical science, but accessible to Reason and/or poetic intuition, is the one from which man acquires his moral bearings.

Indeed, the moral fervor imparted by Transcendentalism to American social thought served to reinforce that aspect of philosophical concern which had been so strong in earlier times. The moral idealism of Puritanism, plus the belief in natural rights of the Enlightenment, combined to give to Transcendentalism a humanitarian drive. These men were consciously revolutionary and often engaged in subversive activities. Parker was indicted for his activities in opposition to the Fugitive Slave Law, and Thoreau not only went to jail for refusal to pay taxes to a government which permitted slavery, but his essay, "Civil Disobedience," inspired Gandhi and has influenced such revolutionaries as Martin Luther King, Jr., down to the present day.

Evolution and Idealism

The Civil War was not only a break in American political life, but also a point of separation in philosophy, for it coincided with the introduction into America of two strains of thought, both European in origin, but which came to represent in America two major philosophical traditions. The one, which was prompted initially by Darwin's theory of evolution, strongly influenced the formation of pragmatism, and has continued to the present as Naturalism. The other, speculative idealism, came to greatest prominence around the turn of the twentieth century, but has continued with diminished prestige until quite recent time.

Evolution.

Darwin's theory of evolution provoked a crisis in American thought, not so much because of its implications for science but because it seemed to many to threaten the foundations of religion and morality. While in America it was attacked on scientific grounds by Jean Louis Agassiz of Harvard (1807-73), most of its defenders as well as its opponents argued its pros and cons in terms of its presumed metaphysical and theological implications. In England T. H. Huxley and Herbert Spencer supported Darwinism, while in America it was defended by the botanist, Asa Gray (1810-88), and by John Fiske and Chauncey Wright. Its defense was taken up also by the pragmatists Charles S. Peirce, William James and John Dewey.

It was Darwin's theory of natural selection which was the focus of philosophical concern, for it seemed that if Darwin was correct in his view that the species of organisms, including man, originated at various points in time as a result of "blind," natural conditions rather than by the work of God in the beginning, then not only is the Biblical account of creation overthrown, but also the received religious view that man and all other forms of life are the result of God's intention or "design." An atheistic naturalism seemed to be the logical consequence of accepting the theory of evolution.

Various writers hastened to argue, however, that such a conclusion was not necessary. John Fiske, for example, in *The Outline of Cosmic Philosophy* (1874), presented a popularized version of Spencer's doctrine of evolution, and sought to show that evolution is a process in which, viewed on a cosmic scale, God uses evil merely as a means to the ultimate end of establishing good, of putting down the dinosaurs, and of installing man and his values in their place. Chauncey Wright presented a much more cautious interpretation of Darwinism, opposing the speculative elaborations of Spencer and his followers, but insisting, as Darwin himself did, that there is no necessity for a conflict between the theory of evolution and religion. Not only does evolutionary theory leave untouched the basic concerns of religion, he argued, but it serves the valuable function of purging religious doctrines of superstition. Wright's views on scientific method were a major influence in shaping the development of the pragmatic naturalistic tradition in America.

Speculative Idealism.

We have previously labeled Transcendentalism as a form of idealism. This it was, in view of its insistence that the Reality behind phenomena is ultimately some form of Divine Mind. But the idealism of the Transcendentalists was not speculative. Such a form of idealism came to expression in America only after the Civil War with the importation of German philosophy in large segments. Many native German emigrants to the United States, settling in the Middle West, brought with them a warm enthusiasm for the philosophy of their fatherland. In turn, many Americans went to Germany to study philosophy. Beginning in the 1830s and continuing into the latter part of the nineteenth century, German thought continued to be perhaps the most important of all the European influences in shaping American ideas.

A group known as the St. Louis Hegelians formed the St. Louis Philosophical Society in 1866, a small division of which was known as the Kant Club, led by William T. Harris and Henry Brokmeyer. These, together with Denton J. Snider, Carl Schurz, Joseph Pultizer, George Howison and Thomas David-son, promoted the study and dissemination of the philosophy of Hegel both in the Middle West and in New England (the Concord School of Philosophy, founded by Alcott and Harris, 1879). This same group also established *The Journal of Speculative Philosophy* (1867-1893). This was the first philosophical journal of this type in America, and indeed the first philosophical periodical in the English language.

The title of the *Journal* provides the key to its philosophic viewpoint. In explicit opposition to the empiricism and agnosticism of current British philosophy, especially that of Spencer, Harris led the fight to establish Reason as the instrument of speculative insight in place of the fragmented and illusory deliverances of sense experience and the understanding. Reason thus establishes itself as the content of Ultimate Reality, which is a self-contained whole of absolute Activity. It is speculative philosophy which provides the basis for our knowledge of "cosmic self-activity," and with it a truly comprehensive grasp of Spiritual Being, of ultimate truth. At the same time, a complete synthesis is achieved of the various insights of science and art, as well as religion, and of the practical demands of ethics, politics and education.

The significance of the *Journal*, however, was not limited to its function as a vehicle of speculative philosophy. It was indeed the main source of idealistic doctrine in America, as far as its initial impetus was concerned, for it provided the first American translations of the writings of Fichte and Schelling, as well as Hegel. But it also provided a new generation of philosophers a vehicle of philosophic expression, and such worthies as Peirce, Royce, James and Dewey sharpened their philosophic teeth in its pages. Largely through its influence, idealism became the dominant school of philosophy in America in the late nineteenth and early twentieth century. With the founding of the *Philosophical Review* at Cornell University in 1892, idealism reached its high point in America.

The Classic Period of American Philosophy

The emergence of idealism in America marks the beginning

of what some historians have called "the golden age" of American philosophy. In the sixty years or so following 1880 there appeared for the first time in America distinctive alternatives to European viewpoints as well as several philosophers of preeminent stature. This was the period when idealism, pragmatism, realism and naturalism came to the fore, and when Royce, James, Peirce, Dewey, Santayana and Whitehead were at the center of attention.

Idealism.

Undoubtedly the outstanding spokesman for idealism in America was Josiah Royce (1855-1916). Royce's "absolute idealism," as it is usually labeled, is in part, a continuation of romantic German idealism, but it also reflects the influence of Peirce and James. As a form of idealism, Royce's philosophy renews the claim that reality is mind, and that Absolute, or Infinite, Mind is the framework within which our finite, human minds are contained and judged. The idealism of Royce, however, while continuous in basic outline with its European antecedents, was developed in view of certain specific problems which he believed it would solve. As his interest in various problems changed, so did the formulation of his idealism. In his *The Religious Aspects of Philosophy* (1885), for instance, a central concern was the problem of error. The problem is solved, he believed, by reference to "the Unity of Infinite Thought," the Absolute Mind, which serves as the standard by which all finite thought is judged and error is exposed. So God conceived as Omniscient Being provides the standard of objectivity, or reality, by which all our finite experience and thought receives its perfect fulfillment.

Royce himself claimed never to have departed in basic outlook from that presented in this early work; indeed, that seems to have been the case. Still, as he moved to consider other than epistemological issues, his Absolute tended to assume corresponding changes in definition. Thus, in considering the problem of evil, man's sufferings are explained as events in the life of God, the Absolute Being, in whose life

man's life is contained, so that man's sufferings are identical
with the sufferings of God. The question then becomes, Why
does God suffer? The answer proposed by Royce is that
suffering is a necessary part of the process by which God
achieves perfection.

In principle, Royce's approach to the solution of all the
philosophical problems with which he dealt was of this sort.
The Absolute is the standard by reference to which truth,
being, goodness and moral excellence are to be determined.
So, toward the end of his career, in *The Problem of
Christianity* (1913), it is the conception of "the beloved
community" which provides the unifying principle of Christian faith: the standard and the goal of all human aspiration.

Royce's absolute idealism did not remain unchallenged,
however, even by other idealists. Personal idealism, for
instance, has held that reality is personal and that the many
persons or selves are unique and irreducible. As developed by
George H. Howison, and continued by Borden Parker Bowne,
this brand of idealism, sometimes called personalism, has had a
long and distinguished career in American philosophy. Recent
versions of it have been presented by E. S. Brightman and
Peter Bertocci. Other idealists, outstanding in their time, have
been James E. Creighton, Mary Calkins, W. E. Hocking and J.
E. Boodin. Brand Blanshard may also be numbered in this
group.

Pragmatism.

The origins of pragmatism in America are usually assigned
to the discussions of the Metaphysical Society in Cambridge in
the 1870s, which included among its members Chauncey
Wright, John Fiske, Oliver Wendell Holmes, William James and
Charles Peirce. It was Peirce who took the lead in formulating
the philosophy to which the name pragmatism came to be
applied.

Peirce.

It was Peirce's article "How to Make Our Ideas Clear"

(1878), which introduced pragmatism to the public. As formulated by Peirce, the rule by which pragmatism proceeds to establish clarity for our ideas is: "consider what effects, which might conceivably have practical bearings, we conceive the object of our conception to have. Then our conception of these effects is the whole of our conception of the object." As applied to concepts employed by the scientist, this rule provides a specific procedure for determining their meaning. Thus a thing is called "hard" if it cannot be scratched by many other substances; or, using the rule of pragmatism, "if a given substance is hard, then it will scratch, but not be scratched by, many other substances." The "scratchability" of a substance constitutes the set of effects in terms of which its hardness is defined. Unless there exists some procedure, such as scratching, by which specific effects may be observed, "hard," and other similar ideas, are without meaning.

The significance of this doctrine of Peirce's is to be measured, however, not only by its application, as proposed by Peirce, to scientific concepts, but also by its employment, in a generalized form, by James, Dewey and others to a wide variety of data, by no means all of which could be called scientific.

James.

Indeed, it was not Peirce but William James (1842-1910) who brought pragmatism to the attention of the public and who provided it with a more broadly humanistic orientation. It was also James's use of the term "pragmatism" which finally led Peirce to call his theory "pragmaticism," a label which Peirce said he hoped was "ugly enough to be safe from kidnappers."

The differences between the pragmatism of James and Peirce stemmed basically from James's attempt to go beyond Peirce's conception of pragmatism as a theory of meaning to the point where it could be viewed, as well, as a theory of truth. Peirce had argued in his essay, "The Fixation of Belief," that the scientific method is the only reliable method for

arriving at beliefs which can be called true, with truth being
conceived as the outcome of scientific inquiry, prolonged,
ideally, to the point where all questions are answered and the
conclusions of all inquirers are the same. James interpreted
Peirce's views on this point, however, as involving essentially
an appeal to "expediency." As James put it in his *Pragmatism*
(1907), and reaffirmed it in *The Meaning of Truth* (1909),
"'The true' is only the expedient in the way of our thinking,
just as the right is only the expedient in the way of our
behaving. Expedient in almost any fashion, and expedient in
the long run and on the whole, of course." So conceived,
"pragmatism" becomes, for James, not only a way of arriving
at the meaning of concepts in general, but also − and most
importantly − at the concept of truth, in particular. An idea
or belief is true, said James, insofar as our holding it yields
results which make a specific difference in experience. Unless a
belief has "cash-value" in experience, and only to the extent
that it has such "cash-value," can it properly be called "true."
Thus, since belief in God, for instance, "works" or produces
results in experience which are, on the whole, satisfactory, this
belief is true, or (if one prefers) pragmatically justified. The
main point for James, however, was that the truth of a belief is
to be assessed, not in terms of some static norm, but in terms
of future experience in a world which is not only "unfinished," but which is in large part a consequence of the beliefs
which we hold about it. Our beliefs, hence, help to produce, as
well as report, the kind of world in which we live and the kind
of experience which we have.

Reactions to James's theory of truth were, predictably,
various. To his critics, such as Russell, Lovejoy and G. E.
Moore, his stated views represented a mare's nest of confusions
and contradictions. To others, however, what James put forth
was suggestive and challenging, and worthy of elaboration. To
the latter group belonged John Dewey.

John Dewey.

Dewey's version of pragmatism was such that he preferred

for it the name "instrumentalism." This was in keeping with his insistence that pragmatism was primarily a method for articulating the claim that the significance of any thought or species of reflection is to be found in its consequences rather than its origins, and that ideas are to be seen primarily as instruments by which man achieves satisfactory relations with various aspects of his experience. With a background shaped both by Hegel and William James's biological construction of experience, Dewey came to insist that human thought is primarily a tool for effecting survival in the struggle for existence and that such a tool is to be measured by its success in proposing means for solving human problems.

A major share of Dewey's polemic was directed against "the bifurcation of nature" into dualisms of various sorts, most of which can be subsumed under the split between thought and action. In opposition to the Greco-medieval ideal of knowledge as a passive contemplation of static forms, or of God, Dewey proposed two major theses. On the one hand, rather than passive, thought is an active grasping and manipulation of the facets of experience for the purpose of synthesizing conflicting factors originally apprehended as "felt difficulties," thus bringing about a satisfactory resolution of the initial conflict. Thought is a problem-solving activity. On the other hand, what is apprehended as "the world," is always a fluid complex within which is to be found a continually shifting variety of relationships with no single end or order which may be viewed as antecedently real, fixed, or permanent. Even as thought is an instrument for the furtherance of human action, so the world of human experience is a never-ending succession of challenges requiring continual revisions of past procedures as guides for future responses.

In moral theory and in his social and political philosophy, it was also Dewey's aim to make ideas relevant to the changing complex of human experience. He saw morality as an achievement of responsible selfhood whereby, in interaction with other selves, the individual achieves freedom from blind habit and irrational impulse, and directs his life by norms which have as their goal the production of conduct which is satisfying in the highest possible degree to all concerned. Democracy in its widest sense would be realized, Dewey felt, when the sharing of experience results in mutual satisfaction of common interests in a society of rational free men.

Pragmatism has continued as a force in American philosophy to the present time, notably in the work of such philosophers as C. I. Lewis and W. V. Quine. Though it is not at present among the influential movements in America, its effect is still noticeable in the form in which philosophical questions are posed and answers presented, mainly among those who are usually classed as analysts.

REALISM.

While some would date the appearance of realism in America as early as the pre-Civil War period when Scottish "Common Sense" realism came in by way of Princeton, the modern form, which flourished in the nineteen-twenties and thirties, was quite independent of the earlier version, and was, moreover, moved by different interests. Twentieth century realism was essentially a protest against idealism. Peirce and James inclined toward realism and both contributed various arguments to its development. Realism was fully launched with Ralph Barton Perry's article, "The Ego-Centric Predicament" (1910). Idealism, Perry argued, is fallaciously established on the fact that we can never examine any instances of a thing outside of its relationship to a consciousness to determine what it "really" is in itself. Since every examination of a thing presupposes a cognitive relationship to an ego, we are caught in the "ego-centric predicament." But, said Perry, this methodological predicament does not warrant the idealistic conclusion that the reality of a thing is constituted by its relationship to a knowing ego. So the way is open to the thesis of realism that there is a "real" world independent of the minds which seek to know it.

Realism itself, however, soon split into two schools. The first school, called "New Realism" — which came to include, besides Perry, W. P. Montague, E. B. Holt, W. T. Marvin, E. G. Spaulding and W. B. Pitkin – held to the reality of objects, both particulars and universals, independently of their being known, and to the claim that such objects are directly apprehended apart from any mediating copies or images. Such a version of realism quickly produced the objection that it is unable to account for error and illusion: if objects are immediately perceived, then what happens when what *appears* to be perceived does not in fact exist?

The other school, "Critical Realism," was also committed to the view that there are real objects apart from any relationship to minds which know or perceive them. However, the Critical Realists sought to meet the difficulty in accounting for error and illusion by holding that the object of perception is not identical with the object known, that there is an "idea object" present to consciousness, and that this "idea object" somehow mediates the mind's apprehension of the external physical, or metaphysical, object. Physical objects are known by inference rather than by direct apprehension.

The Critical Realists came to include a number of prominent American philosophers, such as George Santayana, A. O. Lovejoy, Roy Wood Sellars, J. B. Pratt and Durant Drake, but even the Critical Realists could not agree among themselves. One group, led by Santayana, held that the immediate objects of consciousness are eternal "essences" which are separate both from the mind and from the external things which they represent. Lovejoy and others maintained, however, that there are no such independently real essences, but that the mind knows by means of logical constructs of its own devising, based on sense data, as a bridge to physical reality.

What continued to plague the Critical Realists, however, was what turned Berkeley against Locke: the argument, namely, that if the mind can never know external, real objects directly, but only indirectly (if at all) by means of "essences," percepts or ideas, how can we be sure that there even exist external real objects? Even if we suppose that such objects exist, how can we ever be sure that our ideas or perceptions of them are in any sense accurate? As Santayana and Lovejoy both admitted (in different ways) the required conformity between ideas and things must ultimately rest on an assumption, or faith. Otherwise, it would seem, realism will have made a complete circle back to idealism.

Realism faded from the philosophical scene in America in the late 1930s as other issues seemed to be more worthy of attention and their resolution to promise greater success.

NATURALISM.

While realism in America is *passé*, another movement which emerged about the same time, has continued to show vitality down to the present. This is the view known as naturalism.

Naturalism may be characterized as the philosophical theory that, in principle, any and all data may be understood by means of a single type of explanation, namely that which has been employed most notably in the development of natural science; and that the traditional dualism between the temporal and the eternal, or the natural and supernatural, is to be uncompromisingly rejected. The "natural" alone is real, and natural causes and principles are both necessary and sufficient to explain the world of human experience.

It is important to see that naturalism in America is not to be identified with any of the movements so far considered. Dewey, for example, who is usually identified as a pragmatist, contributed to the development of naturalism. But Santayana, who, as we have seen, was a realist, was also an outstanding naturalist. Indeed naturalism has continued to flourish in various quarters in America while realism and, for the most part, pragmatism have ceased to be vital forces in philosophy today.

Besides Dewey and Santayana, naturalism has included such prominent philosophers as Frederick J. E. Woodbridge, Morris Cohen, W. P. Montague, Ernest Nagel, Sidney Hook, and J. H. Randall, Jr. Obviously, many differences may be found among the views of such diverse thinkers, but they are agreed on several tenets which are usually regarded as characteristic of naturalism in its American setting.

As its name suggests, naturalism is committed to the claim that nature is that by reference to which we may determine what is and what may be known. The scientific method has emerged as that method which, broadly conceived, has provided man with the instrument for gaining whatever insight he can achieve, not only into the workings of physical nature, but also of man and society. It is the one method which has fully and consistently vindicated itself, in contrast to the methods of authority, of mystical experience, and of appeal to self-evident truth, all of which have proved inadequate as bases on which to establish solutions for the problems which have beset mankind from its beginnings. Science has been man's salvation in the past, and it is his only hope for the future.

An important difference between American naturalism and some of its varieties (including materialism, with which it is often confused) is its rejection of "reductionism," the claim that the various qualities of "raw experience" can be reduced to some single quality or kind of thing (such as material atoms). While repudiating the supernatural (or anything non-natural), naturalism is also insistent that all the various qualities of things encountered in human experience deserve to be regarded as equally fundamental. What the physicist studies is no more real than what the painter depicts or the musician tries to capture in his compositions. Indeed the dualism between appearance and reality which has long been a favorite of philosophers has been shown by many naturalists to be simply a function of the context within which a type of data has been placed for the purpose of a given inquiry. There is no absolute context and hence no type of data which enjoys exclusive or even preeminent prestige.

It is along this line that many naturalists have carried out philosophical investigations of religious experience. James, Santayana, Dewey and J. H. Randall, Jr., have all written on this subject, although without any attempt to defend or rehabilitate traditional supernaturalism. Rather, they have attempted to show that religious experience embodies significant moral and aesthetic qualities and that these form a basic segment in man's life. In the same vein, Perry, Dewey, C. I. Lewis and others have argued that moral and other values have a natural basis and are integral components of the human world.

WHITEHEAD.

An important American philosopher of recent years, whose background was British, was Alfred North Whitehead (1861-1947). Unaffiliated with any single school or movement in philosophy, he brought a wide range of scientific knowledge to his philosophic productions, most of which were devoted to the construction of a speculative system. Such a system was necessary, he believed, to do justice to the insights of modern science and also to provide an adequate basis for man's religious, moral and aesthetic interests. These interests are poorly served, he maintained, by traditional concepts and categories derived from outmoted scientific cosmologies and metaphysical schemes. What was needed, Whitehead felt, and what he tried to supply, was a conceptual framework reflecting more accurately recent developments in man's thinking about himself and his world. The result was a series of writings employing, in some cases, a unique terminology, difficult to interpret, but more suitable, in his view, to the revised outlook he hoped to promote. More specifically, what Whitehead offered was a system to replace the mechanistic, absolutistic world view of Newton basic to so much of modern thought by one derived from Einstein's principle of relativity and incorporating an organic conception of nature. The result is a view of the cosmos in which process is a central feature and in which events are constituent elements of each other, as well as of the universe as a whole.

Recent Trends in American Philosophy

With the waning of the classic period in American philosophy, the influence of European movements has again become strong. Logical empiricism (positivism), linguistic analysis, existentialism and phenomenology have come prominently to the fore in recent years, although as often in the past, such British and/or Continental views have frequently been tempered to the American scene.

The brand of European philosophizing most widely accepted by American philosophers in the immediate past is what, broadly speaking, may be called analytic philosophy. This label covers not only linguistic analysis of the Oxford variety deriving from G. E. Moore and the later Wittgenstein, but also the positivism originating in the Vienna Circle of the 1920s. In this country the movement has been strengthened by the presence of expatriates such as Rudolf Carnap and Hans Reichenbach speaking for logical positivism; but at the same time positivism has many affinities with pragmatism and naturalism. C. I. Lewis and C. L. Stevenson, and more recently W. V. Quine and Nelson Goodman, have allied themselves with various facets of the theories of logic, language and the philosophy of science characteristic of the views of the positivists.

On the other hand, analysts opposed to the "formalism" of Quine, Goodman and Carnap, and adopting instead a criterion of meaning purporting to reflect ordinary language usage, have rejected the attempt to devise systems of discourse for the study of traditional problems in philosophy. Instead, they have sought to achieve clarity by exposing pseudo problems arising from various uses of key terms, such as "mind," "matter," and "evidence," with which philosophers have been concerned, and to solve, or understand, the remaining problems through such linguistic analysis. Norman Malcolm and Max Black at Cornell University have been among the more active proponents of this form of analytic philosophy.

Another European import which has attracted some support among American philosophers since the 1940s is existentialism. Its outstanding representative in this country was undoubtedly Paul Tillich, whose brand of existentialism was theistic. The writings of many European existentialists such as Sartre, Camus and Heidegger have also had some impact on American thought in recent years.

Phenomenology, an important school in Europe, also has been building its influence in America since the 1930s and is coming on more strongly, it seems, at the present time. Marvin Farber has been the major American philosopher active in advancing its fortunes on this side of the Atlantic.

It is obvious, of course, that any attempt to identify American philosophy by reference at any school or movement, past or present, is futile. Indeed what is most characteristic of it is its pluralism, and this trait will undoubtedly continue to be attached to it in the future.

On the other hand, it would be a mistake to view American philosophy, and to seek to understand it, as merely an extension of European models. Wherever philosophy having a European origin has taken root in America, it has shown a marked tendency to develop strains which only faintly resemble its parentage. As it continues to grow it also continues to be receptive to influences from all over the world, including the Orient. Indeed, it may be hoped that American philosophy will never manifest the provincialism and chauvinism displayed by many other nationalistically oriented philosophies in the world, past and present.

BIBLIOGRAPHY

Abell, Aaron I. *The Urban Impact on American Protestantism, 1865-1900.* Cambridge, 1943.

Adams, G.P. & W.P. Montague. *Contemporary American Philosophy.* New York, 1962.

Ahlstrom, Sydney E. *A Religious History of the American People.* New Haven, 1972.

-----, ed. *Theology in America; the Major Protestant Voices from Puritanism to Neo-orthodoxy.* Indianapolis, 1967.

Baritz, Loren. *Sources of the American Mind,* 2 vols. New York, 1966.

Barrett, C. *Contemporary Idealism in America.* New York, 1932.

Bentley, J.E. *American Philosophy.* Totowa, N.J., 1963.

Blau, Joseph, ed. *American Philosophical Addresses, 1700-1900.* New York, 1946.

-----. *Cornerstones of Religious Freedom in America.* Boston, 1949.

-----. *Men and Movements in American Philosophy.* New York, 1952.

Brumm, Ursula. *American Thought and Religious Typology.* New Brunswick, 1970.

Carter, Paul A. *Decline and Revival of the Social Gospel,* 2nd ed. Hamden, Conn., 1971.

-----. *The Idea of Progress in Recent American Religious Thought, 1930-1960.* Philadelphia, 1969.

-----. *Spiritual Crisis of the Gilded Age.* De Kalb, Ill., 1971.

Clebsch, William A. *From Sacred to Profane America.* New York, 1968.

Cohen, Morris. *American Thought, A Critical Sketch.* New York, 1968.

Commager, Henry Steele, ed. *Living Ideas in America.* New York, 1967.

Curti, Merle. *The Growth of American Thought*, 2nd ed. New York, 1950.

Dewey, John. *A Common Faith*. New Haven, 1934.

Dohen, Dorothy. *Nationalism and American Catholicism*. New York, 1967.

Dons, Edmund, ed. *Political and Social Thought in America, 1870-1970*. London, 1971.

Dougherty, J.P. *Recent American Naturalism*. Washington, 1960.

Easton, Loyd D. *Hegel's First American Followers—The Ohio Hegelians*. Athens, Ohio, 1966.

Edie, James M. *Phenomenology in America*. Chicago, 1967.

Ekirch, Arthur A., Jr. *American Intellectual History*. Washington, D.C., 1967.

Fisch, H.M., ed. *Classic American Philosophers: Peirce, James, Royce, Santayana, Dewey, Whitehead*. New York, 1951.

Frankel, Charles, ed. *The Golden Age of American Philosophy*. New York, 1960.

Gaustad, Edwin S. *American Religious History*. Washington, D.C., 1967.

Grant, George P. *Philosophy in the Mass Age*. New York, 1960.

Grob, G.N. *American Ideas*. New York, 1963.

Hall, Thomas C. *The Religious Background of American Culture*. Boston, 1930.

Haller, William. *The Rise of Puritanism*. New York, 1938.

Handy, Robert T. *A Christian America*. New York, 1971.

-----. *Protestant Quest for a Christian America, 1830-1930*. Philadelphia, 1967.

Heimert, Alan. *Religion and the American Mind*. Cambridge, 1966.

Herreshoff, David. *American Disciples of Marx*. Detroit, 1967.

Hofstadter, Richard. *Social Darwinism in American Thought*, rev. ed. Boston, 1955.

Hook, Sidney, ed. *American Philosophers at Work*. New York, 1956.

Hopkins, Charles H. *The Rise of the Social Gospel in American Protestantism 1865-1915.* New Haven, 1940.

Howe, Daniel Walker. *The Unitarian Conscience.* Cambridge, 1970.

Hudson, Winthrop S., ed. *Nationalism and Religion in America.* New York, 1970.

Jacobson, J. Mark. *The Development of American Political Thought.* New York, 1932.

James, William. *Varieties of Religious Experience.* New York, 1902.

Jones, Adam Leroy. *Early American Philosophers.* New York, 1958.

Kallen, H.M. *American Philosophy Today and Tomorrow.* New York, 1935.

Kurtz, Paul, ed. *American Thought Before 1900.* New York, 1968.

-----. *The American Philosophers,* 2 vols. New York, 1965.

-----. *American Philosophy in the Twentieth Century.* New York, 1968.

Learsi, Rufus. *The Jews in America.* Cleveland, 1954.

McCown, Chester C. *The Genesis of the Social Gospel.* New York, 1929.

Mann, Jesse. *Pragmatic Man.* Milwaukee, Wis., 1968.

Marnell, W.H. *Man-Made-Morals.* New York, 1966.

Mayer, Frederick. *A History of American Thought.* Dubuque, Iowa, 1950.

Mecklin, John M. *The Story of American Dissent.* New York, 1934.

Middlekauf, Robert. *The Mathers—Three Generations of Puritan Intellectuals, 1596-1728.* New York, 1971

Miller, Perry. *The New England Mind: From Colony to Province.* Cambridge, 1953; rpt. Boston, 1961.

-----. *The New England Mind: The Seventeenth Century.* Cambridge, 1954; rpt. Boston, 1961.

Muelder, W.G., Laurence Sears & A.V. Schlabach, eds. *The Development of American Philosophy,* 2nd ed. New York, 1960.

Niebuhr, H. Richard. *The Kingdom of God in America.* Chicago, 1937.

-----. *The Social Sources of Denominationalism.* New York, 1954.

Niebuhr, Reinhold. *The Nature and Destiny of Man.* 2 vols. New York, 1946; rpt. 1949.

-----. *The Self and the Dramas of History.* New York, 1955.

Novack, M., ed. *American Philosophy and the Future.* New York, 1968.

Padover, S.K. *The Genius of America, Men Whose Ideas Shaped Our Civilization.* New York, 1961.

Perry, R.B. *Characteristically American.* New York, 1949.

Persons, Stow. *American Minds: A History of Ideas.* New York, 1958.

-----. *Evolutionary Thought in America.* New Haven, 1950.

Peterfreud, S.P. *An Introduction to American Philosophy.* New York, 1959.

Reck, A.J. *New American Philosophers.* Baton Rouge, La., 1968.

-----. *Recent American Philosophy.* New York, 1964.

Reiser, O.L. *Man's New Image of Man.* Pittsburgh, 1961.

R   man, David, in collaboration with Reuel Denny & Nathan Glazer. *The Lonely Crowd.* Rev. ed. New Haven, 1969.

Riley, I.W. *American Philosphy, the Early Schools.* New York, 1907; rpt. New York, 1958.

-----. *American Thought.* New York, 1915.

Rogers, A.K. *English and American Philosophy Since 1800.* New York, 1922.

Roth, R.J. *American Religious Philosophy.* New York, 1967.

Santayana, George. *Character and Opinion in the United States.* New York, 1920; rpt. St. Paul, 1973.

-----. *Philosophical Opinion in America.* London, 1918.

Savelle, Max. *The Colonial Origins of American Thought.* Princeton, 1964.

Schneider, H.W. *A History of American Philosophy,* rev. ed. New York, 1963.

-----. *The Puritan Mind.* New York, 1930.

-----. *Religion in 20th Century America.* Cambridge, 1952.

-----. *Sources of Contemporary Philosophical Realism in America.* Indianapolis, 1964.

Sellars, Roy Wood. *Reflections on American Philosophy from Within.* Notre Dame, Ind., 1969.

Shea, Daniel B. *Spiritual Autobiography in Early America.* Princeton, 1968.

Sheldon, W.H. *America's Progressive Philosophy.* New Haven, 1942.

Smith, J.E. *The Spirit of American Philosophy.* New York, 1963.

Smith, J.W., and A.L. Jamison, eds. *Religion in American Life.* 4 vols. Princeton, 1961.

Stelzle, Charles. *The Church and Labor.* Boston, 1910.

Stokes, Anson P. *Church and State in the United States.* 3 vols. New York, 1950.

Sweet, William W. *The American Churches.* New York, 1947.

-----. *The Story of Religion in America,* rev. ed. New York, 1939; rpt. Grand Rapids, Mich., 1973.

Townsend, H.G. *Philosophical Ideas in the United States.* New York, 1934.

Van Wesep, H.B. *Seven Stages.* New York, 1960.

Walton, Hanes, Jr. *The Political Philosophy of Martin Luther King, Jr.* Westport, 1971.

Werkmeister, W.H. *A History of Philosophical Ideas in America.* New York, 1949.

White, M.G. *Social Thought in America,* 2nd ed. Boston, 1957.

Whittemore, R.C. *Makers of the American Mind.* New York, 1964.

Winn, R.B. *American Philosophy.* New York, 1955; rpt. Westport, Ct., 1968.

-----, ed. *Survey of American Philosophy.* New York, 1965.

CHAPTER FIVE

American Studies: The Discipline of Literature

American Literature
Rita K. Gollin

Since American literature offers entry into American life in all the senses in which literature mirrors life, connections between American literature and American studies are dense and extensive. Emerson was right to say that scriptures must be read in the light of the times in which they were written; but it is equally true that reading any "scripture" allows us to see something of the "light" by which it was written.

In obvious ways, literature written about its own time and place conveys homely details about how people lived – their houses, clothing, occupations, pastimes. And clearly, such details can implicitly suggest an author's underlying beliefs – about what men should strive for or take risks for; about what can be changed and what should be changed. Further, even a work not explicitly about its own time and place – a lyric poem, or a historical romance – can lead the student of American studies to valid inferences about the concerns of its author, and of his age. Even essentially formal or aesthetic questions can lead to broader issues: the question of why Charles Brockden Brown resorted to elaborate moral apologetics about his novels, for example; or why the American novel is typically open-ended in structure; or why its hero is usually an "anti-hero." Fiction most obviously lends itself to the American studies approach; but all forms and kinds of American literature can be read both as literature and as information about the civilization that produced it.

The student soon recognizes that American literature articulates the country's most profound intellectual and emotional concerns. One approach to the literature is to pursue a recurring attitude, theme, or technique. The problem of individual freedom and self-fulfillment arrived with the first settlers: they sought the free new world as an alternative to England, with its monarchy and political hierarchy, established religion, and limited economic opportunity; yet they retained respect for social and religious order, the habit of looking to the past for guidance, and a mistrust of emotions and imagination. Writers have articulated this tension from the beginning: they have made the case for the individual's goals and dreams, despite Puritan belief in innate depravity, or more recent assumptions that the universe is meaningless.

Recurrent in our literature is the figure of a lonely seeker, as R.W.B. Lewis describes him in *The New Adam*, trying to make the best of his second chance in the Eden of a fallen world; or as Ihab Hassan follows him into the twentieth century in *Radical Innocence*. He is usually outside organized society, in some sense an alien — an artist, a child, a woman, or an ethnic minority figure. He may select a companion, a teacher, a wife, but never expects to live happily ever after. Leslie Fiedler explores his frustrations in *Love and Death in the American Novel*. Society, which offers safety but imposes conformity, is antagonistic to his goals. If he finally accepts society it is more as a compromise than an achievement: A.N. Kaul, in *The American Vision*, examines the discrepancy between man's vision of an ideal society and his sad acceptance of actuality.

The American writers' commitment to individual freedom and self-fulfillment has led them to condemn exploitation of any human being, whether for financial or psychological gain. They have deplored destruction of nature — the cutting of the trees in the fiction of Cooper and Faulkner, for example; but the real villains of American literature are those who exploit people — Judge Pyncheon in *The House of the Seven Gables* or

Gilbert Osmond in *The Portrait of a Lady*.* Implications of this generalization are important and largely unexplored; and it is equally applicable to literature about southern slavery, industrial wage slavery, or discrimination against minorities.

Focus on the experience of the unique individual necessarily affects style and structure. The language at its best, whether poetry or prose, is colloquial but flexible, ranging from formal to lyric to vernacular speech; this range and its implications Tony Tanner examines in *The Reign of Wonder*. The world the lonely seeker moves through is open rather than closed — the prairie, the forest, the ocean, rather than the town; and the form of the novel or poem that presents him is also typically open rather than closed, experimental rather than derivative. Any plot line tends to be a chronological thrust, a voyage through the real world, often equated with a voyage through the self. The voyage is rarely concluded: one stage may end, but it usually anticipates a further stage of ongoing effort.

Second only to American literature's concentration on the individual search for self-fulfillment is its celebration of the western encounter; that is, confrontation with some frontier not yet shaped by genteel society. From the time of the first settlers, Americans have always had the challenge to action and imagination of vast, unexplored territories. There has always been some invitation for a young man to go west, some opportunity for glory, whether the Indian-filled forest, the central plains, the western mountains, Alaska, or the moon. The effect on literature has been multiple: it has stimulated romance, realism, and humor. Americans have always had a predilection for romance, as Richard Chase describes it in *The American Novel and Its Tradition*, a desire to reach beyond the ordinary to unusual and challenging people, places, and actions, and the West has fed that appetite. From the times of

---

*In later American literature, the "culprits" of exploitation are not necessarily individuals — but sometimes war, society's mores, industrial complexes, etc.

Brown, Cooper, Poe, and Melville to Faulkner, Mailer, and Dickey, American writers have fashioned viable myth from wild nature (an Indian, a bear, a whale, a river). Primitivism is recurrent in American literature, which celebrates wild nature, violent action, strong men, strong emotions. The frontier itself, free from intrusions of gentility and open to physical surprise, resulted not only in romance but also in western humor, long before Twain and continuing after Faulkner. Its characteristic iconoclasm, irreverence, comic exaggeration, colorful dialect, physical violence, and riotous rambunctiousness recur frequently. Selections are found in such works as Walter Blair's *Native American Humor,* and Constance Rourke analyzes these characteristics in her *American Humor.* Further, from the first promotional literature the colonial writers sent back to England, American literature has tried to tell in precise detail about the new world, and in this sense the experience of the West has been a force for realism. Henry Nash Smith's *Virgin Land* is a seminal study of the effects of the idea of the frontier on the popular mind and literature of the nineteenth century; C.L. Sanford's *The Quest for Paradise* studies the Edenic myth in American culture; Edwin Fussell's *Frontier* examines how some major nineteenth century writers used the idea of the West; and Lucy Hazard's *Frontier in American Literature,* though dating from 1927, is still valuable, especially for the "new regionalism" of the early twentieth century.

A third major attribute of American literature is symbolism, a way of rendering a world of meaning and experience beyond nature and "real" experience. The symbolic habit of mind came to America with the first Puritans, who had been taught to read nature as God's book, so a phenomenon such as the celestial A in *The Scarlet Letter* was immediately assumed to be a divine message. Symbolism also flourished in the early and middle years of the nineteenth century, in Poe's poetry and prose, and in the writings of the Transcendentalists, themselves influenced by English and German romantics. The Transcendentalists believed that important realms of subjective and spiritual truths lie beyond the physical surfaces. Thoreau, for example, believing that man is in nature which is of God, and that all are interfused, could learn from Walden Pond about nature, his own nature, and ultimate spiritual truth. In *American Renaissance*, F.O. Matthiessen brilliantly explores the symbolism of some of our major writers; and Charles Feidelson in *Symbolism and American Literature* examines the epistemological and aesthetic implications of the symbolism of the Puritans and nineteenth century writers, carrying his study into the twentieth century.

Though symbolism varies in successive periods of American literature, it reinforces other recurring characteristics. Since symbolic significance necessarily spirals outward, it contributes to the open-ended suggestiveness of American literature, and in its richness and irresoluteness it is a component of romance. Less obviously, it contributes to the essential idealism of American literature, implicitly suggesting that an idea is superior to the material form which embodies it. This in turn is related to the moral bias of American literature, its praise of man's search for perfection. Thus symbolism is integral to American literature's thrust for self-fulfillment, for venture and adventure, on the frontiers of outer and inner experience.

These generalizations apply to the literature of each period of American literature, to each region of the country, and to each genre, despite important differences within each subdivision. They apply not only to the "good" literature but also to the less enduring literature which filled popular magazines and anthologies. For a detailed study of the development and composition of the magazines, see Frank Luther Mott's *History of American Magazines*, covering the period from 1741 to the present. For a study of the phenomenon and compositions of gift-books, see Ralph Thompson's *American Literary Annuals and Gift-Books: 1825-1865*. James D. Hart's *The Popular Book* is a thorough and entertaining study of developments in popular literary taste from the colonial period to the mid-twentieth century.

American literature can also be approached by the

traditional paths of literary history — tracing the varying and successive achievements of each period, its major authors, and perhaps its minor authors as well. Discussions of American literature as a whole must lean on the monumental composite work, *Literary History of the United States*, written by Robert E. Spiller and other distinguished scholars. Spiller's *The Cycle of American Literature* is concise and stimulating; Marcus Cunliffe's *Literature of the United States* is a good short survey. Vernon Parrington's *Main Currents in American Literature* subordinates aesthetic values to interest in social and economic ideas that animate the literature, yet for that reason it is valuable to the student of American civilization. Howard Mumford Jones's *Theory of American Literature* is helpful as a guide to all the successive literary histories; it explains, for example, the Marxism of V.F. Calverton, and the Freudianism of Ludwig Lewisohn.

Traditionally, American literature has been taught and studied in period divisions: early American literature, romanticism, realism, naturalism, modern literature, and contemporary literature. Genre studies necessarily overlap period courses or parallel them, whether in fiction, poetry, drama, or criticism. Study frequently concentrates on particular writers or groups of writers within a period or genre.

Scholarship in all these areas of American literature is proliferating rapidly. James Woodress in *Dissertations in American Literature, 1891-1966* notes that the number of dissertations has nearly doubled since his first compilation in 1957. This in turn suggests not only the increasing number of scholars in the field but the increasing specialization of articles and books offered for publication. Phenomenology, structuralism, and the women's movement have provided new approaches to literature; and textual studies and bibliographical compilations are now making special advances, in contrast to the 1940s and 1950s when "new critical" analyses dominated. But despite variations in technique and emphasis, scholars in every decade have drawn on social and intellectual history and biographical data as well as techniques of formal analysis.

Although most students of American civilization will not themselves engage in textual scholarship, they can benefit from using texts as close to the author's intentions and as free from publication error as possible. A current long-range effort involving hundreds of American scholars on dozens of university campuses is the establishment of definitive texts of major American authors. The Center for Editions of American Authors, through the Modern Language Association, is now sponsoring editions of Emerson, Hawthorne, Howells, Irving, Thoreau, Whitman, and the unpublished works of Twain. Other editions prepared under various academic auspices include the words of Melville, Cooper, Poe, Twain, Edwards, Brown, Simms, Frederic, Dreiser, Cable, and some Southwestern Humorists. Many of these scrupulously edited volumes are already available in paperback; obviously students should use such editions whenever possible.

During the period of early American literature, the term "literature" is applied more loosely than in any other: it includes promotional prose, polemical writing, histories, diaries, letters, and sermons. Little "pure" literature was written in the early days of the colonies: many believed it a waste of God's time to indulge the imagination; and the new country required diligent workers. Further, since books were easily available from England whether in original or pirated versions, whether purchased or borrowed from a library, the American writer could anticipate little social or financial reward. Yet, although seventeenth century writers were not primarily men of letters, but men who for various reasons recorded the facts and wonders of life in the new world, scholars have increasingly recognized that much of this early literature deserves attention not only as record and social fact but also as literature. The student of American studies should read this early literature as a unique response to new experience, which at the same time derives from earlier models. And he can observe how a work is informed by (or departs from) prevailing religious beliefs, such as the belief in innate depravity, or the view of life as a morality play. Students would do well to begin with a study of New England culture such as Alan Simpson's *Puritanism in Old and New England*, Perry Miller's *New England Mind*, or Kenneth Murdock's *Literature and Theology in Colonial New England*, before going on to more specific literary studies, such as Harold Jantz's *First Century of New England Verse* or Kenneth Silverman's *Colonial Poetry*.

The earliest literature both in Massachusetts and Virginia essentially records what American life was like. This took the form of diaries, such as John Woolman's *Journal* and Samuel Sewall's; histories, such as William Bradford's *Of Plymouth Plantation* and Winthrop's *History of New England*; and promotional literature intended to encourage immigration from England, such as John Smith's *The General History of Virginia, New England, and the Summer Isles*. Colonists also wrote documentary narratives, such as Mary Rowlandson's report of her Indian captivity; and social satire, such as Nathaniel Ward's criticism of women's fashions in "A Simple Cobbler of Aggawam." The sermon and the religious treatise are especially important in New England prose; notable are those of Roger Williams and Cotton Mather (also important for his historical and scientific work). And from the earliest colonial days, Americans wrote poetry, personal as well as devotional. Best known are the metaphysical poems of Edward Taylor, the personal poetry of Anne Bradstreet, and the sermonizing verse of Michael Wigglesworth; but there are many engaging minor poets also.

Fervent religious prose continued into the eighteenth century; most important are Jonathan Edwards' rhetorically powerful sermons and essays, building from strong personal conviction and from bases in Lockean psychology and Calvinist orthodoxy. With the development of the Enlightenment in the eighteenth century, distinguished prose is also written for political purpose and to encourage individual self-development. The student should confront the political affirmations of Thomas Paine and the Federalist papers; he will readily apprehend the intrinsic optimism, rationalism, and self-awareness of Franklin's *Autobiography* and *Poor Richard's Almanac*. Letters of travellers of American life, notably Crèvecoeur's *Letters from an American Farmer*, and Bartram's *Travels*, transmit detailed information about changing American life and values. Poetry widens its range to include the patriotic and satirical poetry of Philip Freneau and of the Connecticut Wits – chiefly John Trumbull, Timothy Dwight, and Joel Barlow. Original American drama begins with Royall Tyler's *The Contrast* (appropriately, a contrast of American innocence with European experience), although plays had been produced since colonial times. Most important, prose fiction emerges at the end of the century, not only in short stories but in novels – notably Hugh Brackenridge's satirical romance, *Modern Chivalry*, and – more significant and influential – the moralized Gothic novels of Charles Brockden Brown. Brown's tormented introspective heroes, moving in confusion through the American landscape, are literary ancestors of sensitive young men in the fiction of Poe, Hawthorne and Faulkner.

With the nineteenth century, American literature moves beyond a provincial identity. The preceding two centuries produced some literature of intrinsic interest, but the next half-century gave the country and the world major writers and major works of literature. The reasons for the flowering (especially in New England), and its profound effects on subsequent literature, have engaged the minds of some of our best scholars and critics. (Most of the books in Section E of the bibliography at the end of this chapter concentrate on writers of this period). F.O. Matthiessen's *American Renaissance* is the most probing and suggestive study of the period and some of its major authors; Van Wyck Brooks in *The Flowering of New England* tries to convey the complexity and excitement of the period and its writers.

As the American nation became more firmly established and began its thrust westward, writers became increasingly exploratory and innovative. In part this must be explained in the context of European romanticism, particularly German philosophy and English poetry. Americans felt released from the dogmas of Calvinism, and were optimistic about the country's possibilities for progress and reform. The dominant philosophical approach was idealistic; experiment and organic form characterize the literature. Writers felt encouraged to explore their inner and outer worlds of experience: they trusted the imagination as a valid mode of experience, and with delight and curiosity contemplated the homely details of nature and daily life. Like European romantics, American writers of both prose and poetry also reached into the exotic world of long-ago-and-far-away, and into the facts and legends of the American past.

The early romantic poet, William Cullen Bryant, celebrated both wild and gentle nature, finding moral consolation as well as knowledge and pleasure in the movements of a waterfowl or a violet. Washington Irving, America's first belletrist, produced successful sketches and romantic tales about the Spanish past, and even more firmly made his reputation by his legends of the Hudson Valley. James Fenimore Cooper demands attention as a prolific and successful novelist, especially for his series of Leatherstocking Tales, panoramic novels which convey detailed yet mythic and moralizing versions of frontier life, with its Indians, its buffaloes, its pioneers. Poe is the most quintessentially romantic writer of them all. He exploited the terrors and delights of the individual sensibility in his Gothic tales, his love poems and other lyrics, his detective stories (in which he pioneered), and his one journey novel, as David Halliburton demonstrated in his seminal study, *Edgar Allan Poe: A Phenomenological View* (1973). He opened for Americans new dimensions of intense emotion, yet he also formulated standards for literary criticism that remain valid (despite some curious and questionable specific critical judgments). He was one of the first writers to try to support himself as a man of letters; his meager livelihood as he edited and wrote for southern and northern periodicals suggests important extrinsic questions for study.

Transcendentalism requires separate attention for its influential ideas and its influential writers. Ralph Waldo Emerson, spokesman for the movement, wrote essays which explained his belief in correspondence between the world of nature, God, and the self, and urged self-reliance, individual fulfillment, trust of intuitions and emotions, and the aesthetic criterion of organic growth. His lectures, essays, and poems made him a figure of importance well beyond the limits of his home in Concord, and he was acclaimed as a leading author not only in America but also in England. Henry David Thoreau had little literary fame during his years in Concord, but he has won it since. His experiment in simple living described in *Walden,* continues to win thoughtful readers, as do his journals and poems; and his essay "Civil Disobedience," urging that conscience takes precedence over civic law, has been consistently influential in civil rights movements from Ghandi's through to the present. Other Transcendentalists — the Channings, Bronson Alcott, Jones Very, Margaret Fuller — merit study as their beliefs informed not only their writings but their lives; many worked for reforms in education and women's rights, for abolition, for penal reform; they established the Utopian community of *Brook Farm,* and the high-minded periodical, *The Dial.* Perry Miller's *The American Transcendentalists* is an excellent anthology with discriminating introductions.

The two giants of the period, Hawthorne and Melville, have received and still require meticulous critical and scholarly attention. Critics during the last fifty years have been challenged by their tragic vision, their perception of man's agonies of moral choice. They have been studied in the context of their religious heritage (especially Calvinism), their literary precedents (especially Gothic and sentimental fiction), and their life histories, as well as through their writing. Scholars have investigated their effects on each other and their relationships with other literary men; more can be learned about their involvement with politics and patronage, publishers, and literary coteries. Most helpful are studies like F.O.

Matthiessen's *American Romanticism* or Richard Chase's *The American Novel and its Tradition,* which study the authors' symbolic methods, their heroes' struggles for self-knowledge and metaphysical quests, and their belief that although mortality precludes perfection, the struggle toward the absolute must go forward. The student can test these generalizations against their greatest novels, *The Scarlet Letter* and *Moby Dick;* but they apply equally to all their fiction and their letters, journals, and poetry. Modern awareness of the complexities of man's inner life, as in Simon Lesser's *Fiction and the Unconscious,* has led to new comprehension of Hawthorne's characters and their problems of choice. Melville's poetry has only recently claimed serious critical attention; and studies of point-of-view such as Wayne Booth's *Rhetoric of Fiction* have suggested new ways of comprehending Melville's narrative methods.

The once-famous New England romantics, Longfellow, Lowell, Whittier, and Holmes, still merit study as good craftsmen who celebrated native traditions past and present and criticized human folly. Longfellow was the country's most famous poet; Lowell was a scholarly editor and critic, as well as satirical poet; Whittier, a Quaker who favored the abolitionist cause, wrote poems of rural life; and the urbane Brahmin, Dr. Holmes, wrote witty essays and poems, and novels which draw on his medical knowledge of mental aberration. They have received relatively little recent critical attention, but their urbane confrontations of American life deserve close examination. Among the scores of minor romantics are sentimental regional writers, many of them women, who maintained genteel standards of morality and didacticism. To suggest wide avenues for study, take the example of Sarah Josepha Hale, a successful poet and anthologist who, as editor of *Godey's Ladies' Book* not only instructed women in culture and domestic graces but also published literature by some of our leading authors. Her novel, *Northwood* (1828), celebrates New England village life but at the same time evaluates the morality and economy of southern plantation life. Because she believed

in reform from within the South, led by enlightened plantation owners, in 1852 she expanded and reissued *Northwood* as
an answer to Harriet Beecher Stowe's bestselling novel, *Uncle
Tom's Cabin.*

The Southwestern Humorists, direct precursors of Mark
Twain, also flourished in this pre-Civil War period — Long-
street, Thorpe, Hooper, and most important, George Washington Harris. For the burgeoning newspapers, they wrote short
and energetic vernacular tales, ambivalently celebrating the
adventures of rogues, con men, and mighty hunters, in this
vast and rapidly changing country.

America's great poet, Walt Whitman, belongs to the period
but overstrides it. In many ways he practiced what Emerson
preached: he sang himself and so sang America, trying to omit
nothing, whether sordid or glorious. He celebrated the
continuum of all life: man and all men; nature in all its forms;
and the realm of spirit. He used diction new to poetry and
stretched the poetic line to new lengths, echoing the Bible,
opera, the ocean, and vernacular speech; his poems were
shaped not according to some arbitrary pattern, but followed
the demands of organic form. Yet his poems also chronicle the
agony of the Civil War, and disillusionment with the country's
increasing materialism in the postwar years. He thus looks
backward to the exuberance of the early romantic period and
forward to the tough-minded and experimental poets of our
own day. His prose also looks both ways: the 1855 Preface to
Leaves of Grass is gloriously optimistic about the possibilities
of democracy; while "Democratic Vistas" (1871) somberly
criticizes the country's moral and political corruption.

The Civil War provides a valid beginning date for American
realism; postwar self-consciousness directed writers' attention
to the look and feel of regional life. The realistic writers worry
about man in society and sometimes man in nature, but rarely
about divinity or eternity. They are accurate but selective in
their details of setting, character, action, and dialect, conveying the feeling of what it was like to be an American in the
post-Darwinian world of urban development and industrial

growth, when materialism and political corruption were rampant. Henry Nash Smith's *Popular Culture and Industrialism, 1865-1890* is a useful study of the daily concerns of the period. The major realistic writers — each unique — are Mark Twain, William Dean Howells, and Henry James.

Mark Twain, the first famous American writer born west of the Mississippi, is realistic in his celebration of direct sensual response to experience, especially in his most famous book, *The Adventures of Huckleberry Finn.* His people talk in dialect; they are superstitious, gullible, self-seeking; nature is not always beautiful or helpful to man. Credible people engage in believable actions; and we know just how the sky looked in a thunderstorm. *The Gilded Age,* the novel Twain wrote in collaboration with Charles Dudley Warner, satirically exposes the corruption of the period named by the novel. And in *Roughing It* he conveyed, albeit with the exaggeration of western humor, the sense of life in the "wild West." Only recently have critics begun to comprehend his mastery of narrative point of view, the pessimism implicit even in his early humorous writing, and his profound ambivalence about slavery and about the claims of genteel society. Kenneth Andrews' *Nook Farm* is an excellent study of Twain's life in that culturally elite Hartford community during his most successful years, including the time of his successful reading tour with George Washington Cable. The phenomenon of the reading tour itself, like the Lyceum lecture, requires further study.

William Dean Howells was born in the Midwest but came east to make his long literary career. His fiction unfolds in a more urbane and at the same time more domestic setting than his friend Twain's. In the Boston of *The Rise of Silas Lapham* we observe people from different social levels as they conflict with one another and with their own goals and social mores. We know what kind of conversation characterizes each family dinner table, and are invited to condemn hypocrisy and applaud honesty. As an important theorist and critic of realism in fiction, Howells contended that novelists should stress the "smiling aspects" of American life because they were most characteristic; yet, as in *A Hazard of New Fortunes,* he

introduced sad new problems of city life — slums, impover-
ished immigrants, conflicts between capitalists and workers,
political radicalism, and the corrupting morality of get-rich-
quick businessmen. His novels raise important questions about
individual moral responsibility and social complicity, and his
social satire leads directly through Edith Wharton to Twentieth century writers such as John P. Marquand.

   Although Henry James' fiction concentrates on manners of
the upper reaches of society, James is nevertheless a psychological realist in his unfaltering recognition of human limitations that preclude self-fulfillment, and in his close attention
to subjective response, to nuance of behavior, and to problems
of communication and trust between individuals. His long
career as novelist (as well as critic and, briefly and unsuccess-
fully, dramatist) both in America and abroad, merits even
more analysis than his many astute critics have provided; we
need fuller understanding of the forces which shaped his
imagination, such as art and architecture, the fiction of
Hawthorne, his father's Swedenborgianism, the pressures of his
talented family, and his own neuroses. The many volumes of
Leon Edel's biography of James are only now beginning to
reveal the profound personal problems that help explain his
heroes' anguish. Edith Wharton is one of the important
novelists who learned from James' fictional techniques; Mil-
licent Bell's *Edith Wharton and Henry James* is an exemplary
chronicle of their friendship.

   The fiction of the local colorists, including Joel Chandler
Harris, Bret Harte, Mrs. Stowe, Edward Eggleston, Sarah Orne
Jewett, George Washington Cable, Thomas Nelson Page, and
Kate Chopin, accurately renders the dialect, manners, and
geography of their various regions. The new periodical,
American Literary Realism, has begun to compile bibliographies for authors of the period; now their social and political
assumptions merit further attention. Many attacked the
materialism and corruption of "The Gilded Age": Henry
Adams blasted the hypocrisies of Washington politics in his
novel *Democracy,* and pondered more crucial problems of

American culture in his autobiography, *The Education of Henry Adams;* A.W. Tourgee attacked southern racism in his novels of the Reconstruction. Edmund Wilson's *Patriotic Gore,* concentrating on writers of the Civil War period, has stimulated new interest in these writers and others who had previously received little critical attention (including Harold Frederic and William de Forest), as well as new understanding of such familiar figures as Abraham Lincoln and Harriet Beecher Stowe.

Two unique poets of this period seem alike only in intense dedication to their craft. Sidney Lanier's sufferings and ideals are those of the South: a captured confederate soldier, debilitated by tuberculosis, he was nonetheless a professional flutist who conceived of poetry as a form of music, and wrote poems based on his own metrical theories. In many ways — including his arraignment of trade as the source of evil — he anticipates the Southern Agrarians. The isolated and intense life and poetry of a New England spinster, Emily Dickinson, suggests a wholly different world. She recalls Emerson and Thoreau in stressing the individual attempt at self-fulfillment, pressing beyond time to eternity; yet she looks forward to our own time in her unsentimental confrontation of spiritual anguish, her homely images and diction, and her tight yet metrically experimental lines. Virtually unpublished and unknown until after her death in 1886, Emily Dickinson is now accepted as one of America's major poets. That she won this reputation first in France (as did Poe and subsequently Faulkner) suggests curious questions about literary fame in America.

Of course, there is no sharp division between realism and naturalism; yet naturalism — stretching from the 1890s well into the twentieth century — differs from realism in its greater pessimism and determinism. Man is envisaged as a victim of chance and the forces of heredity and environment, often devoid of will and intelligence. The naturalist feels free to explore themes previously banned from polite literature and to reach into low life for characters, action, even dialogue. An obvious approach to the literature of naturalism is through the history of ideas, especially the theories of Darwin and Spencer; another is through literary history, tracing the influence of Continental writers — Tolstoy, Balzac, and especially Zola; a third is through social history, especially the growth of the cities and industry. The fullest studies of naturalism are Lars Ahnebrink's *Beginnings of Naturalism in American Fiction* and Charles C. Walcutt's *American Literary Naturalism*; but more exact critical distinctions have yet to be made. The major writers — each widely divergent in subject and style — are Stephen Crane, Frank Norris, and Theodore Dreiser; others include Jack London and Hamlin Garland. That some critics stretch the period forward to such proletarian novels of the 1930s as James T. Farrell's *Studs Lonigan* trilogy or John Steinbeck's *The Grapes of Wrath* suggests some problems of definition yet unresolved.

Stephen Crane's tersely ironic fiction and poetry presents individuals unaware of their own pettiness and motivated by group pressures and their own uncomprehended emotions, yet all capable of dignity and generosity. This is equally true of his first novel, *Maggie*, about a slum girl turned prostitute; his most famous work, *The Red Badge of Courage*, about a young soldier undergoing trial by battle; and his short stories and poems. Frank Norris' novels insist on the destructiveness of the animal pressures within man and of the natural and social forces that surround him, notably *McTeague*, about a brutalized San Francisco dentist, and *The Octopus*, which probes economic pressures — especially from the railroad monopoly — on California wheat farmers. Theodore Dreiser's novels, from *Sister Carrie* on, show man as the pathetic victim of social and natural forces, who nevertheless merits compassion. Though stylistically pedestrian and morally enervating, these strong, somber novels remain influential to the present day.

The novel of manners, continuing into the twentieth century, is related to naturalism in stressing the individual's role as victim, though it presents the victim within the context of established society. Thus Edith Wharton's vulnerable heroines in *The House of Mirth* and *The Age of Innocence* are defeated by the social codes of New York aristocracy. Comparable are Willa Cather's social chronicles of Nebraska pioneers, and Ellen Glasgow's about Virginians: each presents morally admirable individuals whose societies offer them no tolerable roles.

Some poets of the early twentieth century also are related to naturalism in their stress on the individual as victim. Edgar Lee Masters' once-famous *Spoon River Anthology* dramatizes the destructive hypocrisies of midwestern villagers. Edwin Arlington Robinson, in his terse vignettes about Maine characters or in his long Arthurian romances, contemplates man's tragic burden of self-knowledge; yet Robinson manages to assert an ultimate cosmic idealism.

Without breaking away from earlier movements, American literature crossed into the twentieth century with new bursts of creative energy in all genres, and from all parts of the country; and American literature itself emerged as a respectable subject for study and criticism. The student of twentieth century literature can choose from vast ranges of primary and secondary sources, including anthologies of critical articles devoted to a particular decade (e.g., the twenties), or to an author (e.g., Fitzgerald), or even to a single work of literature (e.g., *The Great Gatsby*).

The early decades of the twentieth century introduced many distinguished poets, and new magazines devoted either to the new poetry or to experimental literature in general. *Poetry, A Magazine of Verse* was founded in Chicago in 1912 and still continues. A mere list of some of the poets published in early issues suggests the high quality, the range, and experimental diversity of their poetry: they include Ezra Pound, T.S. Eliot, Robert Frost, Hart Crane, Amy Lowell, Carl Sandburg, Vachel Lindsay, and Edgar Lee Masters. The student can easily find secondary materials about particular movements in poetry (e.g. imagism), about particular regional influences, and about particular magazines, as well as about individual poets and their interrelationships. Louise Bogan's

Achievement in American Poetry, 1900-1950 is a useful general study.

The early twentieth century tradition stemming from Ezra Pound and the experimentalism of the twenties is that each poet finds his own voice while working in a tightly-controlled, explicatable rhetorical style. The major poets writing in this tradition are Pound, insisting on words as hard objects; Wallace Stevens, exploring the aesthetic imagination; and T.S. Eliot, writing poems about dissociated sensibility. Others include E.E. Cummings, William Carlos Williams, and the early Robert Lowell. More recently, and especially during the fifties, a new group of poets has been writing in the traditions of Walt Whitman and Hart Crane: they write in an open declarative style, with open indignation about American social injustice and the quality of American life. These poets — Allen Ginsburg, Lawrence Ferlinghetti, and many others — have affected the styles of such older poets as John Berryman and Robert Lowell in ways that remain to be studied, as does the relation of their poetry to the older ideal of genteel self-sufficiency. These poets and trends are the frequent subject of articles in contemporary literary quarterlies.

In 1916 Eugene O'Neill, America's first important playwright, saw *Bound East for Cardiff* produced by the Provincetown Playhouse first on Cape Cod and then in Greenwich Village. For eight more years, until 1924, the Provincetown group produced his experimental plays; subsequently others were produced on and off Broadway even after his death in 1953. During the twenties, small regional and experimental theaters emerged all over the country, and even Broadway welcomed the "new drama." Such young playwrights as Elmer Rice, Sidney Howard, Maxwell Anderson, and S.N. Behrman reached an early maturity. During the depression years of the thirties, a more socially conscious drama emerged, as in Clifford Odets' plays, produced by the Group Theatre, and in the plays of the government-sponsored Federal Theatre. Since the Second World War, three playwrights have joined O'Neill in achieving international fame — Arthur Miller, Tennessee

Williams, and more recently, Edward Albee. At each period
these writers' relationships with theatrical groups and their
concern with contemporary problems need study. Useful
general introductions to these developments are Arthur Hobson Quinn's *A History of the American Drama,* and (more
recent but less detailed) Alan Downer's *Fifty Years of
American Drama.*

The importance of fiction in the early years of the
century, especially after World War I, is suggested simply by
listing novelists whose careers first began at that time: Ernest
Hemingway, F. Scott Fitzgerald, John Dos Passos, William
Faulkner, Sherwood Anderson, and Sinclair Lewis. Their
major achievement has been approached in many ways: for
those who went abroad after the war, there are accounts of
their expatriate existence (e.g., Sylvia Beach's *Shakespear &
Co.,* and Hemingway's *A Moveable Feast),* and accounts of
what happened when they returned home (e.g., Malcolm
Cowley's *Exile's Return),* as well as many judicious critical
assessments of their work. Those who, like Sinclair Lewis,
stayed at home and criticized village and urban stultifying
mediocrity are less glamorous and so have received fewer
separate studies, while Faulkner's magnificent fictional Yoknapatawpha County has demanded astute critical attention;
yet, of course, all figure in such general studies as Frederick
Hoffman's *The Modern Novel in America* and Alfred Kazin's
On Native Grounds. These studies go forward into the
proletarian literature of the thirties and forties; but Walter
Rideout's *The Radical Novel* is a useful special account which
includes many unfamiliar names, and others only recently
familiar, such as Henry Roth. The forties was a period of
moral reassessment, as discussed in essays edited by Scully
Bradley, *The Arts in Renewal,* and in Chester E. Eisinger's
detailed analysis, *Fiction of the Forties.* Fiction of the fifties
and thereafter — by writers including Saul Bellow, Bernard
Malamud, John Updike, and Philip Roth — is still so close that
distinctions are hard to make; yet one may find Marcus Klein's
After Alienation a thoughtful study and Ihab Hassan's *Radical*

Innocence a provocative one.

The regional approach to literature of the twentieth century is most applicable to the South, which for the last half century has been enjoying its own literary renaissance. First came the Vanderbilt-based fugitive poets (their work ably studied by John Bradbury in *The Fugitives* and by Louise Cowan in *The Fugitive Group).* Subsequently some of these poets — including John Crowe Ransom, Robert Penn Warren, and Allen Tate — cooperated as part of a group of thirteen Southerners who urged the South to return to a pre-industrial, agrarian way of life; *I'll Take My Stand* is their manifesto. Most of these writers subsequently left the South for academic careers elsewhere, continuing to write distinguished poetry, fiction, and criticism; but their identity as Southerners remains.

The Southern achievement in fiction is prodigious: it includes the rambling autobiographical novels of Thomas Wolfe, the moralizing romances of Robert Penn Warren, and the richly diverse novels and short stories of a remarkable group of women — Katherine Anne Porter, Carson McCullers, Eudora Welty, and Flannery O'Connor. Most important, of course, is the work of William Faulkner, whose novels of Yoknapatawpha County reach backward in time to include the country's past and deep within the individual mind to engage all readers, so that Faulkner is simultaneously Southern, national, and universal.

Americans in the twentieth century have been taught by many divergent and even antagonistic schools of critics. Some read literature as a reflection of life, including Van Wyck Brooks, Max Eastman; and H.L. Mencken, who acidulously attacked prudery and pretense wherever he found it. The neo-humanists, notably Irving Babbitt and Paul Elmer More, rejected the values of both romanticism and science, turning instead to more traditional humane ethics and classical literary standards. The school whose influence has extended even into the elementary schools is the "New Criticism," formulated by the southern agrarians, Warren, Tate, Brooks, and Ransom.

These critics approach each work of literature as a discrete world of meaning and experience which can be understood through examination of its structure, texture, images, symbols, and diction. Brooks and Warren's *Understanding Poetry* has taught students and teachers the art of such formal exegesis since 1938. At the same time, the Chicago school of criticism offered structural criticism with an Aristotelian base, and many distinguished critics have worked outside these groups — including Edmund Wilson, Yvor Winters, Richard Blackmur, and Kenneth Burke; but all insist on the importance of literature and thus of the act of criticism. There are many good anthologies of American criticism, including M. D. Zabel's *Literary Opinion in America;* and such works as Stanley Edgar Hyman's *The Armed Vision,* Murray Krieger's *The New Apologists for Poetry*, and William Van O'Connor's *An Age of Criticism: 1900-1950* make judicious critical analyses of the critics.

American literary scholarship has changed along with American literature. Early nineteenth century critics measured American literature by English standards, cited the "beauties" of a literary work, and provided details of the author's life. Poe was ahead of his time in seeking the organic unity of a literary work. The cry for a national literature began early in this country, and by the 1830s critics stressed the particularly *American* qualities of a work — its setting, character, dialogue. The criterion of moral decency prevailed into the present century, when it was displaced by interest in literary experimentation. Increasing sophistication of analysis and increasing response to tragic conflicts between man's aspirations and his achievements has led to new appreciation of the writers now considered our classic authors — Poe, Hawthorne, Melville, Twain, Whitman, James, Dickinson and Crane, as well as Eliot, Hemingway, Fitzgerald, and Faulkner. The depression years returned critical attention to the moral attributes of ordinary Americans and led to praise of writers such as John Steinbeck. With the 1940s, the formalist "New Critical" aesthetic prevailed. Currently, critics still seem interested in image clusters and symbolic patterns, but more in the author's voice, consciousness, and point-of-view, and the handling of time structure and chronology.

One notes a resurgence of interest in recent literature now securely in the past — that of the thirties and forties. Widespread literary attention has been given most recently to literature by black writers and about blacks; this is comparable to earlier interest in Jewish literature. For some time now, the mid-twentieth century has seen increasing concern by novelists and critics alike for ethnic and other minority groups comprising the culture; since the early 1940s numerous American writers have depicted meaningfully the contributions of such minority groups and hyphenate Americans to the culture of which they are, whether by birth or adoption, an integral part. More recently, literature by and about women has commanded special attention. It remains to be seen what new directions such interests will take. The only constant is change and diversification, both in American literature and scholarship.

BIBLIOGRAPHY

Aids to Research

Blanck, Jacob. *Bibliography of American Literature.* 10 vols. [In progress] New Haven: Yale Univ. Press, 1955.

Bradbury, Malcolm, *et al.,* eds. *Penguin Companion to American Literature.* New York: McGraw-Hill, 1971.

Evans, Charles. *American Bibliography: a Chronological Dictionary of all Books, Pamphlets and Periodical Publications Printed in the United States ...1639-(1800).* 14 vols. (1903-55) New York: P. Smith, 1941-67.

Gerstenberger, Donna, and George Hendrick. *Third Directory of Periodicals Publishing Articles in English and American Literature.* Chicago: Swallow, 1970.

Hart, James D. *The Oxford Companion to American Literature.* New York: Oxford Univ. Press, 1965.

Harte, Barbara, and Carolyn Riley, eds. *Two Hundred Contemporary Authors.* Detroit: Gale, 1969.

Herzberg, Max, *et al. The Reader's Encyclopedia of American Literature.* New York: Crowell, 1962.

Jones, Joseph, *et al. American Literary Manuscripts.* Austin: Univ. of Texas Press, 1960; rpt. 1971.

Kunitz, Stanley J., and Howard Haycraft, eds. *American Authors, 1600-1900.* New York: H.W. Wilson, 1938.

-----. *Twentieth Century Authors.* New York: H.W. Wilson, 1942. (Supplement, 1955)

Woodress, James. *Dissertations in American Literature 1891-1966.* Durham, N.C.: Duke Univ. Press, 1968.

Bibliographies

American Literature. Quarterly journal since 1929. Durham, N.C.: Duke Univ. Press. Each issue contains "Articles on American Literature Appearing in Current Periodicals." Analytic Index to Vols I-XXX, March 1929-January 1959.

Bryer, Jackson R. *Fifteen Modern American Authors: A Survey of Research and Criticism.* Durham: Univ. of North Carolina Press, 1969.

Charles E. Merrill Checklists. Columbus, Ohio: Charles E. Merrill. (Selected bibliographies of Crane, Dreiser, Emerson, Frederic, Frost, Hawthorne, James, Melville, Mencken, Poe.)

Gohdes, Clarence. *Bibliographical Guide to the Study of the Literature of the U.S.A.* 3rd ed. Durham, N.C.: Duke Univ. Press, 1970.

Goldentree Bibliographies. New York: Apleton-Century-Crofts.

Clark, Harry Hayden. *American Literature: Poe through Garland.* 1970.

Davis, Richard Beale. *American Literature through Bryant.* 1969.

Holman, C. Hugh. *The American Novel through Henry James.* 1966.

Long, E. Hudson. *American Drama from its Beginnings to the Present.* 1970.

Nevius, Blake. *The American Novel: Sinclair Lewis to the Present.* 1970.

Turner, Darwin T. *Afro-American Writers.* 1970.

Jones, Howard Mumford, and Richard M. Ludwig. *Guide to American Literature and its Backgrounds Since 1890.* 4th ed. Cambridge, Mass: Harvard Univ. Press, 1972.

Leary, Lewis G., ed. *Articles on American Literature 1900-1950.* Durham: Duke Univ. Press, 1954. *Articles 1950-1967,* 1970.

MLA International Bibliography. Published each spring as a supplement to PMLA. Sections on American literature.

Rubin, Louis D., ed. *A Bibliographical Guide to the Study of Southern Literature.* Baton Rouge, La.: Louisiana State Univ. Press, 1969.

Spiller, Robert E., *et al.,* eds. *Literary History of the United States: Bibliography.* New York: Macmillan, 1963.

Van Derhoof, Jack W. *A Bibliography of Novels Related to American Frontier and Colonial History.* Troy: Whitston, 1971.

Woodress, James, ed. *American Literary Scholarship: An Annual/1963.* Durham, N.C.: Duke Univ. Press, 1965; and annually since.

----, *et al.*, eds. *Eight American Authors: A Review of Recent Criticism.* New York: Norton, 1972.

Other helpful bibliographies may be found in the University of Minnesota pamphlets on American authors and the Twayne United States Authors Series.

Periodicals

American Literary Realism, 1870-1910

American Literature

American Quarterly

Modern Fiction Studies

New England Quarterly

Nineteenth Century Fiction

Twentieth Century Literature

Other periodicals publishing articles on American literature include *English Language Notes, Modern Language Notes, PMLA, Twentieth Century Literature, English Record, American Notes & Queries.*

Literary History

Cunliffe, Marcus. *The Literature of the United States.* Revised. Baltimore: Penguin, 1967.

Jones, Howard Mumford. *The Theory of American Literature.* (1948) Ithaca: Cornell Univ. Press, 1966.

Mott, Frank Luther. *A History of American Magazines.* 5 vols. Cambridge, Mass: Harvard Univ. Press, 1930-1968.

Parrington, Vernon Louis. *Main Currents in American Thought.* 3 vols. New York: Harcourt Brace, 1927-1930.

Spiller, Robert E. *The Cycle of American Literature.* (1955) New York: Macmillan, 1969.

-----, et al. Literary History of the United States. New York: Macmillan, 1963. Supplement, 1972.

Tyler, Moses Coit, A History of American Literature During the Colonial Time. (1897) Ithaca: Cornell Univ. Press, 1949.

-----. The Literary History of the American Revolution, 1763-1783. 2 vols. (1897) New York: Ungar, 1957.

Special Critical Approaches

Chase, Richard. The American Novel and Its Tradition. New York: Doubleday, 1957.

Feidelson, Charles, Jr. Symbolism and American Literature. Chicago: Univ. of Chicago Press, 1953.

Fiedler, Leslie A. Love and Death in the American Novel. (1960) New York: Dell, 1969.

Fussell, Edwin. Frontier: American Literature and the American West. Princeton: Princeton Univ. Press, 1965.

Hart, James D. The Popular Book: A History of America's Literary Taste. (1950) Berkeley: Univ. of California Press, 1963.

Hassan, Ihab. Radical Innocence: Studies in the Contemporary American Novel. Princeton: Princeton Univ. Press, 1961; rpt. 1971.

Hazard, Lucy. The Frontier in American Literature. (1927) New York: Frederick Ungar, 1960.

Hoffman, Daniel G. Form and Fable in American Fiction. New York: Oxford Univ. Press, 1961; Norton, 1973.

Hubbell, Jay G. The South in American Literature, 1607-1900. Durham, N.C.: Duke Univ. Press, 1954.

Kaul, A.N. The American Vision: Actual and Ideal Society in Nineteenth Century Fiction. New Haven: Yale Univ. Press, 1963.

Lawrence, D.H. Studies in Classic American Literature. (1923) New York: Viking, 1964.

Lewis, Richard W.B. The American Adam: Innocence, Tragedy, and Tradition in the Nineteenth Century. Chicago: Univ. of Chicago Press, 1955.

Marx, Leo. *The Machine in the Garden: Technology and the Pastoral Ideal in America.* (1964) New York: Oxford Univ. Press, 1967.

Rourke, Constance. *American Humor: A Study of the National Character.* (1931) New York: Harcourt Brace Javanovich, 1971.

Sanford, Charles L. *The Quest for Paradise: Europe and the American Moral Imagination.* Urbana: Univ. of Illinois Press, 1961.

Smith, Henry Nash. *Virgin Land: The American West as Symbol and Myth.* (1950) New York: Random House, 1957.

Tanner, Tony. *Reign of Wonder: Naivety and Reality in American Literature.* (1965) New York: Harper and Row, 1967.

Divisions by Period

Early American Literature

Emerson, Everett H., ed. *Major Writers of Early America.* Madison: Univ. of Wisconsin Press, 1972.

Howard, Leon. *The Connecticut Wits.* Chicago: Univ. of Chicago Press, 1943.

Jantz, Harold. *The First Century of New England Verse.* (1944) New York: Russell & Russell, 1962.

Miller, Perry. *The New England Mind: From Colony to Province.* (1953) Boston: Beacon, 1961.

Miller, Perry. *The New England Mind: The Seventeenth Century.* (1954) Boston: Beacon, 1961.

Murdock, Kenneth B. *Literature and Theology in Colonial New England.* Cambridge, Mass: Harvard Univ. Press, 1949.

Piercy, Josephine K. *Studies in Literary Types in Seventeenth Century America (1607-1710).* New Haven: Yale Univ. Press, 1939.

Silverman, Kenneth. *Colonial Poetry.* New York: Hafner, 1968.

Simpson, Alan. *Puritanism in Old and New England.* Chicago: Univ. of Chicago Press, 1955.

Winslow, Ola. *American Broadside Verse (1930).* Detroit: Singing Tree, 1969.

Wright, Louis B. *The Cultural Life of the American Colonies.* New York: Harper & Row, 1957.

Wright, Thomas G. *Literary Culture in Early New England.* (1920) New York: Russell and Russell, 1966.

in between ↗

Romantic Period

Frothingham, Octavius B. *Transcendentalism in New England: A History.* (1876) Philadelphia: Univ. of Pennsylvania Press, 1972.

Gohdes, Clarence. *The Periodicals of American Transcendentalism.* Durham, N.C.: Duke Univ. Press, 1931.

Matthiessen, F.O. *American Renaissance: Art and Expression in the Age of Emerson and Whitman.* (1941) New York: Oxford Univ. Press, 1968.

Miller, Perry. *The American Transcendentalists, Their Prose and Poetry.* (1950) New York: Doubleday, 1957.

Miller, Perry. *The Raven and the Whale: The War of Words and Wits in the Era of Poe and Melville.* New York: Harcourt Brace, 1956.

Realism and Naturalism

Aaron, Daniel. *The Unwritten War: American Writers and the Civil War.* New York: Knopf, 1973.

Åhnebrink, Lars. *The Beginnings of Naturalism in American Fiction: A Study of the Works of Hamlin Garland, Stephen Crane, and Frank Norris... 1891-1903.* (1952) New York: Russell and Russell, 1961.

Carter, Everett. *Howells and the Age of Realism.* Philadelphia: Lippincott, 1954.

Pizer, Donald. *Realism and Naturalism in Nineteenth Century American Literature.* Carbondale, Ill.: So. Illinois Univ. Press, 1966.

Smith, Henry Nash. *Popular Culture and Industrialism, 1865-1890.* New York: New York Univ. Press, 1967.

Walcutt, Charles Child. *American Literary Naturalism, A Divided Stream.* Minneapolis, Minn.: Univ. of Minnesota Press, 1956.

Wilson, Edmund. *Patriotic Gore: Studies in the Literature of the American Civil War.* New York: Oxford Univ. Press, 1962.

The Twentieth Century

Beach, Joseph Warren. *The Twentieth-Century Novel: Studies in Technique.* (1932) New York: Appleton, 1960.

Bradbury, John M. *Renaissance in the South: A Critical History of the Literature, 1920-1960.* Chapel Hill, N.C.: Univ. of North Carolina Press, 1963.

Cowley, Malcolm. *Exile's Return.* New York: Viking, 1951.

-----. *A Second Flowering: Works and Days of the Lost Generation.* New York: Viking, 1974.

Edel, Leon. *The Modern Psychological Novel.* New York: Grosett & Dunlap, 1964.

Hilfer, Anthony C. *The Revolt from the Village, 1915-1930.* Chapel Hill, N.C.: Univ. of North Carolina Press, 1969.

Hoffman, Frederick J. *The Art of Southern Fiction: A Study of Some Modern Novelists.* Carbondale, Ill.: So. Illinois Press, 1967.

-----. *Freudianism and the Literary Mind.* Baton Rouge, La.: Louisiana State Univ. Press, 1957.

-----. *The Modern Novel in America: 1900-1950.* Chicago: Henry Regnery, 1964.

Kazin, Alfred. *On Native Grounds.* (1942) New York: Doubleday, 1956.

-----. *Bright Book of Life: American Novelists and Story-tellers from Hemingway to Mailer.* Boston: Little, Brown, 1973.

Klein, Marcus. *After Alienation: American Novels in Mid-Century.* Cleveland and New York: World, 1964.

Rideout, Walter B. *The Radical Novel in the United States: 1900-1954.* (1956) New York: Hill and Wang, 1966.

Rubin, Louis D., Jr. *The Faraway Country: Writers of the Modern South.* Seattle, Wash.: Univ. of Washington Press, 1963.

Rubin, Louis D., Jr., and Robert D. Jacobs. *Southern Renascence: The Literature of the Modern South.* Baltimore: Johns Hopkins Press, 1953.

Straumann, Heinrich. *American Literature in the Twentieth Century.* New York: Harper and Row, 1968.

Tanner, Tony. *City of Words.* New York: Harper and Row, 1971.

Thorp, Willard. *American Writing in the Twentieth Century.* Cambridge, Mass.: Harvard Univ. Press, 1960.

Divisions by Genre

Novel

Bone, Robert A. *The Negro Novel in America.* New Haven: Yale Univ. Press, 1965.

Booth, Wayne. *The Rhetoric of Fiction.* Chicago: Univ. of Chicago Press, 1961.

Brown, Herbert Ross. *The Sentimental Novel in America 1789-1860.* Durham, N.C.: Duke Univ. Press, 1940.

Cooperman, Stanley. *World War I and the Novel.* Baltimore: Johns Hopkins Press, 1967.

Cowie, Alexander. *The Rise of the American Novel.* New York: American Book Co., 1948.

Eisinger, Chester E. *Fiction of the Forties.* Chicago: Univ. of Chicago Press, 1963.

Frohock, W.M. *The Novel of Violence in America.* (1957) Boston: Beacon, 1964.

Gelfant, Blanche H. *The American City Novel.* Norman, Okla.: Univ. of Okla. Press, 1954, rpt. 1970.

Gerstenberger, Donna and George Hendrick, *The American Novel; A Checklist of Twentieth Century Criticism on Novels Written Since 1789.* Vol. I: *Criticism Written 1900-1959.* Chicago: The Swallow Press, 1961. Vol. II: *Criticism Written 1960-1968.* Chicago, 1970.

Loshe, Lillie D. *The Early American Novel.* New York: Columbia Univ. Press, 1907.

Quinn, Arthur Hobson. *American Fiction: an Historical and Critical Survey.* New York: Appleton-Century-Crofts, 1936.

Rubin, Louis D., Jr., and John Reese Moore, eds. *The Idea of an American Novel.* New York: Thomas Y. Crowell, 1961.

Wagenknecht, Edward. *Cavalcade of the American Novel.* New York: Henry Holt, 1952.

Poetry

Bogan, Louise. *Achievement in American Poetry, 1900-1950.* Chicago: Regnery, 1951.

Bradbury, John M. *The Fugitives: A Critical Account.* Chapel Hill, N.C.: Univ. of North Carolina Press, 1958.

Cowan, Louise. *The Fugitive Group: A Literary History.* Baton Rouge: Louisiana State Univ. Press, 1968.

Gregory, Horace, and Mary Zaturenska. *A History of American Poetry, 1900-1940.* New York: Harcourt Brace, 1965.

Howard, Richard. *Alone with America: Essays on the Art of Poetry in the United States since 1950.* New York: Antheneum, 1970.

Jarrell, Randall. *Poetry and the Age.* New York: Octagon, 1972.

Mills, Ralph, Jr. *Contemporary American Poetry.* New York: Random House, 1965.

Murphy, Rosalie and James Vinson, eds. *Contemporary Poets of the English Language.* Chicago: St. James Press, 1970.

Pearce, Roy Harvey. *The Continuity of American Poetry.* Princeton, N.J.: Princeton Univ. Press, 1961.

Perkins, George, ed. *American Poetic Theory.* New York: Rinehart, 1972.

Waggoner, H.H. *The Heel of Elohim: Science and Values in Modern American Poetry.* Norman: Univ. of Oklahoma Press, 1950.

Drama

Clurman, Harold. *The Fervent Years.* New York: Knopf, 1945.

Downer, Alan. *Fifty Years of American Drama, 1900-1950.* Chicago: Regnery, 1951.

Herron, Ima H. *The Small Town in American Drama.* Dallas, Tex.: Southern Methodist U. Press, 1969.

Himelstein, Morgan Y. *Drama Was a Weapon: The Left-Wing Theatre in New York, 1929-1941.* New Brunswick, N.J.: Rutgers Univ. Press, 1963.

Hughes, Glenn. *A History of the American Theatre, 1700-1950.* New York: French, 1951.

Krutch, Joseph Wood. *The American Drama Since 1918.* New York: Braziller, 1957.

Meserve, Walter J. *An Outline History of American Drama.* Totowa N.J.: Littlefield, Adams, 1965.

Moses, Montrose J., ed. *Representative Plays by American Dramatists.* 3 vols. New York: Benjamin Blom, 1964.

Moses, Montrose J., and Joseph W. Drutch, eds. *Representative American Dramas.* Boston: Heath, 1941.

Odell, George C.D. *Annals of the New York Stage.* 15 vols. New York. Columbia Univ. Press, 1949.

Quinn, Arthur Hobson. *A History of the American Drama from the Beginning to the Civil War.* New York: Appleton, 1944.

-----. *A History of the American Drama from the Civil War to the Present Day.* New York: Appleton, 1937.

Rankin, Hugh F. *The Theater in Colonial America.* Chapel Hill: Univ. of North Carolina Press, 1965.

Rigdon, Walter. *The Biographical Encyclopedia & Who's Who of the American Theatre.* New York: Heineman, 1966.

Weales, Gerald. *American Drama Since World War II.* New York: Harcourt, Brace, and World, 1962.

Criticism

Charvat, William. *The Origins of American Critical Thought, 1810-1835.* (1936) New York: Russell and Russell, 1968.

Frailberg, Louis. *Psychoanalysis and American Literary Criticism.* Detroit: Wayne State Univ. Press, 1960.

Glicksberg, Charles Irving, ed. *American Literary Criticism 1900-1950.* New York: Hendricks House, 1952.

Hyman, Stanley Edgar. *The Armed Vision: A Study in the Methods of Modern Literary Criticism.* (1947) New York: Random House, 1955.

Krieger, Murray. *The New Apologists for Poetry.* (1956) Bloomington: Indiana Univ. Press, 1963.

-----. *Classic Vision: The Retreat from Extremity in Modern Literature.* Baltimore: Johns Hopkins Univ. Press, 1971.

O'Connor, William Van. *An Age of Criticism: 1900-1950.* Chicago: Regnery, 1966.

Stovall, Floyd, ed. *The Development of American Literary Criticism.* New Haven: College and University Press, 1955.

Sutton, Walter. *Modern American Criticism.* Englewood Cliffs, N.J.: Prentice Hall, 1963.

Zabel, Morton Dawen, ed. *Literary Opinion in America.* (1937) New York: Harper, 1962.

CHAPTER SIX

American Folklore

Mary Washington Clarke

American folklore, widely diversified in both content and expression, is an integral part of the fabric of American civilization. The enduring threads of tradition form the warp, inherited and conservative; the varied colors of the present form the woof, as each generation gives to its popular culture a unique blend of innovation and tradition that is endlessly in transition. Folklore is concerned with tradition: since traditional ideas and attitudes manifest themselves in action, and traditional behavior finds its rationale in beliefs and attitudes, American folklore is involved with all the ways of mankind in America, that can be termed cultural.

This universal quality of folklore does not, however, imply that anyone becomes an "instant folklorist" in his moment of discovering this truth any more than a person can qualify as an ethnologist the moment he recognizes that he has grown up in a culture. It does, however, suggest the wide-ranging appeal of a significant area for study in human affairs, an area of special relevance to American studies because of the phenomenal growth of the United States under the influence of so many and such diversified forces.

In the United States, traditions are many instead of one, for their origins were in many other countries. Anglo-American folklore is the most obvious, but Afro-American and Spanish-American come immediately to mind, and as one

141

contemplates the history and geography of the nation, he is made aware of many others. Just as a modern American family may derive from the immigrant stock of Germans, Poles, Italians, and Norwegians, so modern American folklore is a blend of imported materials, native American Indian materials, and the special historical and cultural circumstances which have influenced them.

The Material and its Study: Definitions

The academic discipline of folklore is sometimes called *folkloristics*, the intention being to eliminate the confusion that can develop as a result of using *folklore* to mean either the subject studied or the academic treatment of it. Whether *folklore* or *folkloristics* is the designation of the study, it is the orderly collection, classification, and analysis of the materials of folklore with the purpose of discovering the range of materials and establishing valid generalizations about them. Folklore as an academic discipline leading to both the M.A. and Ph.D. degrees is well established on several university campuses, including Indiana University, the University of Pennsylvania, and the University of California at Los Angeles.

The substance of folklore as it exists in society is somewhat less easy to define satisfactorily, but it may be no more subject to the specialists' perennial preoccupation with definitions than are other related materials such as those of sociology and ethnology. The reason is easy to discern: culture and society exist as complex, protean phenomena, having no neat, natural boundaries suited to the artificial labels of academic specialties. Much is made of the fact that the Funk and Wagnalls *Standard Dictionary of Folklore, Mythology, and Legend* contains not one definition, but many. This does not mean that folklorists despair of finding a satisfactory definition. It does mean that specialists of different kinds (linguists, literary scholars, anthropologists, etc.) see the lore of the folk in the light of their specialized interests, and they vary their emphases accordingly. The multiplicity of definitions in a dictionary is, then, instructive rather than confusing.

It may be observed also that there are ways of defining. A theoretical definition may not agree precisely with a definition based on common usage. The former is an ideal expressed in a logical statement; the latter is a record of usage, regardless of how carelessly the term has been handed around by the people who use it. Simply stated, folklore is made up of the informal knowledge, arts, and skills shared by ordinary people. This is contrasted with knowledge, arts, and skills formally acquired, either by groups or individuals, in a structured, self-conscious, or institutionalized framework.

Theoretically defined, folklore in America has been, until mid-century, keyed largely to verbal expressions: the spoken or sung expression of the common people, passed on by word of mouth, gradually changing as it persists in tradition. *Oral transmission, change,* and *tradition* are frequently cited as critical concepts in discussions of folklore. Since it is not always possible to separate song and music from dance, chant and rhyme from playground games, or verbal formulas from much occupational lore, and since spoken expressions are keyed to many other activities, folklore must extend to games, dances, arts, and domestic skills acquired by imitation and persisting in tradition.

An effort to create a definition based on actual usage as expressed in scholarly journals in the second half of the twentieth century reveals an even wider range of materials and fewer restrictions derived from the critical and theoretical concepts cited above. Much attention has been given to popular materials, without regard for persistence over a span of time, so that *traditional* (continuity in time) materials appear to be confused with *popular* (widely accepted) materials; or, to put it another way, the distinction, if there is a valid one, between popular culture and folk culture has been blurred.

One can hardly overstress the interdisciplinary nature of folklore studies. Where the subject is taught, it is ordinarily attached to an academic department, usually English or anthropology, as an administrative convenience. Only in the

largest and most active centers for graduate studies in this field
has folklore acquired a relatively autonomous status, and even
if separately administered as a department, committee, or an
institute, it must draw talent from representatives of various
academic specialties.

A pie chart with a fairly free-form center or hub provides a
convenient analogy in support of this concept. The lines
radiating from the hub to the outer circumference of the chart
represent the boundaries between academic disciplines, each
"slice" of pie being an area such as literature, medicine, or
history. The larger end of each slice represents the "official"
or commonly accepted, proved, logical textbook content of
the discipline. This is formal knowledge, formally learned,
usually in a classroom situation. As the wedge diminishes
toward the center of the circle, the lines representing
boundaries become less distinct, for the free-form central area
is folklore, unofficial knowledge, the informal arts and skills
unselfconsciously acquired, having no formal areas or disciplines, hence no set boundaries.

For example, a modern university student may enroll in a
course in animal husbandry. During his studies he may inquire
about his grandfather's apparently successful practice of
weaning calves only when the sign of the zodiac is in the feet.
His grandfather maintains that to wean calves when the sign is
in the head will cause them to "bawl their heads off" and to
lose weight. Furthermore, his grandfather will dehorn his
animals only when the sign is in the feet, for to do otherwise
would cause unnecessary bleeding. The student and his
instructor will find in the official knowledge of their textbooks no support for these practices. The student may remark
that his grandfather is superstitious, yet find himself leafing
through the almanac in addition to his textbooks in the future.
The grandfather is mildly suspicious of an educational system
that pays no attention to obviously useful empirical knowledge. We can label his beliefs and practices folklore. They
partake of the primitive science of magic (like things exert an
influence on each other), medicine (control of hemorrhage),

and animal husbandry.

Since the growth of academic institutions is relatively recent in human history, we can observe that the amorphous central area of the pie chart once represented very nearly all of human arts and skills. But in Western culture, especially, with its widespread literacy and technology, the central area has been overshadowed. Literacy and official knowledge, as many scholars have observed, are the "enemies" of folklore. Official knowledge, being more reliable and more useful than unofficial knowledge, has displaced the latter. Creative and experimental arts, unhindered by formula and cliché, have largely displaced traditional narrative and music.

Although folklore appears to play a diminishing role in the daily life of American citizens, it would be an error to overlook its historical role. Folklore has been an important influence in the shaping of the self-image of the people, individually, collectively, and regionally. Attitudes and aspirations develop from much that is traditional, and these grassroots elements project even to the highest councils of official government and diplomacy. Likewise, traditional song and music have provided, and continue to provide, inspiration for more sophisticated composition. The most modern author may utilize archetypal narrative themes as old as the oldest mythology preserved in our culture, or he may rely heavily on the speech, beliefs, and other folkloristic aspects of traditional life to project the characters and situations of his creation.

Applied folklore, still in its infancy and somewhat controversial in the United States in the 1970's, both as to definition and implications, may grow into a fruitful collaboration of folklorists with educators, health officials, urban planners, and others. "The Urban Experience," edited by Ellen Stekert as a special issue of the *Journal of American Folklore*, explores some possibilities for utilizing folklore in dealing with displaced tradition-oriented minorities.

Since folklore readily transcends political and geographical boundaries, generalizations about its nature are equally applicable to European and American folklore. In fact, with the exception of the unwritten literature of the North American Indians, most of the folklore of the United States has its ultimate origin elsewhere. Of particular interest to the student of American materials is the process of local adaptation in the special circumstances of the American setting. As Richard Dorson pointed out in his *American Folklore,* the supernatural beliefs and narratives about supernatural manifestations held by the New England colonists were easily identified as direct importations, but the peculiar and selective emphasis they received in the hyper-religious atmosphere of the Puritan colonies had some shaping influence on the subsequent development of American life and letters.

The westward expansion of the frontier created many opportunities for special blends, brands, and flavors of folklore not to be duplicated elsewhere. There is, for example, a body of folklore of and about the Mormon settlement in Utah, of and about the peoples and events of the Mexican-U.S. border. The gold fever of the 'fortyniners, the great eras of mountain men, riverboats, canal-building, Indian-fighting, and labor strife — these and many more create special opportunities to examine some aspects of folklore as particularly American phenomena.

Genres of Folklore

Spoken Narrative: Traditional forms of narrative include myth, folktale, legend, oral history, fablé, and anecdote. Quite commonly *folktale* is the generic term used to mean any kind of traditional narrative. If it is so used, then what is commonly thought of as a folktale is designated by a more specific term such as fairytale, wonder tale, or *Märchen.* Any of these forms existing in purely oral tradition is subject to change in transmission. Various modifications may be attributed to faults of communication, faults of memory, embellishment, adaptation to a changing environment, adaptation to a particular narrator's skill or understanding, and the pressures of the formulistic elements which appear to exist everywhere in folk literature.

Although *myth* is commonly conceived to be narratives of the supernatural elements of the classical world of Greece and Rome, anthropologists and folklorists are aware of a much larger body of recorded mythology of primitive societies all over the world (including a significant quantity from the American Indians). They turn to these materials for a scientific insight into the nature of myth, more accurate than the insight they get from the relatively sophisticated compositions of classical literature, necessarily one or more steps removed from the antecedent, functioning myth upon which they were based. It has been convenient for scholars in the past to define myth by content (i.e. narrative about gods and their acts). David Bidney proposed a more realistic identification in his *Theoretical Anthropology,* an identification by *psychocultural context.* That is, myth, ancient or modern, in either a primitive or an advanced civilization, is to be identified as that complex of beliefs and attitudes, supported by oral tradition, which the holders believe to be true. The test, then, is the degree of credence given rather than the nature of the content. This can extend the concept of myth, removing it from the classification of the antique curiosity and bringing it into studies of recent or contemporary society. An excellent example of such an effort is *Voices in the Valley: Mythmaking and Folk Belief in the Shaping of the Middle West,* by Frank R. Kramer. In this volume the author conceives of folklore as constantly coming into being among all classes of people, and he quotes Hermann Broch: "The civilization of an epoch is its myth in action."

The *folktale,* here meaning a short prose fiction which is or has been in oral tradition, varies widely in form and content. Evidence suggests that the earliest written literature available to us drew from the oral traditions of the time of its composition. The Jatakas of India, the "Tale of the Two Brothers," of Egypt, and other ancient writings incorporate plots and motifs recognized to be widespread in the oral recitations of tale-tellers over large parts of the world. Hence we have ample evidence of the effect of oral traditions on

written literature from the beginning of the art of writing to
the present. Similarly, the written word, once it developed
into a new convention of communication, has fed back into
oral communication and has created some complex problems
for students of the folktale who wish to follow the development of a particular narrative. It is difficult to determine, for
instance, the source of a modern semi-literate narrator's
version of an analogue of Chaucer's "The Miller's Tale." This
short, bawdy, ever-popular narrative was popular before
Chaucer's time. Has it continued to exist in an independent
oral tradition through the centuries? Has Chaucer's entertaining treatment of a traditional narrative been the literary
device that fed the story back into oral tradition once the
word-of-mouth continuity was broken, if it ever was? Such
questions may be answered by a close examination of the
contemporary text and whatever else is available to the
investigator.

What is generally called a *Märchen,* a fiction about
adventures of stereotyped heroes in an unreal world full of
monsters, magic, and rewards for bravery or constancy, is no
longer a prominent form in the United States. Such tales,
epitomized by the favorite selections from the German
folktales of the Brothers Grimm, are now generally bowd-
lerized for children's books. A few have survived in certain
families or in relatively isolated and backward communities. It
seems quite clear that they play no prominent role in
American folklore now, and it seems unlikely that they could
have had a significant place at any time during the relatively
recent span of history since colonial times.

Nevertheless, we should acquaint ourselves with folktales
as they have appeared in other times and at other places, for
the seemingly recent, native-born tale frequently turns out to
be old wine in a new bottle. The tale of Clever John, the Negro
slave of the Old South who could steal anything, would appear
on first examination to be recent and necessarily local. Closer
examination will reveal that it is merely localized. The master
thief complex belongs to a much older telling in the Old

World.

Some of the hardiest survivors are the so-called "Jack Tales." These have been collected in North Carolina and adjacent areas, and we are fortunate enough to have authentic narrations on recordings if we wish to audit the art of the tale-teller. Among these are the Library of Congress recordings of Maud Long and the Folk-Legacy recording of Ray Hicks. See also the volume entitled *Jack Tales*, by Richard Chase.

The most rewarding avenue for studying the folktale as an aspect of American studies is to examine collections from a regional or ethnic group. Folktales of the American Indians have been widely collected and too little studied in a systematic way. The earliest Negro tales retold by Joel Chandler Harris have been re-examined periodically, but they still need sound evaluation as a collection of African tales persisting in Negro tradition in an environment hostile to their perpetuation. The tall tale has been widely acclaimed as a peculiarly American tradition, but sound analysis to show if, how, or why this is so remains to be done. Much of the early scholarship on folktales in America must be re-evaluated because credulity of collectors and commentators apparently played into the hands of creators of *fakelore*. We have, for instance, an abundance of Paul Bunyan literature, but we have no evidence that there was ever a single traditional narrative upon which the literature is based. The same is true of Pecos Bill, Joe Magerac, Old Stormalong, and other literary imitations of literary imitations. Even the Appleseed legend appears to be largely a journalistic inflation.

Before we retire into complete skepticism, however, we should note that the very fact of journalistic inflation or Chamber of Commerce exploitation represents still another aspect of the American scene and the folklore of folklore — well worth study. Also, we should be aware of some excellent modern collecting and analysis. See, for instance, Richard Dorson's *Negro Folktales from Michigan*. Dorson does much here to dispel the old plantation darkey stereotype and to present the folktale in its contemporary cultural matrix. See also the more recent *100 Armenian Folktales* (collected in Detroit), by Susie Hoogasian-Villa. Much remains to be done on the level of informed, scholarly study as represented in these and similar works.

Legend and Oral History are presented together here because they cannot be completely isolated from each other. The latter, as its designation implies, is the record of events passed on by word of mouth rather than on the written page or in documents. Obviously, not all history is formally recorded. Also, much history that is ultimately recorded derives from the memory of observers, participants, or from people informed by them. The relative reliability of the oral account, especially when considerably removed from the occurrence, is a problem for both the historian and the folklorist. Historians have been able to demonstrate that the folk, given enough time for the retelling, will stereotype their heroes and villains. If the stereotyped account persists, we call it a legend — a narrative about a person, place, or event which is believed to be true. Even when the legend is no longer believed, it tends to persist within a context of pretended belief. It would appear, then, that the degree of skepticism of the auditor might determine whether a given narrative is to be classified as a legend or as oral history.

Kent Ladd Steckmesser, in his *The Western Hero in History and Legend,* demonstrated legend-building according to a stereotyped pattern when he traced the evolution of legends about such men as Kit Carson, General Custer, and Wild Bill Hickok. An amusing aspect of his study is his explanation of the process whereby fictional elements become thoroughly documented as official history once the folklore has intruded and becomes the subject of future footnotes.

A landmark study in American oral folk history is William Lynwood Montell's *The Saga of Coe Ridge.* Here the folklorist-historian combines the insights of both disciplines to record the history of a group of people who are rarely represented in official literature. They are the virtually nameless and inarticulate descendants of slaves in an isolated border-South community.

Anecdotes here designate short, usually humorous narratives which travel by word of mouth and frequently reflect popular beliefs about individuals, places, occupations, races, and nationalities. Some subjects are so popular that a whole series of anecdotes deals with them. The traveling salesman and the farmer's daughter are probably universally known to adult Americans for their sexy misadventures. Some aspects of American history might be illuminated through examination of the rise and decline of cycles of anecdotes. The misadventures of Pat and Mike and the so-called "Dumb Irishman" tales would appear to reflect the impact of Irish immigration. "Pedro" tales are, as one would expect, mostly regional, having their main currency in the Southwest. Yankee peddler tales once reflected provincialism and a possibly well-warranted mistrust of the pack peddler, now a past institution. A study of growing tolerance, especially in modern urban society, may be seen in the cycle of anecdotes about the Catholic priest and his friendly rival, the rabbi. An inquiry into changing literary taste, or possibly into passing fads in oral literature, might begin with the shaggy dog story and extend to other forms of nonsense, non-sequitur, and narrative snipe hunts. If one begins with the premise that significant insights into the taste, morals, self-image, aspirations, and values of the members of a society are reflected in the anecdotal lore people seize upon and perpetuate, then there is unlimited opportunity for investigation.

The most essential bibliographic aids in the study of all kinds of folk narrative are two interrelated works: *Types of the Folktale,* by Antti Aarne and Stith Thompson, and the *Motif-Index of Folk Literature* by Stith Thompson. These are used internationally in folktale scholarship, and they are indispensable for classification of specific tales or for comparative studies involving particular motifs.

Types of the Folktale, usually called the *Type Index,* is a single volume which identifies a large number of European-American folktales. Each narrative which has been identified as one having a traditional life is assigned a number in the index. A brief synopsis of each tale is given, and each principal narrative motif is designated by its number.

The *Motif-Index of Folk Literature*, usually called the *Motif-Index*, is a six-volume work which presents a systematic classification of narrative motifs abstracted from a wide selection of recorded traditional literature of the world. Extensive cross-indexing makes the two works reasonably easy to use in spite of what at first appears to be formidable bulk and complexity.

For American studies, a supplement to the *Motif-Index* and *Type-Index* that greatly extends their utility is Ernest W. Baughman's *A Type and Motif-Index of the Folktales of England and North America*. This extensive survey of British and American materials makes many kinds of comparative studies more convenient to perform than they were before the compilation.

The beginner should acquaint himself with some of the theoretical concepts, definitions, and pronouncements related to studies in folk literature by consulting the following articles in the *Journal of American Folklore:* "Folklore in Literature: a Symposium" (January-March, 1957); Francis Utley, "The Study of Folk Literature: Its Scope and Use" (April-June, 1958); Francis Utley, "Folk Literature: An Operational Definition" (July-September, 1961); Alan Dundes, "The Study of Folklore in Literature and Culture: Identification and Interpretation" (April-June, 1965); Richard Dorson, "A Theory for American Folklore" (July-September, 1959); and the entire issue edited by Americo Paredes and Richard Bauman entitled "Toward New Perspectives in Folklore" (January-March, 1971), in which folklore is viewed as process rather than product.

Song, music, and *dance:* It is convenient to group three entities into one discussion because of their intimate relationship. Folksong may be discussed in terms of content and style, but the presence of music is always implied. Folk music may exist apart from song (as in fiddle tunes), and dance may be performed without song, but in truly traditional performance folk dancing is ordinarily accompanied by music, both vocal and instrumental.

Because of the great popularity of folksong at any time, and especially in the light of the commercial success of recent "revival" and "festival" movements, identification of folksong or distinguishing folksong from popular commercial performance has become quite difficult for the uninitiated. Collecting, publishing, and performing have been so rewarding, both socially and financially, that large numbers of non-academic enthusiasts have presented their opinions in a rather bewildering array of publications. Also, many publications on folksong, ranging from commercial enterprises riding the wave of popular taste (such as *Sing Out!*) to mimeographed newsletters of local societies have provided outlets for pronouncements on folksong that are sometimes too ludicrous for serious comment. They are, however, taken seriously by the uninformed, creating a growing need for sound scholarship to remove the confusion about the nature of folksong and the materials related to it. Such studies as Charles Keil's *Urban Blues* (Chicago, 1966) and Bill C. Malone's *Country Music, U.S.A.*, published by the American Folklore Society in its Memoir Series (1968), illuminate some facets of the interplay between folk and popular music expressions.

The traditional academic definition of folksong conforms to the definition of folklore given above. The criteria of *oral transmission, persistence* in the memories of people, gradual *change* in transmission, so that *traditional life* can be demonstrated hold true for all genres of folklore. Generally, there is little quarrel with these criteria when they are applied to forms of folklore other than song. The commercial aspects of folksong, however, have created kinds of self-interest which seek to extend the magic of the term beyond its accepted points of reference, even to newly composed (and copyrighted) song. Many rationalizations have been employed. The performer of the song, for instance, may be alleged to be a folksinger, hence his song is a folksong. The subject of the song may be alleged to have something in common with accepted folksong (e.g. protest), hence the new song is a folksong. The composer may be alleged to be a member of the folk, hence anything composed by him is a folksong. Or it may be observed that *tradition* is an accepted criterion of folksong, but that there is "vertical" (in time) tradition and "horizontal" (in space, or popular) tradition.

Folksong as discussed here will mean song which can be demonstrated to have enough folk acceptance to persist in oral circulation long enough to permit some modification to occur. This operation of the folk aesthetic on the material of folklore may be demonstrated in a scrutiny of the English and Scottish popular ballads (narrative songs) imported to the United States by early settlers and kept in tradition to the present day.

Traditional ballads have an intrinsic attractiveness. The first great monument of American folksong study was devoted to them, and the quantity of academic literature on the ballad appears to exceed that of any other kind of folklore. Francis J. Child completed his *The English and Scottish Popular Ballads* in 1898. This model of thorough scholarship set the style for many subsequent publications. The critical literature developed in great enough volume and complexity to warrant the 1955 publication of *Anglo-American Folksong Scholarship Since 1898* by D. K. Wilgus.

The first great American field collection of any kind of folksong was made by a visiting English music teacher, Cecil Sharp. His *English Folk-Songs from the Southern Appalachians*, edited by Maude Karpeles, was a reflection of the isolated, self-sufficient era of the Appalachian highlander's tradition-bound culture before the intrusion of modern transportation and communication. The rich collection he harvested, therefore, has not been, and cannot be, equalled. Collecting in the area since Sharp has been fragmentary and anticlimactic, though often interesting in its demonstration of persistence in tradition and continuing operation of the folk esthetic. In 1967 an Eastern Kentucky schoolteacher, determined to find an isolated informant who could give him a rare song, went far enough back in the creek bottoms to be well out of reach of TV antennas. He found an elderly man who did, indeed, sing a version of a Child ballad rarely collected on this continent. The collector was delighted with his discovery until he learned that Sharp had collected the same song from the same informant a half-century earlier. More fortunate have been those who found the old wine in new bottles, songs of recent events in old narrative frames.

Although collecting and scholarship on the ballad may seem disproportionately large, it is not so in reality, for much of the result of ballad research applies readily enough to other forms of folksong. The matter of formulistic re-creation of text, for example, is a principle related to oral transmission, and it is not confined to ballad texts. Fondness for mnemonic phrases and commonplaces extend, not only to other forms of song, but also to the folktale.

Events which stir the sympathy, ire, or imagination of the folk have frequently been celebrated in song. There are, therefore, many opportunities to gain insight into popular attitudes toward events in history through examination of song related to them. A railroad wreck, a maritime disaster, a coal mine explosion, a flood, a battle won or lost – these and many other events have been the subject of song. Undoubtedly many more songs have been composed than the ones that have survived. What is the basis of appeal in the survivors? What was lacking in the discards?

Music did not receive enough attention in early folksong scholarship. One admires the achievement of Francis Child, but his lack of attention to music left a gap in his work, and many of the later collections followed the pattern he set, presenting the songs only as texts (like a species of poetry), without musical notation.

Child's omission has, in a way, procured a delayed benefit for folksong scholarship, for Bertrand Bronson, beginning his project in the 1950s, set out to provide all the musical data available for the Child Ballads. In his *The Traditional Tunes of the Child Ballads and Their Texts*, he has been able to incorporate all the collected data of the intervening sixty years and to utilize the technological aids of his era. With the advent of portable recording devices which provide an opportunity for leisurely transcription and analysis, the music of the songs has emerged as an aspect of folklore that provides new opportunities for scholarship.

In addition to study of the music of the song, the study of traditional instrumental performance, hampered in earlier times by lack of suitable recording equipment, now receives considerable attention. Fife and drum bands, fiddles, banjos, dulcimers, jugs, spoons, harmonicas, singly and in combination, represent some of the grassroots elements of true folk music. Out of the untutored, non-professional performances of "just folks" have sprung the styles of spirituals, hillbilly music, blues, jazz, and bluegrass. Modern hillbilly is, of course, highly sophisticated, professional, and commercial, but there is a continuity tracing back from slick "Nashville sound" to the genuine product of traditional performance.

The folk dance offers some special problems in definition which are similar to the ones suggested above on folksong. It is true that some traditional playparty kinds of homemade diversion have persisted to the present day in an unbroken stream of traditional performance. Such unselfconscious participation is now greatly diminished, and even where it exists, it is likely to be corrupted by spectatorship. It is difficult to imagine anyone so isolated in modern America that he has not had an opportunity to witness a television version of a hoedown or a barndance.

Urban folk dance groups are usually highly promoted. The organizers and instructors may be college professors who studied folkdancing in physical education courses. The dances they teach are as authentic as research can make them. The enthusiastic members willingly attire themselves in costume (sometimes more influenced by hillbilly caricature than by faithful observation). There is no doubt that they are performing a folk dance, but is this an example of folklore in action? Is a factory-made imitation of a handmade Appalachian dulcimer an example of folk art?

The student of folk song should acquaint himself with both Child and Bronson. Child numbers (the numbers Child assigned to the 305 ballads in his collection) are inescapable in folk song literature. For a quick survey of the scholarship, D. K. Wilgus provides the most accessible overview in his *Anglo-American Folksong Scholarship Since 1898.* For a splendid introduction and a convenient set of texts, see *The Ballad Book* by MacEdward Leach. For a systematic classification which has become as indispensable for ballad study as are the Motif and Type Indexes for the folktale, see G. Malcolm Laws, *Native American Balladry* and *American Balladry from British Broadsides.* For a compact general introduction to folk music, see Bruno Nettl, *An Introduction to Folk Music in the United States,* and for a recent and readable text on style, see Roger D. Abrahams and George Foss, *Anglo-American Folksong Style.* Consult especially the topical bibliography in Wilgus for the extensive literature of collection, criticism, and analysis.

Much early research was textual, literary, and historical. Structural and psychological emphases are more prominent in current scholarship. It should be noted here that the apparatus of modern linguistics has given considerable stimulus to structural studies, both in folksong and folktale.

The minor genres of folklore (minor in the relative sense of the amount of scholarly literature devoted to them) include folk arts and crafts, folk games, beliefs and superstitions, riddles, proverbial lore, children's lore, occupational lore, and customs.

Folklife is the term gaining currency in the United States to describe the systematic study of traditional life centered on material culture rather than on verbal traditions. The objects and activities which may be included in folklife studies are very nearly inexhaustible. The most familiar to the average person are such obviously traditional objects as folk toys (willow whistles, etc.) and domestic artifacts (quilt block patterns, etc.). Current literature reveals many other objects of interest: baskets, furniture, farm tools, structures, clothing, decoration, weapons, fences and gates, and so on. Many of these are recognized as objects of curiosity or museum pieces of long standing. The new element in folklife studies is the close, systematic investigation and a developing methodology designed to give more valuable insights into the social, psychological, and historical role of folk arts. See Henry Glassie, *Pattern in the Material Culture of the Eastern United States.*

Traditional games such as marbles, jumping rope, and hopscotch are readily recognized as elements of folklore. Much of the existing scholarship on games concentrates on their associated verbal formulas (such as the rhymes and vocabulary). A much more promising area of exploration is the psychological and sociological impact of games – especially during the most impressionable years of childhood. To what degree do the games of the playground affect enculturation? How do traditional rhymes affect racial awareness and minority prejudice? Little has yet been done to investigate these and similar questions.

Folk beliefs, commonly called superstitions, are easy to collect. The literature of folklore is, therefore, rich in lists compiled in many ways. Folk beliefs have been collected from age groups, ethnic groups, occupational groups, individuals, communities, states and regions. They have been abstracted from the literature of various authors, and to some degree they have been subjected to various kinds of comparative scrutiny. Wayland Hand, who undertook the arduous tasks of classifying and editing the large belief section of the Frank C. Brown Collection of *North Carolina Folklore,* presented an authoritative and perceptive essay on the status of scholarship on beliefs in Vol. 6 of the collection.

Many published collections, especially in regional journals, merely exhibit a compilation of beliefs. Much research remains to be done on such questions as the degree of credence given to them, actions or absence of action deriving from them, the personalities of those who do or do not give credence, and similar related problems.

The general observations above apply similarly to the collection and study of riddles, proverbs, proverbial phrases, and certain aspects of dialect. Archer Taylor provides a survey of the scope and variety of riddles in his *English Riddles from Oral Tradition*. Archer Taylor and B. J. Whiting provide a useful introduction to the study of proverbs and proverbial phrases in *A Dictionary of American Proverbs and Proverbial Phrases 1820-1880*. The student who seeks brief discussions of these and the many other specific areas of investigation can begin with the entries in the Funk and Wagnalls *Dictionary of Folklore, Mythology, and Legend*, edited by Maria Leach.

Formal study of folklore is flourishing in the United States, but it is still so new as a discipline in which one may earn a graduate degree that its national society, its literature, and its curricula, especially on the undergraduate level, are uneven. Research in folklore has attracted some of the finest intellects in the academic world and has resulted in some of the great achievements in our scholarly literature. Conversely, widespread ignorance, even in parts of the academic world, of folkloristics, combined with the attractiveness of the material, have led to a marked degree of amateurism. There is abundant opportunity to contribute to folkloristics, both in new areas of research and in reassessment of much that has been done. Every other aspect of American studies may be related in some way to American folklore. A growing awareness of the relationships will enrich both folklore scholarship and that of its kindred disciplines.

A SELECTED LIST OF
FOLKLORE RESOURCES

General Collections, Archives, and Bibliographies

A resource often overlooked for North American Indian materials is the series of annual reports and bulletins of the Bureau of American Ethnology of the Smithsonian Institution. These have been published by the Government Printing Office, and are available in libraries which preserve government documents.

The Archives of Folk Music in the Library of Congress have issued many LP recordings of story and song. The catalogue is available from the Recording Laboratory, Music Division, Library of Congress.

Among the principal university archives of folklore are those at the University of Pennsylvania, Indiana University, and the University of California at Los Angeles. The UCLA collection contains an especially rich resource devoted to country and western music, the John Edwards Memorial Foundation Collection. The foundation also publishes a newsletter devoted to collections and scholarship. *The Folklore and Folk Music Archivist* is a joint publication of the Folklore Archive and the Archives of Folk and Primitive Music at Indiana University. Files of the *Archivist* contain descriptions of some of the lesser-known collections as well as the better-known archives. The archives at Wayne State University, Detroit, Michigan, contain especially rich resources related to urban and industrial life. The Farmers' Museum at Cooperstown, New York, long recognized for its meticulous historical treatment of material culture, is now integrated with a program of graduate studies leading to a master's degree at the New York State University College, Oneonta, New York. A well-organized and maintained archive (The Western Kentucky University Folklore and Folklife Collection) is developing at Western Kentucky University as one of several adjuncts to a master's degree program in Folk Studies instituted in 1972.

An extensive endowed collection on folklore is the John G. White Collection at the Cleveland, Ohio, Public Library. A special catalogue of a portion of this collection was published in 1966: *Out-of-Print Books from the John G. White Folklore Collection at the Cleveland Public Library*, Bell & Howell Company, Cleveland, Ohio.

Abstracts of Folklore Studies is a quarterly publication of the American Folklore Society (Austin, University of Texas Press). Prior to the beginning of the abstracts publication in 1962, the *Journal of American Folklore* published an annual bibliography of folklore. A special bibliographic aid for locating JAF items is Tristram P. Coffin's *An Analytical Index to the Journal of American Folklore* (vols. 1-67, 68, 69, 70), published as Bibliographical and Special Series No. 3 (1958) by the American Folklore Society.

Publications of the Modern Language Association contain numerous entries on folklore in the annual bibliography issue.

Southern Folklore Quarterly devotes one issue each year to a bibliography of folklore.

The Frank C. Brown Collection of *North Carolina Folklore* contains the scholarship, editing, and bibliographic notes supplied by experts on the various genres of folklore. These seven volumes, then, represent more than just another regional collection. They serve as a convenient reference for examples, comparisons, and additional reading.

Journals

The *Journal of American Folklore* is the official publication of the American Folklore Society. In addition to the quarterly issues of JAF, the Society publishes an annual supplement, *Abstracts of Folklore Studies*, and scholarly books in its "Memoir" series and its "Bibliographical and Special Series" publications.

Other serials which have appeared regularly enough to be stocked in many libraries are the following:
Folklore Americas
Journal of the Folklore Institute
Kentucky Folklore Record
Keystone Folklore Quarterly
New York Folklore Quarterly
North Carolina Folklore
Northeast Folklore
Publications of the Texas Folklore Society
Southern Folklore Quarterly
Tennessee Folklore Society Bulletin
Western Folklore

BIBLIOGRAPHY

Aarne, Antti, and Stith Thompson. *The Types of the Folktale.* FFC 74, Helsinki, 1928. Revised and enlarged, FFC 184, Helsinki, 1961.

Abrahams, Roger D., and George Foss. *Anglo-American Folksong Style.* Englewood Cliffs, N.J., 1968.

-----. *Deep Down in the Jungle.* Hatboro, Pa., 1964.

-----, ed. *Folksong and Folksong Scholarship: Changing Approaches.* Dallas, 1964.

Ames, Russell. *The Story of American Folksong.* New York, 1960.

Bascom, William R. "Four Functions of Folklore," *JAF,* LXVIII (October-December 1954), 333-349.

Bayard, Samuel P. *Hill Country Tunes.* Philadelphia, 1944.

-----. "The Materials of Folklore," *JAF,* LXVI (January-March 1953), 1-17.

Beck, Horace P. *The Folklore of Maine.* Philadelphia, 1957.

-----. *Folklore and the Sea.* Middletown, Conn., 1973.

Blair, Walter, and Franklin J. Meine. *Half Horse, Half Alligator: The Growth of the Mike Fink Legend.* Chicago, 1956.

Boatright, Mody C. *Folklore of the Oil Industry.* Dallas, 1963.

Botkin, Benjamin A. *The American Play-Party Song.* Lincoln, Neb., 1937.

-----. *Lay My Burden Down: A Folk History of Slavery.* Chicago, 1945.

Brewster, Paul G. *American Non-singing Children's Games.* Norman, Okla., 1953.

-----. *Ballads and Songs of Indiana.* Bloomington, Ind., 1942.

Bronson, Bertrand, ed. *Traditional Tunes of the Child Ballads.* Princeton, N.J., 1959-1971.

Brooks, Stella B. *Joel Chandler Harris, Folklorist.* Athens, Ga., 1950.

Browne, Ray B. *Popular Beliefs from Alabama.* Berkeley, 1958.

Brunvand, Jan Harold. *The Study of American Folklore.* New York, 1968.

Campa, Arthur L. *Los Comanches. A New Mexican Folk Drama.* Alberquerque, 1942.

Campbell, Marie. *Tales from the Cloud Walking Country.* Bloomington, Ind., 1958.

Chase, Richard. *The Jack Tales.* Boston, 1943.

Child, Franics J. *The English and Scottish Popular Ballads,* 5 vols. New York, 1965 (reprint of 1884-1898 ed.)

Clark, Ella E. *Indian Legends of the Pacific Northwest.* Berkeley, 1953.

Clark, La Verne Harrell. *They Sang for Horses: The Impact of the Horse on Navajo and Apache Folklore.* Tucson, 1966.

Clarke, Kenneth and Mary. *Introducing Folklore.* New York, 1963.

Coffin, Tristram P. *An Analytical Index to the Journal of American Folklore,* vols. 1-67, 68, 69, 70. Philadelphia, 1958.

-----. *The British Traditional Ballad in North America.* Philadelphia, 1951.

Courlander, Harold. *Negro Folk Music, U.S.A.* (1963) New York, 1970. (Discography and bibliography)

Cox, John Harrington. *Folk-Songs of the South.* (1925) New York, 1967.

Davis, Arthur K. *Traditional Ballads of Virginia.* Cambridge, Mass., 1929.

-----. *More Traditional Ballads of Virginia.* Cambridge, Mass., 1929.

Doerflinger, William. *Shantymen and Shantyboys.* New York, 1951.

Dorson, Richard. *American Folklore.* Chicago, 1959.

-----. *Bloodstoppers and Bearwalkers.* Cambridge, Mass., 1956.

-----. *Buying the Wind.* Chicago, 1964.

-----. *Negro Tales in Michigan.* Cambridge, Mass., 1956.

-----. "A Theory for American Folklore," *JAF*, LXXII (July-September 1959), 195-215.

-----, ed. *Folklore and Folklife: An Introduction.* Chicago, 1972. (Introd. and 26 essays by folklore scholars, each with annotated bibliography)

Dundes, Alan. *The Study of Folklore.* Englewood Cliffs, N.J., 1965.

-----. "The Study of Folklore in Literature and Culture: Identification and Interpretation," *JAF*, LXXVIII (April-June 1965), 136-142.

-----, ed. *Mother Wit from the Laughing Barrel.* Englewood Cliffs, N.J., 1973. (Interpretations of Afro-American folklore)

Emrich, Duncan. *American Folk Poetry: An Anthology.* Boston, 1974.

-----. *Folklore on the American Land.* Boston, 1972.

Espinosa, Jose E. *Saints in the Valleys: Christian Sacred Images in the History, Life and Folk Art of Spanish New Mexico.* Alberquerque, 1966.

-----. *Spanish Folk-Tales from New Mexico.* New York, 1969.

Fife, Austin E. and Alta. *Saints of Sage and Saddle: Folklore Among the Mormons.* Bloomington, 1956.

-----, and Henry H. Glassie. *Folklife Forms upon the Frontier: Folklife and Folk Arts in the United States.* Logan, Utah, 1969.

Flanagan, John T., and Arthur Palmer Hudson. *Folklore in American Literature.* New York, 1958.

Flanders, Helen Hartness. *Ancient Ballads Traditionally Sung in New England*, 4 vols. Philadelphia, 1960-1965.

"Folklore in Literature: A Symposium," *JAF*, LXX (January-March 1957), 1-24.

Frantz, Joseph B. *The American Cowboy: The Myth and Reality.* Norman, Okla., 1955.

Friedman, Albert B. *The Ballad Revival.* Chicago, 1961.

-----. *The Viking Book of Folk Ballads of the English Speaking World.* New York, 1956.

Gardner, Emelyn E. *Folklore from the Schoharie Hills.* Ann Arbor, 1937.

Glassie, Henry. *Pattern in the Material Folk Culture of the Eastern United States.* Philadelphia, 1969.

Goldstein, Kenneth S. *A Guide for Field Workers in Folklore.* Hatboro, Pa., 1964.

Greenway, John. *American Folksongs of Protest.* Philadelphia, 1953.

Griffin, William J. "The TFS Bulletin and Other Folklore Serials in the United States: a Preliminary Survey," *Tennessee Folklore Society Bulletin,* XXV (December 1959), 91-96.

Gudde, Erwin C. *California Place Names.* Berkeley, 1969.

Halpert, Herbert. "American Regional Folklore," in "Research in North America, " *JAF,* LX (October-December 1947), 355-366.

-----. "Some Undeveloped Areas in American Folklore," *JAF,* LXX (October-December 1957), 299-304.

Hand, Wayland D., ed. *American Folk Legend.* Berkeley and Los Angeles, 1972.

Haywood, Charles. *A Bibliography of North American Folklore and Folksong.* New York, 1961.

Herzog, George. "The Study of Folksong in America," *SFQ,* II (June 1938), 59-64.

Hoogasian-Villa, Susie, ed. *100 Armenian Tales and Their Folkloristic Relevance.* Detroit, 1966.

Ickis, Marguerite. *The Standard Book of Quilts and Quilt Collecting.* New York: Dover, 1959.

Jackson, George P. *White and Negro Spirituals.* Locust Valley, N.Y., 1943.

Jacobs, Melville. *The Content and Style of an Oral Literature.* New York, 1959.

Johnson, Guy B. *John Henry: Tracking Down a Negro Legend.* Chapel Hill, 1929.

Kephart, Horace. *Our Southern Highlanders.* New York, 1967.

Kniffen, Fred. "The Folk Housing: Key to Diffusion," *Annals of the Association of American Geographers,* (December, 1965), 549-577.

Korson, George. *Coal Dust on the Fiddle: Songs and Stories of the Bituminous Industry.* Philadelphia, 1943.

-----. *Minstrels of the Mine Patch: Songs and Stories of the Anthracite Industry.* Philadelphia, 1938.

Laws, Malcolm. *American Balladry from British Broadsides.* Philadelphia, 1957.

-----. *Native American Balladry.* Philadelphia, 1951, rev. ed. 1964.

Leach, MacEdward. *The Ballad Book.* New York, 1955.

-----. "Problems of Collecting Oral Literature," *PMLA*, LXXVII (June 1962), 335-340.

Leach, Maria, ed. *Standard Dictionary of Folklore, Mythology, and Legend,* 2 vols. New York, 1950.

Lipman, Jean. *American Folk Art in Wood, Metal, and Stone.* New York, 1948.

-----. *American Folk Decoration.* New York, 1951.

Lomax, Alan. *The Folk Songs of North America in the English Language.* Garden City, N.Y., 1960.

Lomax, John A. and Alan. *Cowboy Songs and Other Frontier Ballads.* New York, 1910; with additions, 1916; revised, 1938.

Mackenzie, William R. *The Quest of the Ballad.* Princeton, 1919.

Malone, Bill C. *Country Music, U.S.A.* Austin, Tex., 1968. (Discography and bibliography)

Montell, William Lynwood. *The Saga of Coe Ridge: A Study in Oral History.* Knoxville, 1970.

Morris, Alton C. *Folksongs of Florida.* Gainesville, 1950.

"Myth: A Symposium," *JAF*, LXVIII (October-December 1953).

Nettl, Bruno. *An Introduction to Folk Music in the United States.* Detroit, 1960.

Newell, W.W. *Games and Songs of American Children.* New York, 1963. (reprint of 1883 edition)

Pound, Louise. *American Ballads and Songs.* New York, 1922.

ᴾrice, Robert. *Johnny Appleseed: Man and Myth.* Bloomington, Ind., 1954.

Puckett, N.N. *Folk Beliefs of the Southern Negro.* New York, 1968.

Randolph, Vance. *Ozark Magic and Folklore.* New York, 1964. (Reprint of *Ozark Superstitions,* 1947).

Raidolph, Vance, and George P. Wilson. *Down in the Holler: A Gallery of Ozark Speech.* Norman, Okla., 1953.

Randolph, Vance, and Floyd C. Shoemaker. *Ozark Folksongs.* 4 vols. Columbia, Mo., 1946-1950.

Reaver, J. Russell, and George W. Boswell. *Fundamentals of Folk Literature.* Oosterhout, The Netherlands, 1962.

Roberts, Leonard W. *Up Cutshin and Down Greasy.* Lexington, Ky., 1959.

Rubin, Ruth. *A Treasury of Jewish Folksong.* New York, 1966.

Sackett, Samuel J., and William E. Koch. *Kansas Folklore.* Lincoln, Neb., 1961.

Saucier, Corrine L. *Folk Tales from French Louisiana.* New York, 1962.

Seeger, Charles. "Professionalism and Amateurism in the Study of Folk Music," *JAF,* LXII (April-June 1949), 107-113.

Sharp, Cecil J. *English Folk Songs from the Southern Appalachians,* ed. by Maud Karpeles, 2 vols. London, 1932.

Sloane, Eric. *A Museum of Early American Tools.* New York, 1964.

Stearns, Marshall. *The Story of Jazz.* New York, 1956.

Stewart, George. *Dictionary of American Place Names.* New York, 1970.

Taylor, Archer. *English Riddles from Oral Tradition.* Berkeley, 1951.

-----. *The Proverb.* Cambridge, Mass., 1931.

-----. *Proverbial Comparisons and Similes from California.* Berkeley, 1954.

-----. "Some Trends and Problems in Studies of the Folk-Tale," *Studies in Philology,* XXXVII (January 1940), 1-25.

Taylor, Archer, and B.J. Whiting. *A Dictionary of American Proverbs and Proverbial Phrases, 1820-1880.* Cambridge, Mass., 1958.

Thompson, Harold W. *Body, Boots & Britches*. Philadelphia, 1940.

Thompson, Stith. "Advances in Folklore Studies," *Anthropology Today*. Chicago, 1953.

-----. *The Folktale*. New York, 1946.

-----. *Motif-Index of Folk Literature*, 6 vols. Bloomington, Ind., 1955-1957.

-----. *Tales of the North American Indians*. (1929) Bloomington, Ind., 1966.

Utley, Francis Lee. "Folk Literature: An Operational Definition," *JAF*, LXXIV (July-September 1961), 193-206.

-----. "The Study of Folk Literature: Its Scope and Use," *JAF*, LXXI (April-June 1958), 139-147.

Vogt, Evon, and Ray Hyman. *Water Witching, U.S.A.* Chicago, 1959.

Welsh, Peter C. *American Folk Art*. Washington, D.C., 1965.

Welsh, Roger L. *A Treasury of Nebraska Pioneer Folklore*. Lincoln, Neb., 1966.

White, Newman Ivey, and Paul F. Baum, general eds. *The Frank C. Brown Collection of North Carolina Folklore*, 7 vols. Durham, N.C., 1952-1961.

Wilgus, D.K. *Anglo-American Folksong Scholarship since 1898*. New Brunswick, N.J., 1959.

Wyld, Lionel D. *Low Bridge! Folklore and the Erie Canal*. Syracuse, 1962.

Yoder, Don. *Pennsylvania Spirituals*. (1951) Hatboro, Pa., 1964.

CHAPTER SEVEN

Aboriginal Cultures and American Anthropology

Bruce Raemsch

America's aboriginal past has been and still is a subject as large as the sea. In many ways it is as mysterious as the abysmal depths, despite all that we claim to know about the subject. It remains, still, for those in generations to come to fully determine the age and distribution, as well as the manifold details of the cultures, of the earliest of Americans. Aboriginal American cultures transcend modern political boundaries and are so complex as to require us to limit treatment to narrow areas of North America, in this discussion.

There is great opportunity for the young student, not so much with respect to unraveling the mysterious past or working the mines of archeological resources, but in work on the meaning of American aboriginal life and culture to mankind itself. We are now at a crossroads, we might say, where some men have stood and looked back, with a keen sense of association between cause and effect, into the meaning of our failure to seize the opportunities presented by five hundred years of contact of Western man with the New World environments and the aboriginal Americans. Gerard Piel has written, for example, "We are waking now from the American Dream to realize that it was a dream few Americans

171

lived in their waking hours. The history of the New World has turned out to be not so different from that of the Old. The peril that threatens the last of the American wilderness [and frontier values] arises not from the reckless dream, but from the same historic forces of rapacity and cruelty that laid waste the land in the Mediterranean Basin, in Arabia, India and the treeless uplands of China."[1]

Coupled with this point of view is another, closely related observation written by a man reflecting upon the American Indian: "They [the Indians] had what the world has lost,...the ancient, lost reverence and passion for human personality, joined with the ancient, lost reverence and passion for the earth and its web of life.... They had...this power for living...as world-view and self-view, as tradition and institution, as practical philosophy dominating their societies, and as an art supreme...."[2]

To understand America's aboriginal past, therefore, requires an understanding of the two observations cited above. When these ideas are put together they suggest the differences that have existed from the beginning between the New World man and the Old World man, between the Indian, that is, and the European and Asiatic. A recognition of the existence of these differences and, further, a need to know more about them in some detail, is reason enough to study the American Indian in the first place. It is also necessary to learn more about the environmental aspect which has played such a large part in the development of man in the New World and the latter's success as a human organism, isolated for thousands of years from other men and other cultures around the world.

The American Indian is a different man from other men. Part of the difference is reflected in his relation to his environment through biological adaptation. The rest of the difference is reflected in his behavior which comes from the cultural value system that develops through the Indian's relationship with his environment. Finally, an intangible hereditary factor, which predisposes the man to respond to the environment in the particular way that the Indian has done, makes him unique.

The peculiar blend of these circumstances that make up the American Indian personality (involving heredity, environmental, and cultural characteristics) has resulted in the large difficulties ever present between him and the New American — that culture bearer from the Old World who, perhaps, met the Indian no later than the fifteenth century. The differences have been due largely to the differences that have existed between the individual and his attitude toward the environment (defined as the physical and biological surroundings of the individual), and the long isolation separating the one from the other. On the Indian's part the point of view of "stewardship" toward the environment has been the predominant attitude. On the other hand, with respect to Western man (with some exception) the attitudes of "aggression" and "conquest" have prevailed in relationships between mind and nature (which includes man himself). In the first view, nature is seen as the source of human vitality; in the second, nature is seen as the hostile to be conquered and subjected to human needs and desires. Both forms of behavior are adaptive mechanisms which have human survival value for the organism. One attitude has led in one direction, and the other over quite a different road. Here is the crossroads, and one of the principal questions anthropology asks is, why do some men go one way and others another? Can we learn something about man, or history, or even the future, in studying such divergence? In the case of American civilization, what meanings are present and where do such answers that we may find lead us?

Another significant feature of America's aboriginal past that is of marked interest is concerned with the antiquity of man in the Americas. Antiquity is important because, as we have said, isolation has played a very large role in culture development where it has not been influenced by outside forces. This subject of the real antiquity of the New World man is one of the most debated issues in American anthropology. It is also one of the most exciting, because so little is really known with certainty of man's appearance for the first time in the North or South American continents; and because at the present time it begins to appear that man's antiquity in the New World is as great as in the Old World.

There are large questions suggested by the knowledge that in spite of such great age as may be represented, no really primitive fossil skulls or related bones have been found that would suggest evolutionary changes that are evident, say, among primates evolving in Africa, Europe or Asia. American culture materials manifested as simple stone tools, now known, are very much like Old World stone tools, and these suggest, always, man's preoccupation with environmental adaptation. Present evidence clearly indicates man's appearance in North America by 40,000 years B.C. at least, and more recent speculations (and evidence incompletely evaluated), suggest that he may have appeared as much as 500,000 years ago.[3] Yet fossil bones, where found, show features essentially modern, and clearly *Homo sapiens sapiens* in kind. The developing field of aboriginal linguistics also indicates great age for man's first occupation of the New World, and is itself an exceedingly important and fundamental field in anthropology.

Such interests as these have been present from the very beginning of Indian-white contact. One needs only to read Jefferson's *Notes on the State of Virginia* or the Lewis and Clark *Journals,* or Benjamin Franklin, to fully realize the extent of interest in the earliest of Americans before the advent of the field of anthropology. Jefferson interested himself in the origin of the Indian and wrote of basic races from which diverse tribes arose. Lewis and Clark, with direct contact experiences, were motivated in their thinking (and behavior) by aboriginal life. And it was Benjamin Franklin, thinking about separation from England before the revolution and reflecting on the League of the Iroquois, who wrote:

> It would be a strange thing if Six Nations of ignorant savages should be capable of forming a scheme for such an union, and be able to execute it in such a manner that it has subsisted ages and appears indissoluble; and yet that a like union should be

impracticable for ten or a dozen English colonies, to whom it is more necessary and must be more advantageous, and who cannot be supposed to want an equal understanding of their interests.[4]

The field of anthropology, as an academic discipline, developed in the United States as a direct outgrowth of experiences similar to those just described. It was the opportunity offered by the presence of aboriginal man living in one's backyard, as it were, that stimulated the development of the field. In the beginning, at least, anthropology (*anthropo* for man, and *logy* for study) was the creation of men of widely diverse interests and training. Besides those already cited, there were figures such as Lewis Henry Morgan, Franz Boas, George Bird Grinnell, and Ales Hrdlička. Morgan began a career as a practicing lawyer, Boas came to America as a German-trained geographer, Grinnell was a geologist, and Hrdlička was a medical doctor. These men brought with them enthusiasm and an ability to excite other individuals with their teachings and writings, about the Indian.

One last example might be the figure of John Wesley Powell (1834-1902), who also was trained in geology, but who, after service in the Civil War, became an outstanding ethnologist, his two most significant anthropological achievements being the founding of the United States Bureau of American Ethnology in 1879 and his original studies and classification of American Indian languages. The highpoint of his geologic career was marked, of course, with his historic trip down the Colorado River and through the Grand Canyon, a three-month journey during which time the Indians as well as the Canyon itself were studied.

We have cited, then, three important historic developments that have evolved with man's interest in man, relative to his New World experiences. The awareness of such developments, and in most cases the actual search for them, has been made possible by careful application of one or more methods in our studies. The principal developments we referred to are: (1) a rebirth of classic Old World attitudes toward the natural environment, (2) a new insight into the antiquity of man in the New World, and (3) the impact of the American Indian on Western man (i.e., man carrying a heritage of Old World cultures), his culture and society.

Now, in each case of recognition of these developments, understanding has come through the application of some kind of orderly response to observed data. Such an orderly response is sometimes referred to as method. A good working method that helps the anthropologist to understand the data, requires one or more points of reference that can be trusted to remain stable, at least during the time of study or investigation. In the search for such constants in the development of American anthropology, we find science playing a large role, perhaps larger than it should, for not everyone feels that we can adopt a method (or points of reference) found useful and even pragmatic in the physical or biological sciences, say, and apply them to an understanding of human behavior, and hence to society and culture. Yet, in anthropology, methods applied elsewhere have prevailed and to a large degree account for development and changes that have come in the field over a period of time. Important ideas such as those of organic evolution and relativity have brought new ways of looking at anthropological data and have left their marks upon the history of the discipline. The student might look for these marks in his studies. We speak and write, for example, of cultural evolution, suggesting that cultures have developed from simpler to more complex stages. For the archaeologist this idea is formulated into ideas of Lithic, Archaic, Form- ative, Classic and Post-classic stages of culture development, each stage having its own definition, its requirements for classification of cultures in one or the other stages. The concept has limitations and many exceptions to the rule. For example, traditions (showing little or no culture change through time) prevail, and the question immediately is why? Why do some cultures show constant change and take directions that, knowing some of the details, make possible some predictions by the anthropologist concerning culture destiny? Why do other cultures remain basically unchanged?

Why does "culture lag" prevail among some peoples where neighboring communities and events are dynamic and changing? The idea of organic evolution is beset by similar questions which are the result of recognition of unchanged forms in nature, sometimes called living fossils.

These and other questions require some system of study, so the anthropologist is very sensitive to procedures of analysis. Through the years, various methods of approach have been tried.

Because anthropology was born at a time when the idea of organic evolution was abroad, the idea of culture evolution developed as an early concept in explaining the presence of cultures with varying complexities, as developing through periods of growth from the so-called savage to the civilized states (the idea of societies being responsible for cultures always understood). This concept, derived from the natural sciences, became the keystone for development of the early phase of the comparative method, the principle by which each culture studied was compared with (or set against for comparison) what passes for the civilized state, in this case Western Civilization. The working part of the method, which was rooted in the premise that a unilinear development of cultures takes place through stages, from savagery to civilization, compared and evaluated all world cultures in terms, characteristics, and values found in Western Civilization. Implicit in the method is the regular need to make value judgments upon other cultures and societies, based upon the belief that Western man has already arrived at the highest possible state of development and his culture represents the ideal state of accomplishment. Also implicit is a strong belief in the idea of progress.

In the American school, Lewis Henry Morgan was the principle force behind this idea and method during the 19th century. Subsequent research among primitives, especially in the New World, and the introduction of ideas of other men, have radically changed this basic approach. Though it survives today, it does so with decided alterations.

In a sense Franz Boas, the principle critic of the Morgan concept, may be said to utilize the comparative method, also, as a way of analyzing culture data. His own methodology, based upon the study of *traits*, as minimum units of culture, emphasizes "the tracing of specific units in cultural settings of past and present [and it]involves constant exercises in cultural comparison."[5]   Boas, however, was a trained geographer, and the impact of that training is evident in his interest in the distribution of culture traits in *space* as well as through *time* so that each culture represents an historical growth through time, and a distribution of culture traits over space, thus making *culture areas*. An analysis of these characteristics of cultures presents the maximum opportunity for understanding cultures. Looking back at the whole idea, it seems to have had only one principle weakness: it was inclined to look upon the individual as merely a kind of mold into which the clay of culture was poured. This made the individual the subject of what is known as cultural determinism. Today we know that forces besides culture make the individual (hence the society and culture) what he becomes; environment and heredity also play significant roles.

Boas had a great deal of success with his historical method, as is evidenced by students such as Alfred Kroeber and Clark Wissler, who amplified his ideas and extended them into working theories and methods of their own. One example is Dr. Clark Wissler and his concept of a *culture area,* which is a measure of the spatial dimension representing a geographic region where common culture traits are found. In a culture area we find the center at or very near the region where the greatest concentration of type traits exist, and the margin of the culture area is bounded by the disappearance of these traits. Kroeber was successful in showing that culture areas and natural areas correspond very closely, hence one can (in the Americas) understand cultures as adaptations to natural areas, in part. We have, therefore, designations such as Plains Tribes (peoples dependent on the horse and bison which themselves are dependent upon the grasslands of a prairie or steppe environment; and even these physiographic regions are dependent for their characteristics upon rainfall, hence climate), Wild Rice Gatherers (Indians of the Great Lakes region), the Desert Farmers (Pueblos) and the Northwest Coast Fishermen (Haida, Tlingit and Tsimshian, as examples). The *age-area* is a closely related concept of the culture area which Wissler and others used, to add the dimension of time to the historical framework. The idea states simply that older traits in any given culture will be found to be more widely distributed than more recent traits, and the application of this idea serves best where materials dealt with are scanty in number. It is an idea borrowed from biologists, and is another instance of the impact of science on anthropology.

These two working methods, comparative methodology and historicalism, are only two of a number of more or less successful methods that have concerned anthropologists as the field has developed. Other working models used to help explain culture are Diffusionism, Functionalism and Configurationalism. Since they are rather complex approaches, it is advisable for students to look into these individually and study them carefully. There are others in culture studies, especially in ethnology.

One last method example might be cited, largely because of its successful application to historic writings which enable us to examine cultures of which we would be largely ignorant had it not been for men such as the Jesuit missionaries, travelers to the West after the return of Lewis and Clark, who, like the latter, kept daily journal notes; military men on campaigns against the Indians; and scientists recording data from their explorations of the land, who also made notes on Indians as well as on the environments that seemed to be their principle interest. The method of study is known as ethnohistory, which simply enables us to study or analyze cultures that no longer exist (or exist markedly changed), through a study of historical documents that were written at a time when cultures were still alive and vital, and observations were being made and recorded on the spot. These observations amount to primary source material. A succinct but complete description of this method is found in *American Indian and White Relations to 1830* by William N. Fenton [Chapel Hill, 1957] pp. 19-21. This method reminds one of the frequent use of autobiography, dictated by Indians to ethnographers and ethnologists, who then frequently apply ethnologic methods to the resulting material for purposes of culture analysis. Paul Radin's editorial work titled, *Crashing Thunder: The Autobiography of an American Indian* (New York, 1926), is a good example of this approach.

American archaeology also demonstrates a precise approach to prehistoric materials. This branch of American anthropology has its special problems, too, which involve interpretation of limited culture inventories: that is, artifacts that were cast away by primitives having no more use for them. There is no living man who can interpret for the archaeologist the meaning of some obscure design on a clay pot fragment (sherd), or explain the origin of the Iroquois. The archaeologist must piece together the past from human remains found in soils where they were usually left for trash. Nevertheless, a method may be applied to even these scant traces, permitting the maximum reconstruction of prehistoric cultures. In spite of the fragmentary nature of most of the culture remains in North America, students usually find this kind of research endeavor exciting beyond expectation. The reconstruction of such cultures by application of strict method stimulates the same kind of excitement (and under field conditions that are usually exciting in themselves) which results from the study of a good mystery story, especially where solutions to problems of culture are forthcoming and add to our basic knowledge.

We walk on the past every step we take — history, men's lives, and critical events of the past are entombed in the earth where they preserve unique histories of the unknown past, and where they await only the proper application of a careful method to resurrect them, to bring them to life again, to make them a part of our own lives. The method that resurrects the past for the American archaeologist is not unlike the historical method of the ethnologist. As a matter of fact, it is much more satisfactorily applied, and results are more tangible in spite of the scant remains with which we often deal. The method is somewhat easier to grasp than other anthropological methods, largely because the approach used by the archaeologist utilizes actual field conditions on a site once occupied by the society producing the culture. Stable points of reference are still important because of unique field conditions that place sharp restrictions upon deviations that might creep into methods of investigation.

In this discussion it should be remembered that one of the most fundamental of discoveries at the very dawn of science (some three or more thousands of years ago) was the fact that we have no immutable points of reference on the earth. Mountains form and are worn down (peneplaned) by forces of erosion, lakes and rivers develop and dry away. Life is born, and dies. Change is everywhere around us. One of the reasons for the early development of astronomy was the search for permanent reference points – which, of course, do not exist. With the success of astronomy, then, and the application of prediction as one of the ends of careful observation, what better dimensions could we use than those that have borne successful results for so long a time?

The principle dimensions are (1) *space,* which attempts to measure culture trait distribution geographically, (where common traits appear regularly over an area at a given depth, we speak of a culture horizon); (2) *time,* a vertical line crossing the horizontal one (for space) on the model, and representing the age and development of culture; finally, (3) the *formal content* of the culture represented, and distributed in space at a particular time. The formal content represents specific characteristics (the ethnologist's traits) found in any recognized culture complex. The total picture, represented by an integration of the time and spacial dimensions of the culture with the understanding and addition of the formal content, gives us what Willey and Phillips describe at the cultural-historical integration.[6] This synthesis, theoretically, reconstructs as nearly as is possible the total description of a culture in its temporal and spacial perspective. In doing so it describes the society; and, by focusing on units of material culture and relationships that exist there, it treats human behavior and the individual producing the culture.

This broad outline might be improved by the addition of the diagram shown in Fig. 1.

In archaeology *time* is determined by radiocarbon dating of charcoal from old fire hearths, or bone, or vegetable fiber making up wearing apparel, or any other organic remains containing carbon; or by dendrochronology (tree ring dating); by potassium-argon determinations, if the human remains or artifacts are very old; or by geochronology (that is, by dating culture materials relative to the age of sediments in which they are found). These represent only several of many methods used in archaeology to arrive at the ages of what we might call temporal sequences for cultures of prehistoric character.

Space is evaluated in terms of the distribution of cultural traits (type of pottery, designs on pottery or textiles, or even in terms of projectile point types, where material culture development has not proceeded very far). Perhaps the most significant variable determining the distribution of societies of men (represented by cultures) is environment again — that is, the distribution of men possessing different cultures throughout different geographic regions can often be accounted for in terms of adaptation of a primitive people to specific ecologic zones, such as the case with the Wild Rice Gatherers of the Great Lakes region, or the so-called Anasazi culture to the southwest of the United States. In these different regions, men have learned to adapt to specific conditions of environments and, to the degree that these environments differ from one another, the cultures will differ also. Examples of studies along this line are Alfred Kroeber, *Cultural and Natural Areas of Native North America* (Berkeley, 1953); and Clark Wissler, *The Relation of Nature to Man in Aboriginal America* (New York, 1926).

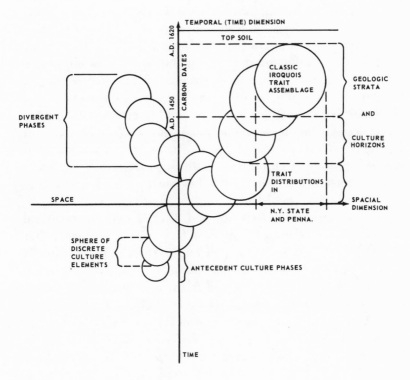

Fig. 1. Idealized model (modified from Willey & Phillips) of the theoretical development of culture (represented here by the Iroquois) through time, as found in temporal sequences exposed in archaeological field work. Classic Iroquois is characterized, through studies in ethnography, by development of the Longhouse, the League, false face societies, matrilineal descent and maize economy. Radiocarbon dates represent absolute times given by Isotropes, Inc. after analysis of charcoal from two different hearths associated with type Iroquois artifacts.

There are other variables: culture influences culture, as where two cultures (societies) meet and one influences the other through social impact. Sometimes the influence of one is greater than another and we find mixed traits, with one or more traits predominating in what is usually considered a marginal area. Internal political or religious strength may carry ideas (hence cultural traits found woven into textiles by way of military or religious motifs) far and wide, crossing mountains, or passing through geographic filters (such as the Isthmus of Panama) or even the oceans (such as has been demonstrated in Ecuador by Evans and Meggers in showing the markedly similar features between the Valdivia pottery of Ecuador and the Jomon of Japan). In any event, the study of the distribution of cultural traits throughout geographic space is an important reference point that usually contributes to the understanding of prehistory.

Formal content is that body of discrete culture traits and relationships (collectively referred to as phase, or focus) that are specific to a society at any given time and/or place. Formal content manifests itself as the hardcore remains of human behavior in whatever form, and frequently deals with subjective concepts, such as religious views that are objectified by way of designs, and art styles incorporated within the material remains of the culture. Formal content *is* culture, which, in turn, is patterned human behavior discovered by archaeological method, and recorded as ethnographic material derived from a people no longer surviving to relate the information. It incorporates material culture, suggests economic, political and social organization, as well as ideas of cosmogony and cosmology. It includes language and play. Formal content distinguishes all of these culture universals insofar as they can be discovered through archaeological method. When the field work is finished and when the formal content is understood in terms of its time-space relationships, the culture-historical integration is complete and, presumably, the prehistory is known.

Applying such a method to prehistoric New World sites has

made possible the construction of some theoretical generalizations about cultures known in this hemisphere. These generalizations are not always entirely accepted, but nevertheless do
supply tentative explanations for cultural phenomena.

The first generalization having considerable influence and
some validity emphasizes that, with due consideration given to
gradations at each level, cultures develop in, and proceed
through, stages in an evolutionary fashion. Hence it is possible
to see culture change leading from the Lithic Stage to the
Archaic Stage (from a nomadic life where game and plant food
are sought, to a sedentary way of life where various foods are
collected, respectively). The Archaic Stage evolves into the
Formative with the domestication of plants and the development of agriculture. The Classic Stage is marked by the
development of urbanization (as among the Inca, Maya, Aztec
and Pueblo) attended by increased political influence and
cultural expansion. The fifth and final stage is referred to as
the Post-classic and is marked by shrinkage of political and
cultural influence along with the decline of regional styles in
such materials as pottery, painting and textiles, where the
latter are present. This stage is regularly associated with the
development of militarism and a significant attention to
secularism.

This stepwise progression is marked with difficulties that a
little reflection on the part of the student may well make
clear. It represents, above all, an oversimplification of complex
cultural phenomena having their roots in even more complex
human behavior, which we are all too quickly inclined to
believe to be regularly predictable.

Stage development is often characterized by incomplete
development of the total cycle. The Iroquois, for example,
never developed a culture (by definition) more complex than
that which we have referred to in the Formative Stage. There
are reasons for this trend — and well known to the Iroquois —
which careful study of the political structure of the Iroquois
will make quite clear. Other examples of living cultures could
be cited as well. The Sioux Indians are cultural nomads and to

this day have had great difficulty in adapting to any other life-way. There are characteristics in their culture so precisely geared to the nomadic way of life, with its freedom and rugged individualism, that individuals regularly suffer shock when attempting to change, or are driven to change by others.

This tendency to move through time without the development of significant change in culture is referred to as tradition. Big Game Hunting was once a tradition persisting over a period of thousands of years in the face of opportunities that might have made culture changes advantageous to the people confronting them. The concept of tradition brings us back to the temporal dimension of our working diagram and, when looked at in terms of this vertical line representing time, it (tradition) is seen as a continuity of persistent culture characteristics through time. Big Game Hunting has been a culture tradition in the New World, but so has the continued use of maize (Indian corn) as a staple crop, and elaborate religious ceremonials associated with its planting and harvest. Should one distinguish between different kinds of traditions? It is significant that these traditions, having historical depth, have been the most successful of adaptive mechanisms, and they have carried with them guarantees of culture survival not seen among cultures where change, often taking place rapidly, continually carries the latter through stages of development (making for increasing complexity and associated instability).

When we write about the American culture we think in social, economic and political (mostly political) terms, not of people indigenous to North America but of people recently arrived, who have developed a somewhat new life-way, after the era of Columbus. In point of fact, the unique unawareness to opportunities presented to migrants from the Old World, and the inability of the immigrating people to seize upon apparently unique conditions to create a truly new society and culture, is what Gerard Piel refers to in his statement cited earlier in this chapter. This Old World pattern, he says, of human exploitation and conquest of our resources, both human and environmental, is our failure. For example, we seldom, if ever, think of the Indian and the possible impact of his ways of life on the newly arrived western man. We speak of the frontier's impact on westward migrating people, but forget that the Indian was the personification of that frontier spirit which contributed to the new nation. We speak of the wilderness as producing experiences never known before to people whose limited exposure to such a phenomenon did not prepare them for the impact of an environment so exotic as to "strain the imagery of the travelers," as one writer put it in commenting on the western landscape. The Indian is not recalled, nor is his unique cultural adaptations to the various environments considered much more, in most instances, than a struggle for survival. We do not think of corn or potatoes, squash, beans or quinine as products introduced by Indians; nor do we think of the political impact of the League of the Iroquois upon such an influential man as Franklin. We have overlooked the impact of the boyhood experiences of Thomas Jefferson with the Indians, with whom his father had to deal on the Virginia frontier. It is an historical omission of great magnitude that captive whites, more often than pleased the civilized, could not be persuaded to return to white society when "rescued."

In working with such knowledge and attempting to understand it, anthropologists today have had their first real opportunity to apply knowledge acquired from their science to human problems, hence the special area known as Applied Anthropology begins to make possible the use of detailed information about culture; heretofore, because of extreme reticence on the part of the anthropologists about making value judgments, the application of anthrological knowledge was largely bypassed.

What we see is a wall being erected between man and his natural environment that increasingly removes man from that environment and substitutes the cultural in its place. Sometimes the natural environment is referred to as the "primary," and the cultural environment the "secondary," for convenience. Whatever the case, as the cultural more and more replaces the natural, man's problems increase in geometric progression, in a direction toward structural crisis of the society as a result of too rapid a change; and aggression directed against the earth and forces within the cosmic framework that enabled man to evolve into a lifeform capable of maintaining unprecedented positions within the larger framework of nature.

The field of applied anthropology, therefore, appears at this time to be one of increasing importance as a result of the many problems that have developed in the course of man's momentary successful adaptation to his environment, and because of serious problems now facing us, such as overpopulation, pollution of air and water, of foods, and even pragmatic human values. The direction which the applied anthropologist will take will not be simply that of coping with these problems, for that would be merely symptomatic treatment!

Though no anthropologist for a moment pretends that even the most successful Indian cultures were without major problems, many of the Indian cultures nevertheless present much that American culture might emulate, as recognized by John Collier, and others. We have cited the League of the Iroquois and its political structure, which involved orderly and successful government, yet did not greatly limit individual autonomy. The Pueblos are recognized as having constructed the world's first true democracy (the Greeks, of course, held slaves). The Plains Tribes doggedly protected the freedom of the individual and, above all, perpetuated the concept of "stewardship of the earth" and incorporated values derived from the relation of man to nature into every aspect of their cultures. In fact this is true of most American Indians, and that characteristic has made them at once the most successful in developing life of great quality, and the most vulnerable to other peoples who carry with them the aggressive instinct directed especially toward the environments of the earth.

It is very late. Extinction of the human species seems a very real possibility at the present time, through multiple causes, but all of them are of man's own making. It is this simple fact that becomes apparent as the anthropologist compares cultures of the New World. If we are to survive as a society and culture, applied anthropology will be one of the specialized fields in the larger whole which will contribute most, and probably by some not now apparent method of restructuring our value system; perhaps in part, so far as the environment is concerned, by pointing out what is needed within the American character that will motivate it toward the stewardship value rather than the spirit of conquest.

It is not a peculiar deficiency in the Indians north of Mexico that civilization, as we understand it, was not created. Every evidence indicates that high civilization was in every case avoided, simply because of the Indian recognition of its meaning. The great period of time of occupancy of North America which the archaeologist is discovering, by the man we call the Indian, together with the low level of quantitative culture development, suggest not only great culture success (good adaptation) among Indians of northern America but also the traditional patterns needed in culture which intends to survive in the face of rapid change.

To close this chapter by stressing and illustrating the value of the field of applied anthropology one could do no better than to quote the eminent anthropologist, Loren Eiseley, as one of the best examples of the thinking leading toward the outright application of anthropological knowledge:

> If we are to build a stable cultural structure above that which threatens to engulf us by changing our lives more rapidly than we can adjust our habits, it will be by flinging over the torrent a structure as taut and flexible as a spider's web, a human society deeply self-conscious and undeceived by waters that race beneath it, a society more literate, more appreciative of human worth than any society that has previously existed. That is the sole prescription, not for survival — which is meaningless — but for a society worthy to survive.[7]

NOTES

1. *The Dynamics of Change*, ed. Don Fabun, (Englewood Cliffs, 1967), part II, p. 11.

2. John Collier, *The Indians of the Americas*, (New York, 1947), pp. 15-16.

3. C. Vance Haynes, Jr., "The Earliest Americans," *Science*, 166: 3906 (November 7, 1969), 713. See also, B.E. Raemsch, "Artifacts from Mid-Wisconsin Gravels," and "Pleistocene Tools from the Northeast of North America," *Yager Museum Publications in Anthropology Bulletin*, Nos. 1 and 3, respectively, 1968 and 1971.

4. Carl VanDoren, *Benjamin Franklin* (New York, 1938), p. 209.

5. Felix M. Keesing, *Cultural Anthropology* (New York, 1964), p. 146.

6. *Method and Theory in American Archaeology* (Chicago, 1958), p. 12.

7. *The Firmament of Time* (New York, 1962), p. 147.

BIBLIOGRAPHY

Resource Bibliographies

Bibliographic Index: A Commulative Bibliography of Bibliographies. New York, 1937.

Butler, Ruth Lapham. *A Bibliographical Checklist of North and Middle American Indian Linguistics in the Edward E. Ayer Collection.* 2 vols., Newberry Library. Chicago, 1941.

Dockstader, Frederick J. comp., *Graduate Studies; A Bibliography of the American Indian in Theses and Dissertations.* Museum of the Amer. Indian, Heye Foundation, *Contributions.* 15. New York, 1957.

Fenton, William N., L.H. Butterfield and Wilcomb E. Washburn. *American Indian and White Relations to 1830.* Chapel Hill, 1957.

Gommer, George Laurence. *Index of Archaeological Papers, 1665-1890.* London, 1907.

Hodge, Frederick Webb. ed., *Handbook of American Indians North of Mexico.* Bur. Amer. Ethnol. *Bull.* 30, pts. 1-2 Washington, 1907-1910; repr. 1912.

Keesing, Felix M. *Culture Change: An Analysis and Bibliography of Anthropological Sources to 1952.* Stanford, 1953.

McCoy, James C. *Jesuit Relations of Canada, 1623-1673.: A Bibliography.* Intro. by Lawrence C. Wroth. Paris, 1937.

Murdock, George P. *Ethnographic Bibliography of North America.* Yale Univ., *Anthropological Stud.* I. 3rd ed.; New Haven, 1960.

Rouse, Irving and John M. Goggin. eds., *An Anthropological Bibliography of the Eastern Seaboard.* Eastern States Archaeological Federation, *Research Pubn. I.* New Haven, 1947.

Swanton, John R. *The Indian Tribes of North America,* Bur. Amer. Ethnol., *Bulletin 145.* Washington, 1952.

Willey, Gordon R., and Philip Phillips. *Method and Theory in American Archaeology.* Chicago, 1958.

Serials

American Anthropologist, Washington, D.C.

American Antiquity, Washington, D.C.

American Museum of Natural History, *Anthropological Papers,* & *Memoirs,* New York.

American Philosophical Society, *Transactions, Proceedings,* Philadelphia.

Anthropologica, Ottawa.

Bureau of American Ethnology, *Annual Reports,* & *Bulletin,* Washington, D.C.

Current Anthropology, Chicago.

Ethnohistory, Bloomington.

Exploration: Studies in Culture and Communication, Toronto.

Field Museum of Natural History, *Publications,* & *Anthropological Series,* Chicago.

Harvard University, Peabody Museum of American Archaeology and Ethnology, *Papers,* & *Memoirs,* Cambridge, Mass.

Heye Foundation, Museum of the American Indian, *Contributions,* & *Indian Notes and Monographs,* New York.

National Museum of Canada, *Bulletin,* Ottawa.

Southwestern Journal of Anthropology, Albuquerque.

University of California *Anthropological Records,* Berkeley.

Wenner-Gren Foundation for Anthropological Research, *Viking Fund Publications in Anthropology,* New York.

Yager Museum Publications in *Anthropology Bulletin,* Oneonta, New York.

Yale University, *Publications in Anthropology,* New Haven.

Archives

(Little used, but important depositories offering unique opportunities for research.)

FRANCE

Paris: ARCHIVES OF THE QUAI D'ORSAY (missionaries of the Northeast).

SPAIN

Barcelona: CITY HALL LIBRARY (California Indians).
Seville: ARCHIVES OF THE INDIES *(ARCHIVO GENERAL DE INDIAS)*
            (a) *Casa de Contratación de las Indias* Section.
            (b) *Gobierno* Section (Puebla de Los Angeles in the *Audiencia).*
            (c) *Correos* Section.
            (d) *Ultramar* Section.
            (e) *Mapas, Planos, y Dibujos* Section.

MEXICO

Mexico City:
            1. NATIONAL ARCHIVES (ARCHIVO GENERAL DE LA NACION)
            (a) *Ramo de Mercedes.*
            (b) *Ramo de Indios.*
            (c) *Ramo de Tierras.*
            (d) *Ramo de Historia.*
            (e) *Ramo de Padrones.*
            (f) *Ramo General de Partes.*

            2. ARCHIVES OF THE NATIONAL MUSEUM OF ANTHROPOLOGY
            (a) *Anales de Puebla y Tlaxcala.*
            (b) *Fondo Franciscano.*
            (c) *Mapas y Planos.*

UNITED STATES

Berkeley: BANCROFT COLLECTION OF THE UNIVERSITY OF CALIFORNIA.
Austin: UNIVERSITY OF TEXAS LIBRARY.
Chicago: AYER COLLECTION OF THE NEWBERRY LIBRARY.
New York: 1. NEW YORK PUBLIC LIBRARY
            2. CONWAY COLLECTION
Washington: LIBRARY OF CONGRESS

Texts and General Information

Brace, C.L. and M.F. Montagu. *Man's Evolution: An Introduction to Physical Anthropology.* New York, 1965.

Heizer, Robert F. *Guide to Archaeological Field Methods.* Palo Alto, 1958.

Herskovits, Melville J. *Man and His Works: The Science of Cultural Anthropology.* New York, 1948.

Hoebel, E. Adamson. *Man in the Primitive World.* 2nd ed.; New York, 1958.

Hulse, Frederick S. *The Human Species.* 2nd ed. New York, 1971.

Jennings, Jesse D. *Prehistory of North America.* New York, 1968.

Keesing, Felix M. *Cultural Anthropology.* New York, 1958.

Kluckhohn, Clyde. *Mirror for Man.* New York, 1960.

Kraus, Bertram S. *The Basis of Human Evolution.* New York, 1964.

Kroeber, Alfred L. *Anthropology.* New York, 1964.

Pelto, Pertti J. *The Nature of Anthropology.* Columbus, 1966.

Willey, Gordon R. *An Introduction to American Archaeology, Vol. I, North and Middle America.* Englewood Cliffs, 1966.

Wissler, Clark. *The American Indian: An Introduction to the Anthropology of the New World.* 3rd ed.; New York, 1938.

Related Readings

Adair, James, *The History of the American Indians, Particularly Those Nations Adjoining to the Mississippi, East and West Florida, Georgia, South and North Carolina, and Virginia....* London, 1775.

Boas, Franz, *The Mind of Primitive Man.* New York, 1938.

Butzer, Karl W. *Environment and Archaeology: An Introduction to Pleistocene Geography.* Chicago, 1964.

Carver, Jonathan. *Travels through the Interior Parts of North America, in the Years 1766, 1767, and 1768.* London, 1778.

Chard, Chester S. "The Old World Roots: Review and Speculations," in "Early Man in the Western American Artic: A Symposium."

Frederick H. West, ed., *Anthropological Papers of the University of Alaska*, Vol. 10, No. 2, pp. 115-121. College, 1963.

Charlevoix, Pierre F. X. de. *History and General Description of New France*. trans. John Gilmary Shea. New York, 1866-1872.

Colden, Cadwallader. *The History of the Five Indian Nations Depending on the Province of New York*. ed. John Gilmary Shea. New York, 1866.

Collier, John. *The Indians of the Americas*. New York, 1947.

Cornwall, I.W. *Bones for the Archaeologist*. London, 1956.

Curtis, E.S. *The North American Indian*, 20 vols. Cambridge, Mass., & Norwood, 1907-1930. Johnson Reprint, limited ed.; New York, 1970.

Darwin, Charles. *The Origin of Species*. New York, 1958.

Eiseley, Loren. *Darwin's Century*. New York, 1958.

-----. *The Immense Journey*. New York, 1957.

Fabun, Don. *The Dynamics of Change*. Englewood Cliffs, 1967.

Jefferson, Thomas. *Notes on the State of Virginia*. Ed. William Peden. Chapel Hill, 1955.

Murdock, George P. *Our Primitive Contemporaries*. New York, 1934.

Owen, Roger C., James J.F. Deetz and Anthony D. Fisher. eds., *The North American Indians, A Sourcebook*. New York, 1967.

Powell, J.W. *The Exploration of the Colorado River and its Canyons*. New York, 1961.

Radin, Paul. *The Story of the American Indian*. New York, 1927.

Tax, Sol, gen. ed. *World Anthropology*. 80+ vols. The Hague: Mouton (in press). (Recent research by world scholars presented at IXth Internat. Congress of Anthropological and Ethnological Sciences, Chicago, 1973)

Thwaites, Reuben G., ed., *Original Journals of the Lewis and Clark Expedition, 1804-1806*. New York, 1904-1905.

Underhill, Ruth Murray. *Red Man's America: A History of the Indians in the United States*. Chicago, 1953.

Vallois, Henri V. and Marcellin Boule. *Fossil Men*. New York, 1957.

Zeuner, Frederick E. *Dating the Past: An Introduction to Geochronology*. 4th ed.; London, 1958.

Representative Materials

A sampling of representative materials by subject-area of probable interest to the student of American civilization.

General

Childe, Gordon V. *Piercing Together the Past: The Interpretation of Archaeological Data*. London, 1956.

Driver, Harold E., William C. Massey. *Comparative Studies of North American Indians*. Amer. Phil. Soc. *Transactions*. Vol 47, Pt. 2. Philadelphia, 1957.

Haag, William G. "The Bering Strait Land Bridge," *Scientific American*, 206 (1962), 112-123.

Hallowell, A. Irving. *Culture and Experience*. Philadelphia, 1955.

-----. "The Backwash of the Frontier: The Impact of the Indian on American culture." *The Frontier in Perspective*. Ed. Walker D. Wyman and Clifton B. Kroeber. Madison, 1957. Pp. 229-257.

Hoebel, E. Adamson, *The Law of Primitive Man: A Study in Comparative Legal Dynamics*. Cambridge, Mass., 1954.

Kroeber, Alfred L. *Cultural and Natural Areas of Native North America*. Berkeley, 1953.

Moorehead, W.E. *The Stone Age in North America*. Boston, 1910.

Putnam, F.W. *Reports*. as Curator of the Peabody Museum of Harvard University. Cambridge, Mass., 1876-1919.

Sorokin, Pitirim A. *Social and Cultural Dynamics*. Vol II: *Fluctuations of Systems of Truth, Ethics, and Law* and Vol. III: *Fluctuation of Social Relationships, War, and Revolution*. New York, 1937.

Wissler, Clark. *The Relation of Nature to Man in Aboriginal America*. New York, 1926.

Northwest North America Coast Area

Anderson, H.D. and W. C. Eells. *Alaska Natives*. Stanford, 1935.

Barnett, H.G. *The Coast Salish of British Columbia*. Eugene, 1955.

Boas, Franz, *"The Kwakiutl of Vancouver Island,"* in American Museum of Natural History, *Memoirs*. III. New York, 1909, 307-515.

Cook, S.F. "The Conflict between the California Indians and White Civilization," *Ibero-Americana*. Berkely, 1943, XXI, 1-194; XXII, 1-55; XXIII, 1-115.

Drucker, P. *Cultures of the North Pacific Coast*. San Francisco, 1965.

Krause, A. *Die Tlinkit-Indianer*. Jena, 1885.

-----. *The Tlingit Indians*. tr. by Erna Gunther. Seattle, 1956.

Nelson, E.W. *The Eskimo about the Bering Strait*. The Bureau of American Ethnology, *Annual Report*. XVIII: 1. Washington, 1899.

Swanton, J.R. *Contributions to the Ethnology of the Haida*. Memoirs of the American Museum of Natural History, vol. VIII. New York, 1909.

Western U.S.

Carter, George F. *Pleistocene Man at San Diego*. Baltimore, 1957.

Cressman, Luther S. *Archaeological Researchs in the Northern Great Basin*. Publication 538, Carnegie Institution of Washington, 1942.

-----. *et al., Cultural Sequences at the Dalles, Oregon,* American Phil. Society, *Transactions*. Vol. 50, Pt. 10. Philadelphia, 1960.

Goddard, P.E. *Life and Culture of the Hupa*. Vol I. Berkeley, 1903.

Heizer, R.F., J.T. Davis, A.L. Koreber and A.B. Elsasser. *Aboriginal California: Three Studies in Cultural History*. Berkeley, 1963.

-----. and M.A. Whipple. *The California Indians: A Sourcebook*. Berkeley, 1951.

Merriam, C.H. *Studies of California Indians*. Berkeley, 1955.

Ray, V.F. *Primitive Pragmatists: The Modoc Indians of Northern California*. Seattle, 1963.

Rogers, M.L. *Early Lithic Industries of the Lower Basin of the Colorado River and Adjacent Desert Areas.* No. 3, San Diego Museum Papers. San Diego, 1939.

Southwest Area

Bandelier, Adolph F.A. *The Delight Makers.* New York, 1918.

Eggan, F. *Social Organization of the Western Pueblos.* Chicago, 1950.

Forbes, J.D. *Apache, Navaho, and Spaniard.* Norman, 1960.

Goodwin, F. *The Social Organization of the Western Apache.* Chicago, 1942.

-----, and E.B. Sayles. *An Early Pit House Village of the Mogollon Culture, Forestdale Valley, Arizona,* Univ. of Arizona, *Bulletin.* 18:4. Tucson, 1947.

Haury, Emil W. *The Excavation of Los Muertos and Neighboring Sites in the Salt River Valley, Southern Arizona.* Peabody Museum *Papers.* 24:1. Cambridge, 1954.

-----. *The Stratigraphy and Archaeology of Ventana Cave.* Albuquerque, 1950.

Joseph, A., R. Spicer, and J. Chesky. *The Desert People.* Chicago, 1949.

Kluckhohn, Clyde, and C. Leighton. *The Navaho.* Cambridge, 1946.

Parsons, E.C. *The Pueblo of Jemez.* New Haven, 1925.

Thompson, L. *Culture in Crisis: A Study of the Hopi Indians.* New York, 1950.

Plains and Prairie Area

Bowers, A.W. *Mandan Social and Ceremonial Organization.* Chicago, 1950.

Catlin, George. *Illustrations of the Manners, Customs and Condition of the North American Indian.* 2nd ed.; New York, 1842.

Clarke, W.P. *The Indian Sign Language.* Philadelphia, 1885.

Denig, E.T. and J.C. Ewers, eds., *Five Indian Tribes of the Upper Missouri: Sioux, Arickaras, Assiniboines, Crees and Crows.* Norman, 1961.

Dunning, R.W. *Social and Economic Change Among the Northern Ojibwa.* Toronto, 1959.

Ewers, J.C. *The Horse in Blackfoot Indian Culture.* Bureau of American Ethnology, *Bulletin* 159. Washington, 1955.

Fletcher, A.D. and F. LaFlesche. *The Omaha Tribe.* Bureau of American Ethnology, *Annual Report*, No. 27. Washington, 1906.

Grinnell, George B. *The Cheyenne Indians.* New Haven, 1923.

Lowie, Robert H. *Indians of the Plains.* New York, 1954.

Marriot, A. *The Ten Grandmothers: A Contribution of the Ethnology of the Kiowa Indians.* Norman, 1945.

Schoolcraft, Henry R. *Historical and Statistical Information, respecting the History, Condition and Prospects of the Indian Tribes of the United States....* Philadephia, 1851-1857.

Spier, Leslie. *The Sun Dance of the Plains Indians: Its Development and Diffusion.* American Museum of Natural History *Anthropological Papers*, Vol. 16, Pt. 7. New York, 1921.

Thwaites, Reuben G. ed., *The Jesuit Relations and Allied Documents: Travels and Explorations of the Jesuit Missionaries in New France, 1610-1791. The Original French, Latin, and Italian Texts with English Translations and Notes.* Cleveland, 1896-1901. 73 vols. in the original.

Eastern Woodland Area

Abbott, C.C. *Ten Years' Diggings in Lenape Land.* Trenton, 1912.

Fenton, William N. *Parker on the Iroquois.* Syracuse, 1968.

Foreman, Grant. *The Five Civilized Tribes.* Norman, 1934.

Griffin, J.B. ed., *Archaeology of Eastern United States.* Chicago, 1952.

Howley, J.P. *The Beothucks or Red Indians.* Cambridge, 1915.

Morgan, Lewis H. *League of the Ho-De-No-Sau-Nee or Iroquois.* 1901; rpt. New Haven, 1954.

Peithmann, I.M. *Red Men of Fire: A History of the Cherokee Indians.* Springfield, 1964.

Quimby, George I. *Indian Life in the Upper Great Lakes 11,000 B.C. to A.D. 1800.* Chicago, 1960.

Raemsch, Bruce E. "Preliminary Report on Adequentaga," *The Yager Museum Publications in Anthropology Bulletin,* No. 2. Oneonta, 1970, 1-19.

-----. "Pleistocene Tools from the Northeast of North America," *The Yager Museum Publications in Anthropology Bulletin,* No. 3. Oneonta, 1971. 1-21.

Ritchie, William A. *The Archaeology of New York State.* 2nd ed.; New York, 1969.

Speck, Frank G. *Midwinter Rites of the Cayuga Longhouse.* Philadelphia, 1949.

-----. *Naskapi.* Norman, 1935.

-----. *Penobscot Man; the Life of a Forest Tribe in Maine.* Philadelphia, 1940.

Swanton, J.R. *The Indians of the Southeastern United States.* Bureau of American Ethnology, *Bulletin,* 137. Washington, 1946.

Volk, Ernest. *The Archaeology of the Delaware Valley.* Peabody Museum *Papers.* Vol. V. Cambridge, Mass., 1911.

Documentary

Blair, Emma H. *The Indian Tribes of the Upper Mississippi Valley and Region of the Great Lakes....* Cleveland, 1911.

Boyd, Julian P. and Carl Van Doren. eds., *Indian Treaties Printed by Benjamin Franklin, 1736-1762.* Philadelphia, 1938.

Nasatir, Abraham P. ed., *Before Lewis and Clark: Documents Illustrating the History of the Missouri, 1785-1804.* St. Louis, 1952.

New York State. Secretary of State. *Journals of the Military Expedition of Major General John Sullivan against the Six Nations of Indians in 1779.* Auburn, 1881.

Pike, Zebulon M. *An Account of Expeditions to the Sources of The Mississippi, and through the Western Parts of Louisiana, to the Sources of the Arkansas, Kans. La Platte, and Pierre Jaun Rivers; Performed by order of the Government of the United States during the years 1805, 1806, and 1807.* Philadelphia, 1810.

Thwaites, Reuben G., ed., *Early Western Travels*, 1748-1846....
Cleveland, 1904-1907.

U.S. Treaties. *A Compilation of All the Treaties between the United
States and the Indian Tribes, Now in Force as Laws. Prepared under
the Provisions of the Act of Congress, Approved March 3, 1873.*
Washington, 1873.

CHAPTER EIGHT

American Studies: The Discipline of Art and Art History

The Study of American Art

James K. Kettlewell

The beginning student of American art faces the subject
with one or two strikes against him. The chances are that he
knows next to nothing about art. American literature and
history are taught almost at the kindergarten level. Art enters,
too, at this level of learning, but it is taught as a craft, not as
one of the humanities. Recently, so-called "humanities programs" have been introduced in our high schools; but in these
the brush with art is slight, and American art rarely makes
more than a brief appearance. So the student really does not
get a good crack at American art until he arrives at college,
where he will have an opportunity to take a one-semester
course in the subject. Yet American art is rarely a part of the
background knowledge of even cultivated and generally
knowledgeable people in this country, let alone students. The
beginning student, then, starts more or less from scratch. He
will have to learn the names of the key artists. It will be
necessary for him to familiarize himself with the paintings in
the museums and with the architecture in the streets. The
important bibliographical titles will be new to him. Finally,
he will have to master the techniques of analyzing works of
art. This last is of major importance if works of art are to
become for him what in actual fact they should be, unique and
illuminating original documents. So, in approaching the

subject of American art, one must not only introduce American art, but also the field of art history itself.

The subject of American art, like our political institutions, begins with and develops from the English colonies of the eastern seaboard. The interesting contributions of the Dutch, the French and the Spanish are important sidelights, but they do not belong to the main theme of artistic evolution in America. Therefore the general observations made here about American art will not apply to them.

It should be explained now that this consideration of American art includes the arts of painting, sculpture, and architecture.[1] The decorative arts in America are also an important subject: they should be dealt with as an adjunct of architecture.

Style and the Analysis of Art

Books and periodicals constitute a serious danger for the student unfamiliar with the ways of art, for they tempt him from the works of art themselves. It is so much easier to sit in a quiet library reading about pictures than it is to go across town or to a distant city to a museum, then to walk a long distance over hard marble floors and to stand stiffly, uncomfortably, and perhaps blankly before the real thing. The habit is ingrained in us to do our intellectual work seated, surrounded by silence, facing a verbal stream or spewing forth a verbal stream as we write down our notes or thoughts. It takes a real effort, a concerted self-discipline (even on the part of the art historian himself), to face the work of art in all its difficult originality. But it is necessary. We in the field of art history recognize and work with the fact that an immense amount of nonsense has been written about art by people who have failed to take a close and careful look at what they are writing about. Writings in American art particularly, have to be approached with more than a moderate degree of caution. The field is notorious for its inadequate and inaccurate scholarship. The student is advised to check everything he reads against other written sources and against those most sturdy of all documents, the original works of art. The problem is that a great deal of the writing in the field has been done by amateurs or by self-styled scholars from the local historical society who lack the proper techniques to separate fact from fancy. At the same time, these people deserve credit for unearthing and preserving much that might have been lost. One's skepticism should be balanced with respect.

The techniques of the modern art historian are psuedo-scientific. They imitate the techniques of the botanist and the zoologist. Something resembling biological morphology has been developed for the study of art. The scholar begins by classifying works of art into categories and sub-categories according to their formal or structural characteristics. The procedure is very objective. The analysis of the work of art (the art historian uses the word "analysis") is like a dissection: formal qualities are precisely isolated and described.[2] If there is a weakness in this procedure, it is that it places too much emphasis on the formal structure of works of art. This reflects a twentieth century bias, that the essence of art is form. Subject matter and meaning, which are equally essential to the classification and understanding of art, are excluded. On the other hand, the great value of this kind of formal analysis is that it locks the attention of the scholar to the true physical properties of the work of art, which tends to preclude idle speculation about things that do not actually pertain to it.

Stylistic analysis and classification are necessary if art forms are to become useful documents. By this method works of art are dated and located in space and time. It separates authentic works from works that are dubious for one reason or another. It reveals the artist's sources and associations. In the study of American art it is particularly important for the scholar to perceive foreign influences. Only after these are discerned can the true American ingredients be identified. There is, then, a continuing obligation on the part of the student of American art make stylistic comparisons with the art of other countries.

Stylistic characteristics, while simply visual and objective, do reveal much of the meaning of the work of art. Form also carries much of the burden of the work's aesthetic import, so even though the analysis of style is a professional technique of art historians, it would be of great use to students of American studies who are directing their attention to art. Therefore, reading at least the opening chapters of Wölfflin's *Principles of Art History* will prove helpful. Wölfflin's system is very formal and abstract. His famous stylistic contrasts between Renaissance and Baroque art apply primarily to the structuring of space and composition. In his daily dealings with American art the things the art historian finds useful to take note of do not lend themselves very well to systematic organization. Brush stroke and surface texture, color, outlines, the modelling of forms with shadow, and the character of the picture space — these are the stylistic elements that attract one's attention first when he confronts a painting. In sculpture one observes immediately to what degree the form occupies space and how much it is penetrated by space. Then his attention will focus on the smaller aspects of the sculpture's surface: one will observe its texture, its relative simplicity or complexity, and the degree and extent of the modeling.

One useful, personal technique in analyzing representational art is to make judgements about how far forms in a particular work depart from reality, and exactly in what ways the form might differ from the real thing. If the observer's impression of reality is correct, then he will have a relatively clear idea of what the artist has actually done. The catch here is that one's impression of the real thing is often faulty. To be functional, this technique requires an extremely observant eye.

In architecture what attracts one's attention first are, often, superficialities. One sees the small things: the windows, the doors, the brickwork, and the ornamental embellishments. These things date American buildings with unerring precision. It is in the larger aspects of architectural compositions, in the planning of space and in the overall form of the building, that one discovers the philosophical connotations that are of importance to the cultural historian. For example, the complicated, broken shapes of Victorian buildings demonstrate the architect's desire to achieve a form system like the form system of divine nature. These stylistic factors are of great importance for the student of art. Stress must be placed on this, since in what is usually written about art, particularly American art, references to artistic style are rare. The writer gives us his conclusions, not his methods. Methods, however, are our immediate concern.

As a demonstration of how style and subject changes occur in art, consider the three major phases in the evolution of America's great art form of the last century, landscape painting. To date these phases approximately, the first begins in 1835 and ends with the Civil War. The second continues after the Civil War to 1880. The final phase terminates perhaps around 1900. There is, of course, a great deal of overlapping. Artists working at a certain time are not cognizant of the art-historical phases we place them in.

At the beginning (the conspicuous artist is Thomas Cole) compositions are dark. Masses of dark trees or rock in the foreground frame a more luminous central opening into space. This dark proscenium effect makes it evident that our early landscapists are building their styles on the old European Baroque tradition; that, following an 18th century English enthusiasm, they admired the landscape paintings of the 17th century artists Claude Lorrain and Salvator Rosa. In the early American landscape style, brush work is concealed; the artist is naively devoted to the rendering of all details with correct precision. (From time immemorial simple souls have expressed admiration for paintings with the exclamation, "Look at the detail.")

For all the Baroque darkness of the general tone of these early landscapes, the artist exhibits an inclination to use strong and bright hues. Even at this early date the American artist indicates his taste for positive color. A landscape painting by Jasper Cropsey can come close to being gaudy in effect. This taste for color is a distinguishing feature of the American landscape style. It separates it from the landscape painting of Eng-

land and Europe during the same period. Strong color in landscape painting usually indicates that the artist made many of
his observations out of doors. Even though large landscape
paintings were worked up in the studio, it had become
standard procedure for American painters to make small oil
studies in the field. Right from the start our artists wanted to
be true to the nature that they loved, but they still did not
trust nature enough to allow it to stand entirely on its own as
the total artistic expression. Literary themes were usually
illustrated in the action of the figures; this literary bent was
present everywhere in international Romanticism, the great
movement in art history to which our early landscape painting
belongs. Romantic, too, is the "sublime" character of the
nature portrayed.[3] Grandiose, vast, and powerful, this vision
of landscape reflected the growing American feeling that
nature was the embodiment of God.

In the paintings of Church, Bierstadt, and the other artists
of the second phase of American landscape painting, the
sublimity of nature becomes the only theme. Literary associations are dropped; nature stands alone in all its grandeur.
Vast spaces with mighty mountains rising in them overwhelm
the onlookers like Jehovah at the creation. Always the artist
portrays true places, while earlier, more often than not the
landscape was a construction of the artist's imagination. Now
the old European conventions for composing landscapes give
way to the American passion for voluminous and unrestricted
space. Brush work remains tight and details are still rendered
with cautious care, but color and its product light pull the
picture surface together into tighter unity. Color and light
become all-important in establishing in the landscape an
overriding, compelling mood. In their marvelously illuminated
landscapes the Americans of the time achieved something truly
great and, for the first time, American art was recognized and
respected abroad. European landscapes of the period would
appear, in contrast to the American style, more muted and
neutral in tone.

The style of the third phase of American landscape

painting seems almost to be a reaction against earlier tastes. To describe the style is to describe a later work of George Inness. Nature becomes simple and undramatic. Close rather than distant views are preferred. Space is restrained. The quantity of sky is greatly reduced and strong shapes are avoided. The dramatic trees and great mountains of the first two phases are banished from the scene. What you see expressed, rather, is the peace and unity of ordinary fields and trees. Brush work, far from being concealed, now becomes quite broad. The painting surface acquires a distinct overall texture; it appears to be a continuous, unbroken fabric; all this for the sake of unity. For unity, too, the artist will spread the same dominant color tone over every part of his canvas. This style is extremely subtle, sophisticated and artistic. In this final style of 19th century landscape painting, American art arrives at a climactic point.

The student of American culture who has learned to perceive these changes in style through three generations of landscape painting will be able to recognize, classify, and date works of art by artists with whose work he is unfamiliar. Still more important for the art historian and the student of American studies is to account for these changes. Art presents highly visible symptoms of major cultural developments. How do these transformations in landscape painting correspond to other things that were happening in this country? The cultural historian immediately turns to literature and philosophy, but art is affected equally by developments in transportation, by economic changes and by political events. The student who learns how to use works of art as indicative documents could be said to have his fingers on the pulse of history.

The path is clear, I think, for the person in American studies. His role in scholarship is to stand astride of history, observing the interaction of different kinds of occurences at a single time. In art he should notice style changes as a physician observes changes in the color of the skin. Accounting for these changes, tying them to other events, should be his major task. I think it is apparent why a consideration of style is so important. More normally, the person unfamiliar with art sees just the subject matter, which is only a minor part of what art has to offer. When in front of a painting, a work of sculpture or a work of architecture, the student is obliged to observe objectively and record all of its characteristics.

Still, one does not want to play down the importance of subject matter. It often gives the clue to the philosophical ideas that are extended in the style. The great space in a second generation American landscape painting is a component both of the subject and the style. Style and subject interact in other ways. Romantic images in art, for example, are often rendered in a blurred, indistinct manner. Classical images are sharp, clear and definite. In good art one rarely sees highly tangible forms conveying highly intangible feelings. When emotional expression is strong, the style exhibits strong contrasts of shapes and of light and dark. When emotion is restrained, harmonies of form and light prevail.

Just to indicate the kinds of things to observe, and not to suggest any real system, the following list of formal elements are generally most indicative in one's experiences with American art.

In the art of painting, note:

> Brush work and paint texture
> Color (strong or weak; dominant tonality)
> Light and shadow
> Outlines (the edges of shapes)
> Modelling (shading to achieve an illusion of bulk)
> Space (degree of; how achieved; how organized)
> Design structure (the pattern of the form)
> Scale (the actual size of the work of art)

In sculpture, take note of somewhat different effects:

> How the form occupies space
> > Is it frontal or does it face a number of directions?
> > How much is the form penetrated by space?
> > How much does the form penetrate space?
> Movement: what is the degree of motion implied?

Modelling of surface

Texture of surface

In architecture, observe:

The degree of symmetry or asymmetry

Materials

Structural method

Plan

Effects of light and shade

Ornament and details:

Entranceway

Fenestration

Eaves

Wall surface

Subject categories in American art

The art of painting and sculpture in America did not come into its own until after 1800. It was only from that date on that we find American artists working in all the traditional subject matter categories of religious painting, portraiture, landscape, genre (themes from ordinary life) still-life, historical subjects, subjects from literature, poetic allegory; and that later nineteenth century development in artistic subject matter, social realism. Before 1800 American art began and ended with portraiture. Art was functional in the narrowest sense. Colonial patrons wanted to see themselves in art and nothing else. It was this narrow taste that drove Benjamin West and John S. Copley to England; they were our only pre-revolutionary artists whose styles were sufficiently sophisticated to free them from a primitive classification. Could our aversion to other subjects be a result of the Protestant ethic, which inclines toward iconoclasm? God's pronouncement against representational art in the Second Commandment was all too well remembered: "You shall not make yourself a graven image, or any likeness of anything that is in heaven above, or that is in the earth beneath, or that is in the water under the earth."

It is perhaps not correct to say that Colonial Americans

were too busy or too practical to spend money for the
frivolities of art. The splendor of Georgian interiors would
suggest that the opposite was true. Paintings and engravings
were purchased in England by wealthier Americans of the
period. It may simply be that artists of sufficient quality to
produce imaginative works of art were not present in America
until later.

In the nineteenth century, when our art came of age and
artists began to devote their attention to a variety of subjects,
the significant thing that occurred was the rapid rise of
landscape painting. By 1850 it dominated the field of artistic
subject matter and held that position until the close of the
century.[4] Our interest in nature became an obsession.

At this point a word of warning is in order. The student of
American art encounters everywhere certain deeply ingrained
misconceptions about the subject preference of American
artists. There is this persistent idea of the American artist as a
straight-forward, unsophisticated realist who is only interested
in representing the scenes and subjects of American life. This
point of view is aided and abetted by museum curators who
tend to leave in storage works of art that do not conform with
preconceived notion of what American art should be.

As to the artistic lack of sophistication, it should be
pointed out that a great number of our artists of the last
century were thoroughly trained in Europe and that most had
received, through travel, a thorough exposure to European art.
The majority studied in more than one center, moving from
London to Paris to Rome, and later to Munich and Düsseldorf.
The tastes of these artists were international in scope, and
much of their artistic production was not concerned with
native American subjects. The student of American art always
has to deal with this question of European influence. From
Thomas Cole on, painters of the so-called "Hudson River
School" did imaginative landscapes, countless scenes of Italy,
of the Rhine, of England, wherever there were "picturesque"
views, though they may have expressed a preference for the
greater naturalness of American scenery.

Poetic allegory was another type of subject that attracted the American artist. Themes with recondite and often moralistic meanings were conveyed by a variety of idealistic winged beings and mythological gods and goddesses. This artistic tradition goes back to the elaborate allegories of Benjamin West, survives in the neo-classical sculpture of Powers and others, and, in the last quarter of the nineteenth century, in the decorative art and monumental sculpture of William Morris Hunt, John La Farge, Augustus Saint-Gaudens, and Daniel Chester French. This last was an extremely significant episode in American art. The great mural paintings and sculpted monuments of the later nineteenth century are two of the important unexplored subjects in the field.

This is not to say that real themes presented in a real way were not an important aspect of American art. Two of America's greatest painters, Thomas Eakins and Winslow Homer, did many naturalistic paintings in which sections of American life are reproduced with brilliant authenticity. A number of their works belong to the category of subjects known as "social realism." Social realism becomes very important in American art at the beginning of the twentieth century in the works of Robert Henri and the "Ash Can School." It may be said that in the nineteen twenties and thirties themes of social realism dominated American art, having something like a heyday in the government-sponsored art of the depression years, when most of our artists were inspired by socialist ideas.

Mention should be made of another kind of naturalistic subject of American art that does not belong in the traditional categories of painting. Americans were prone to do pictures that could be described as ethnic and geographical anecdotes: pictures of Indians and views of far-off parts of the United States. The paintings by George Catlin of American Indians are an invaluable historical record. Lesser artists did similar descriptive accounts of Indian life. At times, when these were made into impressive works of art, the painter was thinking of a European, not an American, market. Curiosity about the

American Indian was very great in Europe in the nineteenth century, while the Indians were still too close to home at this time to serve as a desirable attraction for art consumers.

Great achievements in American art

Though we should know better by now, there still persists feelings of inferiority about American cultural achievements; we have always been too conscious of the grand monuments of European art and literature. At the same time, when it comes to the visual arts, most Americans are quite unaware of what our great achievements are. It is very curious that they are usually known only to specialists in the field. One would think that every school child should be aware of who were America's genuises in the arts, but it is a rare elementary or high school pupil who can even give the name of an American painter.

It often happens that students of American studies do not realize that our greatest art was the art of architecture; American architecture in the nineteenth century may have been the most important in the world. We first received international recognition for structural innovations and for the invention of new architectural types such as the radial prison plan, the hotel, the department store and the skyscraper. In the 1880s and 90s the incredible artistry of architects such as H.H. Richardson, Louis Sullivan, and Frank Lloyd Wright exalted American building to a position internationally comparable to the importance of French painting. History will probably recognize Wright as the Michelangelo of our epoch. The 1880s was the single most important decade in this evolution. The architecture of the time was both a climax of earlier developments and a beginning, and great quality in building was present everywhere in the nation. This is the period of the Richardsonian Romanesque, of the Queen Anne or "Shingle" style in domestic architecture, and of the Chicago School, internationally famous for its skyscrapers. But the importance of American architecture goes back long before this, even to the brilliant designs of Charles Bulfinch in the Federal Period. While the beautiful buildings of our Colonial period are rather too simple and primitive to be ranked as a fully developed art, again the widespread quality in architecture of the period would indicate that Americans had already demonstrated their talent in this branch of the arts.

Important architects abound in the Greek Revival, the Victorian and the modern periods of American architecture — Benjamin Latrobe, Robert Mills, Alexander Jackson Davis, John Notman, Richard Upjohn, Frank Furness, John Root. It is like the study of English literature; wherever one turns one finds excellence. The history of American architecture is a subject students of American culture should know much more thoroughly than they do. Fortunately, acquiring the background is possible because of the excellent publications in the field. The same, unfortunately, cannot be said of the history of American painting and sculpture. Scholarship in the latter field is spotty. Even important artists are relatively unknown; one discovers who they are by going to the museums and by reading earlier publications about American art.

A point of view, which may be shared by some art historians, is that the two periods in American painting that will leave a major mark in art history are nineteenth century landscape painting and post World War II Abstract Expressionism. It is recognized everywhere today that, with Abstract Expressionism, our country took the lead in world art. The important artists of the movement are Jackson Pollack, Franz Kline, and Willem de Kooning.

In the 1890s, Baedeker's guides of America claimed that our landscape painting put American art in a position second only to the French school. Because the art upon which this opinion was based went completely out of favor, few critics today would place the importance of American landscape painting so high. However, a reassessment is in the process of taking place, spurred on, as is so often the case in the art world, by the extraordinary increase of sale prices for paintings by Cole, Bierstadt, Church, Inness, and the other prominent landscape painters of their age who had long been ignored. Works by these artists that might have sold for $1,000 in the early 1960s now sell for more than $50,000. (It might be added that scholarship in art history often follows closely the movements of the art market.)

Listed below are the names of those American architects, sculptors, and painters who should be known to anyone familiar with the subject of American art. Artists of exceptional importance for historic or artistic reasons are indicated by italics. It is not necessary to point out that such a list must be arbitrary to an extent; anyone knowing American art would question why certain artists are included and certain excluded. On the other hand, probably ninety percent of these artists would be present on any list put together by a specialist in the field. Such lists serve as handy tools. At a glance one can assess one's knowledge of a field and discover areas for further study. The American studies student will be able to see quickly what artists were practicing in a particular period in American history.

Architects and Architectural firms[5]

Peter Harrison, 1716-1775
Thomas Jefferson, 1743-1826
Pierre-Charles L'Enfant, 1754-1825
Samuel McIntire, 1757-1811
William Thornton, 1759-1811
Charles Bulfinch, 1763-1844
Benjamin Latrobe, 1764-1820
Asher Benjamin, 1773-1845
Alexander Parris, 1780-1852
Robert Mills, 1781-1855
Russell Warren, 1783-1860
Ithiel Town, 1784-1844
William Strickland, 1787-1864
John Haviland, 1792-1852
Isaiah Rogers, 1800-1869
James Bogardus, 1800-1874
Richard Upjohn, 1802-1878
Alexander Jackson Davis, 1803-1892

Thomas U. Walter, 1804-1887
John Notman, 1810-1865
Andrew Jackson Downing, 1815-1852
Samuel Sloan, 1815-1884
James Renwick, Jr., 1818-1895
Calvert Vaux, 1824-1892
Richard Morris Hunt, 1827-1895
William Le Baron Jenney, 1832-1907
Henry Hobson Richardson, 1838-1886
Frank Furness, 1839-1912
Louis Sullivan, 1856-1924
Burnham and Root
    Daniel H. Burnham, 1846-1912
    John W. Root, 1850-1891
Holabird and Roche
    William Holabird, 1854-1923
    Martin Roche, 1855-1927
McKim, Mead, and White
    Charles Follen McKim, 1847-1909
    William Rutherford Mead, 1846-1928
    Stanford White, 1853-1906
Cass Gilbert, 1859-1934
Bernard Maybeck, 1862-1957
Ralph Adams Cram, 1863-1942
Frank Lloyd Wright, 1869-1959
Greene and Greene
    Charles S. Greene, 1868-1957
    Henry H. Greene, 1870-1954
Eliel Saarinen, 1873-1950
Raymond Hood, 1881-1934
Walter Gropius, 1883-1969
Ludwig Mies van der Rohe, 1886-
Richard Neutra, 1892-1970
Richard Buckminster Fuller, 1895-
Louis Kahn, 1901-1974
Marcel Breuer, 1902-
Philip Johnson, 1906-

Skidmore, Owings and Merrill
    Louis Skidmore
    Nathaniel Owings
    John O. Merrill
Eero Saarinen, 1910-1961
Paul Rudolph, 1918-

Painters

John Smibert, 1688-1751
John Singleton Copley, 1737-1815
Benjamin West, 1738-1820
Charles Willson Peale, 1741-1827
Gilbert Stuart, 1755-1828
John Trumbull, 1756-1843
Raphaelle Peale, 1774-1825
John Vanderlyn, 1775-1852
Rembrandt Peale, 1778-1860
Washington Allston, 1779-1843
Thomas Sully, 1783-1872
John J. Audubon, 1785-1851
Samuel F.B. Morse, 1791-1872
George Catlin, 1796-1872
Asher B. Durand, 1796-1886
Thomas Cole, 1801-1848
John Quidor, 1801-1881
William Sidney Mount, 1807-1868
George Caleb Bingham, 1811-1879
John F. Kensett, 1816-1872
Jasper F. Cropsey, 1823-1900
William Morris Hunt, 1824-1879
Eastman Johnson, 1824-1906
George Inness, 1825-1894
Frederick E. Church, 1826-1900
Albert Bierstadt, 1830-1902
John La Farge, 1835-1910
Winslow Homer, 1836-1910
Thomas Moran, 1837-1926

Thomas Eakins, 1844-1916
Albert P. Ryder, 1847-1917
Ralph Blakelock, 1847-1919
William M. Harnett, 1848-1892
William Merritt Chase, 1849-1916
John H. Twachtman, 1853-1902
John F. Peto, 1854-1907
John Singer Sargent, 1856-1925
Maurice B. Prendergast, 1859-1924
Childe Hassam, 1859-1935
Henry O. Tanner, 1859-1937
Frederick Remington, 1861-1909
Arthur B. Davies, 1862-1928
Robert Henri, 1865-1929
George Luks, 1867-1933
William J. Glackens, 1870-1938
John Marin, 1870-1953
John Sloan, 1871-1951
Ernest Lawson, 1873-1939
Marsden Hartley, 1877-1943
Joseph Stella, 1880-1946
Arthur G. Dove, 1880-1946
Walt Kuhn, 1880-1949
Hans Hofmann, 1880-1956
Max Weber, 1881-1961
George Bellows, 1882-1925
Edward Hopper, 1882-1967
Rockwell Kent, 1882-1971
Charles Demuth, 1883-1935
Charles Sheeler, 1883-1965
Georgia O'Keefe, 1887-
Joseph Albers, 1888-
Thomas H. Benton, 1889-
Mark Tobey, 1890-
Grant Wood, 1892-1942
Charles Burchfield, 1893-1967
Stuart Davis, 1894-1964

Reginald Marsh, 1898-1954
Ben Shahn, 1898-1969
Adolph Gottlieb, 1903-
Mark Rothko, 1903-1970
Arshile Gorky, 1904-1948
Willem de Kooning, 1904-
Barnett Newman, 1905-1970
Peter Bloom, 1906-
Franz Kline, 1910-1962
Morris Graves, 1910-
Jackson Pollock, 1912-1956
Philip Guston, 1913-
Jack Levine, 1915-
Robert Motherwell, 1915-
Andrew Wyeth, 1917-
Roy Lichtenstein, 1923-
Kenneth Noland, 1924-
Andy Warhol, 1925-
Richard Anuskiewicz, 1930-
Jasper Johns, 1930-

Sculptors

William Rush, 1756-1833
Horatio Greenough, 1805-1852
Hiram Powers, 1805-1873
William Rimmer, 1816-1879
Erastus Dow Palmer, 1817-1904
John Rogers, 1829-1904
John Q.A. Ward, 1830-1910
Augustus Saint-Gaudens, 1848-1907
Daniel Chester French, 1850-1931
Gaston Lachaise, 1882-1935
Elie Nadelman, 1885-1946
Paul Manship, 1885-1966
John B. Flannagan, 1898-1942
Alexander Calder, 1898-

Isamu Noguchi, 1904-
David Smith, 1906-1965
Richard Lippold, 1915-
Claes Oldenburg, 1929-

Resources of American art

Books and written documents are only part of the research materials used in the study of art history. Works of art are primary documents. Artifacts — machines, furniture, tools, etc. — are also significant visual documents; these should be of particular interest to the American Studies student. For the study of American art it is necessary, then, to be familiar with the following:

The art museums with important collections of American Art.
House museums: houses that have been turned into museums for historical or artistic reasons.
Historical restorations and outdoor museums.
Private art galleries.
Depositories of prints: engravings, lithographs, woodcuts, etc., illustrating American city scenes, buildings, landscapes, art, and aspects of American life.
Depositories of photographs of American art.
Communities with particular architectural distinction.

All of the art museums, house museums, historical museums, historical restorations, outdoor museums, depositories of prints and most of the historical societies are listed, with a brief description, in the *Official Museum Directory, 1973*. A much more detailed account of the museum collections in New England and in New York, where the bulk of American material can be found, are the two museum guide books written by S. Lane Faison, Jr.; *A Guide to the Art Museums of New England* (1958) and *Art Tours and Detours in New York State* (1964).

Museums of particular importance in the field of American art are:

The National Collection of Fine Arts of the Smithsonian Institution. The largest collection of American painting and sculpture with a rapidly developing library devoted to American art.

The Whitney Museum of American Art, New York City, features painting and sculpture with an emphasis on 20th century art.

The Metropolitan Museum of Art, New York City. Most of this large collection of American art is not on display, though a new wing for American art has been proposed. The Metropolitan has many very fine "period rooms," rooms removed intact from earlier American buildings, from the study of which the student can acquire a complete visual impression of the artistic tastes and life styles of earlier periods of American history.

The Addison Gallery of American Art, Andover, Massachusetts, offers a rich and complete collection of every phase of American painting, sculpture, and the decorative arts.

The Museum of Fine Arts, Boston, Massachusetts. The Museum of Fine Arts has what is probably the best collection anywhere of early American painting, furniture, and silver. There are also fine period rooms.

It should be noted that most museums exhibit examples of American art. In the eastern United States many small museums contain American painting and sculpture collections of high quality. For example, the Montclair Art Museum, Montclair, New Jersey, or the Canajoharie Art Gallery in Canajoharie, New York. The best display of early American sculpture is at the Shelburne Museum in Shelburne, Vermont. One discovers where these museums are by noting the collection references beneath illustrations in books on American art.

In the field of American Studies, house museums, historical restorations and outdoor museums are of the greatest importance. If one is able to "read" artifacts as documents, one can see in these places those cross sections of American life that are the particular concern of the American Studies student. The value of many house museums is that they often include undisturbed and unselected material, and therefore can reflect no scholarly prejudices or incorrect notions. Examples of house museums exist from every period of American history from the Fairbanks Homestead in Dedham, Massachusetts, built in 1636 to great modern designs like Frank Lloyd Wright's "Falling Water" in Bear Run, Pennsylvania.

Historical restorations that present a particular time in history are scholarly productions and are only as accurate as the research that went into their formation. At the same time, they are great sources of not very carefully organized information. They are the result of careful archaeological efforts. While the research is visible in restored details, much of the accumulated data has not been published. The student either works with the records of these restoration organizations or gathers information by interviewing those in charge. The art historian's purpose would be to discover the interaction of art and life at a particular time in American history. The most famous of the historical restorations is Colonial Williamsburg. One of the oldest is George Washington's Mt. Vernon. Other examples would be Old Deerfield Village in Deerfield, Massachusetts, and Sleepy Hollow Restoration, Inc., in Tarrytown, New York.

Restored villages are related in character to what we call "outdoor museums," but outdoor museums are far less limited in scope. Great examples like the Henry Ford Museum and Greenfield Village (this last a historical restoration) in Dearborn, Michigan, and the Shelburne Museum, Shelburne, Vermont, present marvelous though unselected cross-sections of American art and culture. Again the issue is one of seeing and studying what may be generally called "artifacts," something the student of American Studies must learn to do. Until recently, most serious scholars tended to avoid outdoor museums because of their popular character.

Historical societies fall in a somewhat different category, since they are not primarily museums. All of them have their collections of artifacts, but one goes to them for their documents, pictures, old books, and accumulated information about the community in which they are located. If one wanted to survey the architecture of a particular town, he could approach the local historical society for dates, names and other facts. If one desired information about an important personality in the arts in America, he might find that the historical society in the person's home town has gathered a quantity of unsifted material about him. One can never be sure what historical societies have to offer; it is wise not to overlook them.

Historical museums come in the same variety and almost the same quantity as historical societies. Because most of them contain works of sculpture and painting as well as artifacts and examples of local products of the decorative arts, we must be aware of them and make use of them.

Under the heading of "private art galleries" as a resource of American art, only two need to be mentioned: Kennedy Galleries, Inc., which has been in operation since 1874, and Hirschl and Adler Galleries, both in New York City. These galleries, where art is for sale, have large collections of American art and of documents pertaining to American art. The dealers who manage Kennedy's and Hirschl and Adler's are perhaps as knowledgeable as anyone in the field, and they seem to be willing to help those who are seeking information.

Depositories of prints (engravings, lithographs, woodcuts, and wood engravings) one usually finds in the big-city libraries. The greatest in the country may be that of the New York Public Library. Through reproductive processes artists copied American paintings and made pictures of American sculpture; they executed landscape views, pictures of cities, of individual buildings, of interiors and of scenes of American life. These prints were made from the late eighteenth through the later nineteenth century, when photography replaced them as a popular source of pictures. Prints provide a remarkable visual record of American art and life. Since they are in most instances exactly dated and have a descriptive label, prints are useful documents for dating and identifying works of art and architecture.

Photographs of American art made for art historical studies are most useful. Two major depositories are available to the serious student: the collections at the Fogg Art Museum at Harvard University and at the Frick Art Reference Library in the Frick Collection in New York City. A number of large universities have similar though less complete collections. By working with many photographs of an artist's work the student of art history can quickly acquire an awareness of the total *oeuvre* of an artist, of the variety of his subject themes, of the evolution of his style, and of his relationships to other artists and styles. If the researcher requires photographs for his own work or for publication, these usually can be purchased from the Fogg Art Museum or the Frick Art Reference Library. Otherwise he must send to the museums where the works of art are located.

A special category for art historical research must be made for architecture. Here the streets of American towns and cities constitute the museums, and the student travels to see significant buildings. Certain communities are more rich in surviving architecture than others. Newport, Rhode Island, includes important examples of American architecture from its beginning through the early twentieth century. Chicago must be visited for the great skyscrapers of the "Chicago School" and for the architecture of Frank Lloyd Wright. A choice example for a nineteenth century industrial community surviving intact is Cohoes, New York. Salem, Massachusetts, is a center of Colonial architecture. The astute student will consider every community a museum of sorts, for buildings are the most revealing of all artifacts. Economic, social, artistic, literary, even political factors can shape their forms. Of all nonverbal documents, they are the most available.

The Archives of American Art

As for verbal documents, the student of American art has available for use the extraordinary collection of the Archives of American Art. Quoting from their brochure, "The Archives of American Art is a national research institute established for the purpose of collecting basic documentary source materials on American painters, sculptors, and craftmen." In the Archives are "original letters or notebooks; unpublished notes of historians or correspondence of art dealers; documents of an ephemeral nature and difficult of access; reproductions by microfilming, tape recording or other processes of such records preserved permanently in other collections — in other words, whatever may throw light upon the arts in America." There are also photographs of works of art. (It should be noted, however, that architecture is excluded from the Archives.) Located in Detroit, with a branch office in New York City with a card catalogue and over five million microfilmed items for viewers,[6] the Archives of American Art provides an invaluable resource.

NOTES

1. This chapter is written both for the beginning student of American art and for the student who has had some experience in the field. For the former it will be an introduction; for the latter, a summary with some original thoughts, since my procedure will be something of a critical analysis of the study of American art history with my own point of view uppermost.

2. The technique was devised by the famous Swiss art historian Heinrich Wölfflin in his work, *Principles of Art History*.

3. American artists were very aware of the popular aesthetic theories of Edmund Burke, expressed in his *A Philosophical Enquiry into the Origin of Our Ideas of the Sublime and Beautiful*, first published in 1757.

4. Some may dispute this generalization. From what is contained in art books and exhibited on museum walls the dominance of landscape painting is not such an evident thing. I base my observation not only on what can be seen in museums, but also upon what is in museum storerooms. I also find what I think are more unselected cross-sections of American art in small museums, historical museums, antique shops and, most important, on the walls of houses that remain intact from Victorian times.

5. Architectural firms are placed in their general historical location in relation to individual architects.

6. Detroit office at 5200 Woodward Avenue, Detroit; New York branch at 41 East 65th Street, New York.

BIBLIOGRAPHY

General

Dunlap, William. *A History of the Rise and Development of the Arts of Design in the United States.* 2 Vols., 1834; rev. ed., ed. Frank W. Bayley and Charles E. Goodspeed, 3 Vols. Boston, 1918; rpt. New York, 1969. This early publication is something of an original source as well as a history of the beginnings of American art.

Larkin, Oliver. *Art and Life in America,* rev. ed. New York, 1960. This work must lead every bibliographical list of publications on American art. The author surveys the entire field of architecture, sculpture and painting from its early beginnings to the present. There is a complete critical bibliography organized by historical periods. This bibliography would be of great value in the field of American Studies because it includes historical, literary and other works that were related to, or aid in the understanding of, the arts in a particular period.

Arts of the United States, A Pictorial Survey. Ed. William H. Pierson, Jr. and Martha Davidson. New York, Toronto, London, 1960. Small pictures of over four thousand works of architecture, sculpture and painting with brief text by important scholars in the field.

Methods of research

See *Art in America,* vol. 33, October 1945, ed. Lloyd Goodrich. The entire issue is devoted to problems of research in the field of American art.

Reference

American Association of Museums. *The Official Museum Directory.* Skokie, Ill.: National Register Publishing Co., 1973.

American Federation of Arts. *Who's Who in American Art.* Washington and New York, 1935. Valuable for information about contemporary artists.

Appleton's Cyclopaedia of American Biography. Ed. James Grant Wilson and John Fiske. New York, 1888. Particularly useful for biographies of earlier architects.

The Art Index. A cumulative author and subject index to a selected list of Fine Arts periodicals and museum bulletins, New York, 1929 to the present.

Benezit, E.(mmanuel). *Dictionaire des Peintres, Sculpteurs, Dessinateurs et Graveurs de Tous les Temps et de Tous les Pays,* Nouvelle Edition, Libraire Grund, 1960. Though in French, this is a most complete listing of American artists. Notices are usually very brief, though data is sufficient to make a beginning in research on artists unrecorded elsewhere.

Chamberlin, Mary W. *Guide to Art Reference Books.* Chicago, 1959.

Faison, S. Lane, Jr. *A Guide to the Art Museums of New England.* New York, 1958.

-----. *Art Tours and Detours in New York State.* New York, 1964.

Fielding, Mantle. *Dictionary of American Painters, Sculptors and Engravers.* New York, 1945.

Groce, George C. and Wallace, David H. *The New York Historical Society's Dictionary of Artists in America, 1564-1860.* New Haven, 1957. Lists between ten and eleven thousand artists.

Hitchcock, Henry-Russell. *American Architectural Books; Publications Before 1895.* Rev. ed. Minneapolis, (1962). Very important. The books listed were written by and continually used by American builders and architects.

The Institute of Early American History and Culture. *The Arts in Early American History.* Chapel Hill, 1965. Includes an essay by Walter Muir Whitehill, "The Needs and Opportunities for Study." An excellent account of the problems of scholarship in the field. Should be read by every student of American studies. Bibliography.

Lucas, Louise E. *The Harvard List of Books on Art.* Cambridge, 1952. The most complete listing of art books.

Monro, Isabel S. and Monro, Kate M., *Index to Reproductions of*

American Painting. New York, 1948. First supplement, New York, 1964. A guide to pictures appearing in more than eight hundred books.

Thieme, Ulbrich and Becher, Felix. *Allegemeines Lexicon der Bildenden Kunstler,* 1907-1948. The basic reference work for art historical research. Includes the biographies, brief listings of works and bibliographies for artists of every country and period. Many American artists are included. In German.

Withey, Henry F. and Eloie R. *Biographical Dictionary of American Architects Deceased.* Los Angeles, 1956.

Periodicals

Art Bulletin, New York, 1912-. America's leading journal of art history. Subjects are international with American arts included.

Art Quarterly, Detroit, 1938-. International, but with much that is American.

Art in America, New York, 1913-.

Journal of the Society of Architectural Historians. International with an American emphasis.

Architecture

Andrews, Wayne. *Architecture in America, a Photographic History.* New York, 1960.

-----, *Architecture, Ambition and Americans.* New York, 1955; rpt. New York, 1964. A history of American architecture emphasizing the cultural and social background, with a valuable bibliography.

Downing, Andrew Jackson. *The Architecture of Country Houses.* New York and Philadelphia, 1850; rpt. New York, 1969. The original source of Victorian architectural aesthetics.

Fitch, James Marston. *American Building: The Forces that Shape It.* Sec. ed., rev. and enl. Boston, 1966; rpt. New York, 1973.

Giedion, Sigfried. *Space, Time and Architecture.* 5th ed., rev. and enl. Cambridge, 1967. International in scope, this book contains the most thorough account of commercial and structural developments in American architecture.

Gowans, Alan. *Images of American Living: Four Centuries of Architecture and Furniture as Cultural Expression.* Philadelphia, 1964. This survey of American architecture would prove most useful to students of American studies.

Hamlin, Talbot Faulkner. *Greek Revival Architecture in America.* New York, 1944. Paperback ed., New York, 1964. The best work published on American architecture, 1820-1860.

Historic American Buildings Survey. Historic American buildings catalogue of the measured drawings and photographs of the Survey in the Library of Congress, March 1, 1941.

Kimball, Sidney Fiske. *Domestic Architecture of the American Colonies and of the Early Republic.* New York, 1922; rpt. 1966. The great classic in the subject.

Morrison, Hugh Sinclair. *Early American Architecture.* New York, 1952. The definitive work in the field.

Ware, William Rotch, ed. *The Georgian Period; being photographs of measured drawings of Colonial work with text.* 3 vols., New York, 1923. The basic work on eighteenth century architecture in America.

Sculpture

Gardner, Albert Ten Eyck. *Yankee Stonecutters, the first American school of sculpture, 1800-1850.* New York, 1945; rpt. Metropolitan Museum of Art, 1965.

Schnier, Jacques Preston. *Sculpture in Modern America.* Berkeley, 1948; rpt. Westport, Conn., 1972.

Taft, Lorado. *The History of American Sculpture.* 1903; new ed. with a supplementary chapter by Adeline Adams, New York, 1930. This is the only work that surveys the subject.

Painting

Flexner, James Thomas. *American Painting.* Vol. I, Boston, 1947. Vol. II, New York, 1954. Flexner is a leading writer in the field.

-----. *That Wilder Image. The Painting of America's Native School from Thomas Cole to Winslow Homer.* New York, 1962; rpt. 1970.

Goodrich, Lloyd. One of the most important scholars in the field. See his monographs on Winslow Homer, Thomas Eakins, museum catalogues and articles in periodicals.

Hunter, Sam. *Modern American Painting and Sculpture.* New York, 1965. The best work on the subject.

Richardson, Edgar Preston, *Painting in America.* New York, 1965. The best and most complete survey of American painting.

Tuckerman, Henry Theodore. *Book of the Artists.* New York, 1867. An early source of information about American painters.

CHAPTER NINE

American Studies: The Discipline of Music

American Music

Mark Sumner Harvey

American music is a Sousa march, a Broadway show tune, or a popular love song. It is jazz played in nightclubs, folk music sung in coffeehouses, and symphonic works performed in concert halls. It is urban blues and country ballads, patriotic ditties and protest songs, rock music and rocking-chair music. It is the enormous spectacle of Boston during the National Peace Jubilee and Great Musical Festival of 1869 when Patrick S. Gilmore amassed thousands of choristers and bandsmen to "Commemorate the Restoration of Peace Throughout the Land,"[1] or it is the elegant simplicity of Atlanta in 1968, during the funeral service for Dr. Martin Luther King, Jr., when a soloist from the Ebenezer Baptist Church Choir sang the lovely spiritual "My Living Would Not Be in Vain," both to mourn the tragic death of a national leader and bewail the fragility of that hard-won peace. It is the fervor and vibrancy of a Billings' "fudging tune" during Colonial days, a "Turkey in the Straw" fiddled away on the frontier, or an Ivesian "America" reminiscent of turn-of-the-century Columbia, and predictive in its dissonances of an impending loss of gem-like lustre around the oceans of the world.

In the music of America is reflected the development of a people and a civilization. The lyrics tell only a part of the story, for the music itself conveys the uniquely human struggle involved in this growth process, both in the way it springs forth in creation and expression and in the response which is made to it. Perhaps no other aspect of our experience would be missed so greatly as music were we simply to remove it from our daily life. And it may well be that in American Studies, we would miss a great deal of the culture which we study were we to ignore the musical contributions.

To explore, understand, and appreciate America's living musical heritage requires an open ear and, in John Dos Passos' words a "camera eye," a sense of kaleidescopic vision that discerns the many facets of experience singly and in combination as larger, patterned wholes. No words, however poetic and descriptive, can adequately express the grandeur and glory that is music. Therefore, before, during, or immediately following a reading of this chapter, one should plunge headlong into a listening spree guided by the discography noted at the conclusion. Close investigation and weighty analysis can take place then, but what is essential at the outset is a total immersion in the seas of sound which together constitute the music of America.

THE PROBLEM OF AN "AMERICAN MUSIC"

The question of whether or not we may even presume to speak of an "American music" deserves consideration before we proceed further. In one sense, there can be no such discussion; for music, and indeed any art-form, defies containment within national boundaries and subverts all attempts to serve the ends of either nationalism or politics. One cannot self-consciously set out to create "American music;" one can only create music. History, geography, and social and political crises may provide stimulus to creative individuals, and certainly the totality of American life and experience will influence an individual's expression in the musical form; yet the expression stands primarily as an intensely personal or social creative act. Music must be regarded ultimately as an essence which encounters man in the twin realms of spirit and feeling. It does indeed speak a universal language — to the common humanity which we Americans share with every other person in the world. However, as philosopher Ernst Cassirer has noted, the universal must be manifested in particular situations and human experiences; so, notwithstanding what has been said above, a case may be made for an "American music" which in its particularity demonstrates qualities of music as a universal phenomenom and allows us to apprehend something of that universality as a vital element of our own culture.

Another objection to the claim of an "American music" that must be dealt with, however, is the criticism of some, such as Edward N. Waters, an eminent musicologist, who argue that all so-called "American music" is ultimately derivative from European and African sources, that it is not pure indigenous creation, and therefore cannot bear the title of "American music."[2] This amazingly myopic reasoning, if applied to other aspects of our civilization, would prevent us from admitting any distinctive Americanisms at all. To be sure, we are a polyglot culture and have always held in esteem the image of the melting-pot; we take pride in the mix of influences foreign to our own shores, often to the extent of masking our guilt for injustices perpetrated upon the only truly indigenous population, the American Indians. Yet the mixture − not the disparate constitutive elements − is the important thing. It is in the relationships between the multiple and wide-ranging strands of musical experience in America that we can begin to discern an American music. Music itself is thought to be the arrangement or organization of sound; the sounds are derivative from a host of sources, but it is in their combination, shaping, and ordering that music emerges. In like manner, the American experience has transformed and transmuted the cosmopolitan wealth of influence into a new creation, a music with an identity of its own, yet reflective of its roots.

Related to this concern about American music's derivative nature is a third objection to the basic affirmation of an "American music." This criticism is perhaps the most debilitating and deadly because it is more often than not expressed

subtly rather than articulated openly. It is a variation on
Henry James' theme regarding the interplay of American
innocence and European experience. In his story of an
American traveler abroad, *Daisy Miller,* James portrays a naive,
guileless innocent in quest of some higher virtue or truth than
America of the Gilded Age could provide. This same view of
England and the Continent as the ultimate arbiters of taste and
culture for America continues to exercise influence in the
sphere of music. So pervasive has it been that only recently
have fissures in the crust of European domination begun to
develop. It may be that the argument against an "American
music" on grounds of its derivative nature is as much due to
trepidation in the face of European majesty as it is to
nearsightedness on the American scene.

    We Americans have a difficult time accepting our own
musical endeavors as significant in the light of the accumulated
burden of "culture" across the pond. We have been long in
coming to the realization which anthropology achieved early
on: that culture is not an elitist excess, an ornament separate
from the business of living; but rather that it is precisely the
stuff of life, and is concerned with the processes, products,
and behavior of all the people in a given social and cultural
context. Culture is not the creativity of a few raised to
Olympian heights; it is rather the "totality of the arts of
living"[3] and comprises the creative expression of an entire
people. Yet the old notion of "culture" remains.

    The concert hall and the symphony orchestra, both
patterned on the European model, along with a slavish
devotion to the notated page, remain the dominant musical
value-centers in America, perpetuating an Anglophobic and
Teutonic standard of excellence and achievement. America is
presently acknowledged to be the center of musical activity in
the Western world, as Nicholas Slonimsky has observed,[4] and
yet curiously enough, the percentage of works by American
composers represented among the repetoire of major American
orchestras is shamefully small (not to mention the percentage
of twentieth century works by composers of whatever

nationality).

In terms of jazz and popular music, the dream of success was thought for many years to be consummated when the musician was finally invited to perform with a symphonic ensemble, attired, of course, in full concert dress; recording with strings has also exerted influence as a standard of musical respectability and maturity. And the black musical experience, as well as the white folk heritage, comprised largely of oral traditions, are barely admitted to the canon of music at all, American or otherwise, by those in control of the so-called "serious music" establishment. Yet popular music, jazz, soul, blues, rock, folk, and country and western music are all recognized as solid cultural contributions by the people in the entertainment industry who annually gross several billion dollars as purveyors of this "American music." (Interestingly enough, all the major orchestras are rapidly approaching severe financial crisis.)

This situation indicates that not only are our values misplaced, but that we allow ourselves to be victimized by an ideal and a myth which even the great majority of us no longer believe. The values are misplaced not because they emphasize "serious music" or sanction the concert hall; I have tried to suggest that American composers of symphonic and chamber works have no easy time getting these works performed, and that this is an unhealthy situation. The values are misplaced rather because they are oriented to a bygone age of European romanticism and drawing-room mannerism and appeal to the American nostalgia for less troubled times, when the goodness of rural America seemed to assure the continued success of a nation and a people. By maintaining a standard of "culture" from a past era, a superficial kind of stability and security is sought in the midst of the dizzying change and seeming chaos of the present. Yet the price to be paid is exacted in the violence which we do to musicians who do not conform (or who do not even care to make the effort to conform) to this inauthentic norm. Duke Ellington presents a prime example. This gifted black musician is acknowledged by many to be

America's greatest living composer, and yet in 1965 when the Pulitizer Prize for music went begging, Ellington was recommended for a special citation, as if to imply that someone less identified with the jazz world and perhaps more European than African influenced — in a word, someone more "serious" — would have been named directly to the prize itself. For the record, even the recommendation for special citation was rejected by the advisory board. However, the then sixty-six year old Ellington took it all in stride with great equanimity and grace, quipping "Fate's trying to keep me from becoming too famous too young."[5]

It must be pointed out that the listening public pays a great price, too, in terms of the musical riches which it either ignores or is unknowingly deprived of. The music of Charles Ives, one of America's great composing talents, is slowly gaining respect (and performance). Soul music, a direct descendent of urban rhythm and blues, would probably never have gained exposure on AM radio stations had not a white disc jockey named Allan Freed begun to play, in 1955, "race records" — usually obtainable only in black ghetto record stores and played only on black radio outlets; he discovered that white teenagers literally went wild over them, and started into gear the vast business of rock and roll. Curiously, rock finally progressed beyond the elemental beat and harmony of Elvis Presley only when English musicians, heavily influenced by American black bluesmen (as Presley had been), re-introduced to America in their brand of rock, musical elements which had been here all along as a well-hidden undercurrent.

Americans need to explore their own musical heritage. Times are changing. The old European ideal is losing favor in some quarters: Zubin Mehta invited Frank Zappa and the Mothers of Invention to concertize with the Los Angeles Philharmonic, *au naturel*; Michael Tilson-Thomas in the 1971-72 season initiated the "Spectrum Series" with the Boston Symphony in an effort to attract a younger and more diversified audience to the concert hall; and jazzmen Ornette

Coleman, Gil Evans, Jimmy Giuffre, George Russell, Charlie Haden, and Charles Mingus have all received Guggenheim grants in the last few years.

Musical styles are changing also. Composers are searching for new notational techniques, while some are abandoning all but a minimum of notation in an attempt to rediscover improvisational music; Duke Ellington asked his fan club in New York City, the "Duke Ellington Jazz Society," to drop the word jazz a few years ago — not in any sense as a recantation of his past, but simply because he did not want to be limited in the public view to one category of music; and increasing numbers of conservatory trained musicians are capable of playing many kinds of music — thus, Buell Neidlinger has appeared with Billie Holiday, Cecil Taylor, the Boston Symphony, rock and blues bands, and most recently has performed with the El Monte Art Quartet while teaching at the California Institute of the Arts in Valencia, California.

If we would look for an "American music," we must look at this changing scene as an indication of its reality. The patterns and relationships of diverse influences and styles hold the clues for determining what an "American music" is and might become. It is necessary now to sketch some of these influences and styles.

ORIGINS AND DEVELOPMENT OF AMERICAN MUSIC

American music is fed by tributary streams from two main traditions, the European and the African. As already indicated, in a general sense the European models and values are venerated, while the African influences are either undervalued, patronized, or discretely ignored. I have suggested that this emphasis on the European tradition is somewhat unrealistic, escapist, and detrimental to the growth of American music. I should not like to be misunderstood as critical of European music; there is, beyond question, a rich heritage in this music, which, as we shall see, has played an important part in the development of American music. What I am critical of is the apparent idolatry which American musicians and musical public alike seem to manifest with regard to this tradition. This idolatry is all the more odious in consideration of the neglectful and deprecatory attitude which it fosters toward the other principal source tradition, the African, and the attendant racist overtones which are generated. However, the most curious dimension to this idolatry, as I have suggested, is that while the idol is broken, Americans, rather than elevate the African tradition to its deserved place — not as a substitute idol, but rather alongside of the authentic European influence as another equally significant influence — choose either to ignore the reality of the situation or to wring their hands as if in some imaginary wasteland, too blinded by self-indulgent tears to admit of such a solution. But the European and the African traditions have made solid contributions to our musical culture, and both merit our attention and appreciation.

The European tradition

The music of Europe came to these shores with the early explorers and was largely of a religious cast. In Florida, the Southwest, and California, Spanish missionaries taught the ritual chants of Catholicism to the native Indian populace. New Englanders — both Pilgrim and Puritan — kept alive the psalmody which had nurtured their religious life in the struggle with the kings and the Church of England. In Jamestown, Virginia, psalm singing also probably accompanied Anglican worship observances, although written records of such activity are not extant.

John Tasker Howard makes the claim in his volume, *Our American Music*, that

> The earliest European music to be heard upon either coast of North America north of the Spanish settlements was the French psalmody sung by the Huguenots on the Carolina Coast in 1572, before their brief settlement was wiped out by the Spaniards; and the English psalmody sung by Drake's seamen during their stay of several weeks in June, 1579, at what is now known as Drake's Bay on the California Coast....[6]

The implication here is that the music of the Spanish was heard at least at about the same time as that of the French and English, and the fact that Spanish exploration antedates both these nations' efforts raises the possibility that simple precursors of the "mission music" of the Southwestern United States may have actually constituted the first European music heard here.[7] At any rate, the transplantation of European music to America via the vehicle of religion was not only a most natural process but a most auspicious one as well, for developments occurring first within the religious community soon spread to influence the musical life of the whole country.

As settlements sprang up, the musical seeds planted by the first immigrants took root and began to grow. It was in New England that this development was most marked and remarked upon, thereby ensuring that future generations would be made aware of this important aspect of community life. Psalm singing provided the only means of relaxation and entertainment – along with preaching – available to the New England mind, body, and soul. It was an activity primarily set aside for the Sabbath Day, although it was likely not unusual for a passer-by to hear psalms emanating from this or that house, as women and children went about their daily round of activity – all for the sake of practice, mind you, never (at least not admittedly ever) purely for pleasure.

The early days of colonial life were harsh and left little time for a serious regard for music. Thus at the beginning of the eighteenth century when several prominent divines set about the up-grading and development of the art of psalmody, the common people were suspicious and ill at ease. They regarded the new refining interest as tantamount to witchcraft and objected to it on grounds that "it was needless, the old way being good enough," "it required too much time to learn it, made the young disorderly, and kept them from the proper influence of the family," and "it was only a contrivance to get money."[8] (These arguments seem to have a familiar ring about them for those of us who grew up with the sounds of rock 'n roll, or for those who grew up with the sounds of swing music, or ...etc.)

The furor soon subsided, however, and the people began to appreciate the reforms that were taking place. Before this time, there had existed no written music, only the texts of the psalms having been printed and bound into book form. Singing was led by a precentor who "lined out" the psalm literally line by line, and waited for the congregation's response in like fashion before proceeding to the next line. Needless to say, this method was tedious and the music entirely dependent for its quality upon the ear and sense of pitch of the precentor. With the introduction of musical notation with the psalm texts, an entirely new mode of singing had to be learned, and to this end, singing societies or schools, as they later came to be called, were established throughout New England and the other colonies as well. These singing schools eventually branched off from church influence and became the stimulus to public school singing and the community chorus movement of later years. As David Ewen has said in his highly enjoyable book, *Music Comes to America,* "Choral singing formed the foundation of American musical culture....choral organizations scattered throughout the country, prepared the ground for our musical emergence, educated our first music audiences and set the stage for our early concert life."[9]

The American singing heritage is a long and proud one, but a tradition perhaps past its prime, due to the changing nature and role of the family, the process of urbanization, and the technological revolution which has replaced the piano in the parlor with the juke box in the corner restaurant or tavern, the stereo record player in the game room, and the radio seemingly everywhere. Throngs of spectators at athletic events do not bellow the words of the National Anthem as did their forefathers the texts of the *Bay Psalm Book,* and school-children seem more intent upon identifying the vocalizations of "Top Forty" superstars than upon developing their own vocal cords. Yet, this heritage continues to be expressed in not only high school choruses of the South and Midwest and in the large choirs of black urban churches, but also in new forms as smaller groups of teenagers band together in imitation of their favorite performing star or group; and the folk music renascence of the sixties may certainly be counted as a significant part of this heritage of American music in song.

Even as Europe planted the seeds of future musical growth in America, she also saw to their nurture — but in Continental gardens. Before the First World War, American students were obliged to seek their musical training abroad if they desired a career in music. To be sure, the New England composers, Horatio Parker and Edward MacDowell, taught many aspiring musicians during the late nineteenth and early twentieth centuries, but the European conservatories attracted even these students who sought the confirmation of Europe's high priests, notably Vincent d'Indy in Paris, as the authentic ratification of their musical education.

The first American composer to receive a completely American training was Henry Franklin Gilbert (1862-1928), a pupil of MacDowell, and the first great music school in America was the Institute of Musical Art, founded in downtown New York in 1905 and headed by Frank Damrosch. Soon thereafter followed the Eastman School in Rochester in 1918, the Julliard School in New York and the Curtis Institute in Philadelphia, both in 1924. Several years later in 1940, Serge Koussevitsky, then conductor of the Boston Symphony Orchestra, opened the Berkshire Music Center at Tanglewood, providing still another high calibre training ground for young musicians.

It must be remembered, however, that these were comparitively recent developments, and that American music and musical taste had been largely dependent upon the Europophiles, those sophisticated American world-travelers who dominated the cultural life of Philadelphia and Boston. Wilfred Mellers has written of this American music that, "it manifested a passive veneration for the Teutonic, which represented Art; and was usually well written, cheerful, and agreeable: a pretence that the wilderness did not exist, that the heart was not a 'lonely hunter'."[10] This American music relied upon a complement of European forms and a European standard of virtuosity and technical excellence. It would someday be forced to confront that music which had been growing on American soil and which embraced not only the wilderness, but also the New World of music which that wilderness promised.

The African tradition

Of equal importance as an influence upon American music is the tradition of Africa. Seldom given more than cursory treatment in treatises on American music, the story of this music's significance for our musical life is little known and even less appreciated.[11] Since the American conservatories and schools of music by and large continue to pay homage to European standards, their lists of required texts rarely include such essential works as *Slave Songs of the United States* by Allen, Ware, and Garrison; or *The Story of Jazz* by Marshall Stearns. There are exceptions, of course, and the advent of black or Afro-American studies programs on many campuses has been a hopeful sign in this regard. However, this second great influence on American music remains fairly well hidden from view.

If the implantation and nurture of the European tradition can be seen as the result of trans-Atlantic voyages as the crow flies between Europe and America, then the sowing of New World fields of music with the African tradition may be thought of as a one-way trip from West (and Central) Africa to America, the route of the profitable colonial slave trade. The African tradition did not come into direct contact with the colonial population as did the European tradition, for it remained the cultural province of the slaves. This tradition was constantly fertilized by the arrival of new slaves either directly from Africa (even after the practice had been officially outlawed) or from the West Indies where many had sojourned on Portuguese, Spanish, or French plantations; but there was not the contact back in the other direction to the source as there had been with the European tradition. African music became assimilated into the American experience of the slaves and thereby transmuted into something distinctively other than what it had been.

Interestingly, the vehicle of religion acted here, as in New England, as the primary carrier of this musical tradition, but in a radically different manner.[12] In the colonies under British-Protestant hegemony, this carrier function of religion was negligible except for those occasions when slaves were allowed to attend and participate in revival meetings. Dancing and drumming, two elements of African religious practice, were strictly forbidden by the Baptists and Methodists, but at these revivals, the display of ecstasy on the part of the whites as they shouted their hymn tunes, writhed uncontrollably on the ground, and otherwise drove themselves to a frenzied pitch gave license to the blacks to follow suit. However, the usual concern of southern Protestants — primarily the Anglicans — was for the state of the slaves' souls, perhaps not so much motivated by desire for their salvation as by desire for their social control by means of the promise of heavenly salvation. Conversion was meant to be not only to the white master's religion, but to his customs and traditions as well, and since British-Protestant masters owned fewer slaves, the possibility of closer contact with them — especially house slaves — facilitated the success of this conversion.[13] Thus, for many slaves, to become "washed in the blood of the Lamb" was to become "white-washed" as well — to the great debilitation of the music and their true souls.

The Latin-Catholic controlled colonies presented a different environment, however, one in which it was possible not only for the culture of Africa to survive, but to flourish. The Catholic planters of Portuguese, Spanish, or French lineage were not much concerned with the religious beliefs of their slaves, nor with much else that did not bear directly on production. In contrast to British plantations, where the Protestant hymns were often "droned out...like the braying of asses" according to John Adams,[14] and where only occasional access to revival ceremonies was permitted, the Latin plantations provided a scene in which all of the darkly rich music of

Spain and Portugal could be heard on the many Catholic
festival days. Most important, however, was the ease with
which African religions and customs fused with Catholicism.
This process of syncretism allowed the African to accept many
of the ceremonies and saints of the Church because they
paralleled those of his own religion. Thus, St. Patrick,
reknowned for his feat of driving the snakes out of Ireland,
reminded the Dahomean slave of his god, Damballa, the snake
god; and as Marshall Stearns relates a common practice: ". . .
on St. Patrick's day the slaves played the drum rhythms sacred
to Dumballa and worshipped both Dumballa and St. Patrick at
the same time and on the same altar."[15] The African tradition
thus was carried on with the help of the religious climate, but
was certainly not exclusively dependent upon it for its
development and continued influence in America.

The back-breaking condition of toil in the plantation fields
generated a music which consisted of rhythmic grunts and
groans and occasional melodic fragments. Gradually evolving
into recognizable shape and form, these utterances became
known as work songs. Simultaneously, spirituals began to
emerge, taking as their ostensible subject the promise of a
better life than they knew as slaves, but often serving as
surreptitious communication devices among diverse groups of
slaves. Both work songs and spirituals followed a call-and-
reponse format not dissimilar to the "lining out" method of
Massachusetts Bay psalmody, yet embodying a rhythmic
vitality which only a suffering and captive people could
express since they had so much to gain by freedom. The blues
developed as still another kind of music of the African
tradition, providing a secular counterpart to the spirituals, yet
actually arising out of and expressing similar concerns. The
blues were sung and played after work-a-day tasks were done,
and acted as a kind of meditation on the daily struggle that
was slavery.

With Emancipation and urbanization, many blacks mi-
grated to the large northern cities such as New York, Chicago,
and Detroit, and took their music with them. There the field

cries and hollers characteristic of the work songs blended with the rude country blues to become eventually "rhythm and blues" or just "urban blues," a hard pulsing music, vividly descriptive of the pain and violence of ghetto life. Soul music later arose out of this matrix as a "hymn of hope" and an "unbridled affirmation of dark defiance."[16] Also in the urban centers the new sophisticated spirituals of the Fisk Jubilee Singers were further transformed into the powerful "tambourine shaking hell-defying sound of gospel music."[17] Especially in New York City, the white musical businessman would notice the market possibilities inherent in a musical tradition which minstrelsy had only suggested.

At the turn of the century, New Orleans became the incubator of perhaps the most significant development of the African tradition, namely, jazz. This city at the mouth of the Mississippi had from the start differed greatly from the rest of the country. It had been under both French and Spanish rule before being sold by Napolean to the United States in 1803. Thus, its inhabitants had known the marches of the French military bands, the flamenco and *paso doble* of the Spanish guitarists and dancers, and the rhythms of the African drums at *vodun* ceremonies in Congo Square.

All of these elements fused, first in the large brass bands which were employed frequently by the secret societies and fraternal orders to play at funerals and parades, and later in smaller combinations of players hired to play in saloons and at dances and parties. Pianists such as Jelly Roll Morton found work in the redlight district of Storyville until the Department of the Navy closed it down in 1917. Eventually, New Orleans musicians found work on the riverboats that plied the murky waters of the Mississippi. As the sounds of this melting-pot music called jazz drifted into St. Louis, Kansas City, Chicago, and finally New York — always the "apple" of every musician's eye — cross-fertilization with music of the Southwest and the Southeast occurred. Equally important was the fact that people in general and the songwriters of Tin Pan Alley in particular began to move with the rhythms they heard.

The fusion of traditions

New Orleans was unquestionably the setting for the marriage of these two traditions, the European and the African, to take place. That its offspring, jazz, has prospered through the years is attested to by the enormous popularity which it enjoys the world around, largely as a result of United States State Department sponsored tours and Willis Conover's radio programs on the Voice of America. Yet this same offspring is regarded by many Americans and certainly by the American musical establishment as illegitimate, a step-child of the arts.

To be sure, it was primarily European folk music — ballads, dance music, and hymns — along with extracts from military marches, rather than the high-art music, that represented the European tradition in the match, but could this fact alone be enough to foster such an attitude? Certainly not, for even if the mighty cadences of Beethoven were to be incorporated with a jazz beat (and, sad to say, they have been, to the detriment of both) the result would still not be embraced. The crux of the matter lies deeper than that; it rests in the fact that we are presently witnessing the emergence of a new period in musical history, "what future musical historians may well designate the Afro-American epoch."[18]

The highly controversial critic Henry Pleasants has attempted to explicate this phenomenon in his recent book, *Serious Music and All That Jazz*. He notes that every successful musical epoch has been dominated by one national entity and cultural ethos: "The Renaissance, for instance, was dominated by the Netherlands, the Baroque by Italy, the Classic by Austria-Bohemia and the Romantic by Germany." The present (and long established) refusal to recognize jazz and other musics of African heritage is the result of an inability on the part of the musical establishment to admit that such significant music could arise outside of the family, so to speak, outside of the European tradition; for the participants in this new drama were "for the first time in the history of Western music...a new continent and a new civilization — Africa and America." As Pleasants relates: "Appearing as it did without credentials, either of precedent or of pedigree; its validity and possible ascendency were — and, for most people — still are unthinkable."[19] Yet underneath the incomprehensibility exhibited toward this emerging phenomenom is the very real fear that this new music may, in fact, be as potent as its fanatical followers maintain. It is thus not a lack of clarity in this situation which prevents acceptance of this music, but rather too clear a view of its vitality which threatens the very life of the older tradition and idiom. However, if we accept Henry Pleasants' prophecy of the coming Afro-American epoch in music, we run the risk of commiting over again the same error of judgment which for so long has forced all "American" music to be seen through European opera glasses: that of raising one of the two source traditions to a position superior to the other, and in so doing, proceeding to wreak havoc upon both. The point is that one is not better or worse than the other, but simply different from the other. While we must not lose sight of the needed corrective to the European bias which the notion of an Afro-American epoch provides, a more balanced and wider perspective suggests that each tradition be evaluated on its own terms, though this reasoning may result in either an uncritical and effete aesthetic relativism or merely a heightened awareness of the parts comprising the whole. What we seek is a glimpse of the whole, as well as the constituent parts.

AN "AMERICAN" MUSIC?

The hard task before us is that of defining the focal points of this fusion of source traditions; once again, we are confronted as at the outset, with the problem of an "American" music. In examining the music written by American composers in the classical or serious vein (read European), Charles Ives looms large on the horizon as the seminal figure. English writer Wilfred Mellers in his thoroughly engaging and well-balanced work *Music in A New Found Land,* describes Ives as the archetypal American pioneer, venturing out into the wilderness and reflecting the rawness of this vast unknown in his music. Mellers writes,

> If he was to be an honest creator, he had to take his materials from the world around him: which was the provincial community of the hard-bitten farmer, the small business-man, and tradesman. Here was a certain measure of pioneering vitality, mixed with a somewhat blighted religious ethic; of refinement or 'culture' there was no trace. In musical terms, this life meant the town band (which Ives' father directed), ragtime, the corny theatre tune, the chapel hymn. All these were crude but full of conviction, since they were aspects of a way of life.[20]

If Ives was the pioneer, the prophet in the wilderness, then Aaron Copland can be seen as the cultic priest, building upon Ives' example of engagement with the American scene, the firm basis for an American musical tradition. It is significant that Ives grew up in small town America, while Copland was born in Brooklyn, in New York City: "The ragbag of the past is no longer relevant. The American Jew, expatriated and alienated, accepts the life of the big city and of a machine-made civilization."[21] Mellers does not proclaim him a great composer ("perhaps not even a great composer *in potentia* like Ives") but rather a very important composer in twentieth century history and for the reason that "he is the first artist to define precisely, in sound, an aspect of our urban experience...his experience belongs...to the Big City which emerged out of Ives' America."[22]

In whatever geographic locale, it is the courage to forsake the kind of dependence on the past that debilitates, to explore the unknown present, and to pursue a vision of what the future might be, that characterizes, for Mellers and for this writer, the composers of "American" music. If these criteria should seem somewhat foreign to music criticism, I submit for consideration still another quotation from Mellers,

> All this is at once music and life; the only criterion of 'correctness' is the music's truth to experience. On a wider and deeper scale we have here an extension of the phenomenon we

referred to in the American primitives such as Billings: the 'mistakes' may be, musically and experientially, more interesting than the art-creation. Ives would have agreed with his father, who when asked how he could stand hearing Old John (the local stonemason) bellowing off key at camp-meetings replied: 'Old John is a supreme musician. Look into his face and hear the music of the ages. Don't pay too much attention to the sounds. If you do, you may miss the music.'[23]

Ives and Copland represent the European tradition in so far as their styles and those of other American composers incorporate European elements and methods, yet they are synthesizers drawing upon the sounds and experience around them. Their musical colleagues such as Samuel Barber, Milton Babbitt, Leonard Bernstein, John Cage, Elliott Carter, Norman Dello Joio, Morton Feldman, Lukas Foss, Roy Harris, Lou Harrison, Alan Hovhaness, Leon Kirchner, Harry Partch, Vincent Persichetti, Walter Piston, Mel Powell, Wallingford Riegger, Carl Ruggles, Gunther Schuller, William Schuman, Virgil Thomson, and Edgar Varese, while differing markedly as regards style and method still share this common American quality of seeking the new and the unknown. They also, to one degree of another, like Copland, portray the "neat, bland-eyed, rugged-souled Americans of a Copley portrait — when they have lived through the nervous and physical stresses to which a machine-age has submitted them."[24]

When we turn to the so-called "non-serious" musics, folk, blues, jazz, gospel, soul, rock and popular, we may apply the above criteria with confidence. For in these musics, the attributes of courage and honesty are perhaps more important than in the so-called "serious" musics. Whether considering a soft Appalachian ballad plucked on dulcimer, a brash Memphis or Motown funk tune shouted by voices and horns, or a scintillating Broadway show tune crooned to the accompaniment of a pit orchestra, the quest for an authentic American music true to its peoples and situations will be apparent.

Popular music, in its development through minstrelsy, vaudeville, and Tin Pan Alley, includes also the Nashville sound of slick, saleable (to urban America) country music, the

world of musical comedy, and all other forms of "commercial" music found at dances, restaurants, or on airwaves of
radio and television — forms which are all primarily European
influences. At their best, they reflect and help to sustain the
vitality of various aspects of American life; at their worst, they
degenerate, are diluted, and congeal into the odious plague
known as "muzak," the servant of behaviorists and industria-
lists dedicated to increasing the Gross National Product and
decreasing aesthetic sensibility. As Victor Borge put it, "I
know it was developed to make chickens lay more eggs and
factory workers produce more, but how much more can they
get out of you in an elevator? "[25]

While much of this European-influenced popular music
does seem to settle at the level of banality, nonetheless certain
aspects are worth noting. George Gershwin has undoubtedly
contributed much to our musical life (although the "lady" he
made of jazz is so heavily cosmeticized as to be nearly
unrecognizable), and he may be seen as the counterpart-
catalyst in the arena of popular music that Copland was for
"serious" music. Certainly his "Porgy and Bess" remains both
the first and the benchmark American opera, although
significant efforts in this area have been made by composers
such as Leonard Bernstein with "West Side Story," Marc
Blitzstein with "Regina," and Gian Carlo-Menotti with "The
Consul," "The Medium," and "The Telephone."

The light opera and the musical theatre provided a wealth
of material for our popular musical culture which was
augmented by the output of Tin Pan Alley and continues to be
fed' by the composers of Hollywood soundtracks and television underscores. Names such as Irving Berlin, Hoagy
Carmichael, Rudolf Friml, Victor Herbert, Jerome Kern, Cole
Porter, Sigmund Romberg and Vincent Youmans, along with
the famous teams of George and Ira Gershwin, and Richard
Rodgers (first with Lorenz Hart and later with Oscar Hammer-
stein II) were those to conjure with during the heyday of Tin
Pan Alley. These and their descendents reflect in their musical
poetry a distinctive sketch of American life and the American

experience evaluated in the light of middle-class virtues.

Folk and rock music, while properly counted with the European tradition, share a commonality with the music of the African tradition: jazz, blues, gospel and soul. This unitary element is that of improvisation. As opposed to the written notation of "serious" and, to a great extent, popular music, these musics generally depend only upon sketches acting as blueprints for the musical construction; another metaphor might be that of the nautical chart indicating the course of the musical voyage. In the art of jazz, the performer is simultaneously composer and arranger, responsible for his own creative efforts in relation to those of others with whom he is playing. In other musical forms, and to varying degrees, the sketch or chart is likely to be much more complete, yet the execution remains largely dependent upon collective effort. In still other cases, the framework may be that characteristic of a purely oral tradition as in the blues where a chord progression and a *codex* of melodic and rhythmic nuances known by the practitioners operates. As might be inferred, this art of improvisation is no primitive indulgence, but rather a highly sophisticated and demanding skill; a lack of courage or of concern for authenticity soon becomes evidenced as cliché.

The key element in improvisation is spontaneity, that sense of vitality which guides the music and the musician on their way. It is the *élan vitale* of these musics, which in its sometimes imperfect ebullience is little different from the rawness of Ives' exaltation of small-town America or the nervous tension of Copland's struggle with the urban *daimonic*. The pursuit of this vitality, through whatever form, is the essence of the quest for an American music.

There is no one brand or form of music which may lay exclusive claim to the title of an "American" music. Rather, a rich variety of musics present themselves and their historic traditions to us as representative, in varying degrees, of the American experience. Yet, having said this, we must argue for the possibility of certain elements within this large mixture becoming molded into just such an American music. Insisting upon the criteria of "music's truth to experience" and the honesty, integrity, and courage in creation of the composer and performer, all in pursuit of the vital essence, we may cite certain key figures as visionaries and trail-blazers of such an American music. Ives and Copland would be among their number, as would Duke Ellington and Charles Mingus. George Gershwin and Leonard Bernstein bear consideration, and there can be no question as to the place of John Cage and Lukas Foss. All of these, and others, have given us music which is distinct and identifiable as both characteristic of and an achievement in American culture and civilization. This American music is still quite young but promises magnificent riches to the soul, if we will only open our ears.

NOTES

1. Patrick S. Gilmore, *History of the National Peace Jubilee and Great Musical Festival held in the City of Boston, June, 1869 to Commemorate the Restoration of Peace Throughout the Land* (Boston: Lee and Shepard, 1871).

2. Edward N. Waters, "Music and Musicians," in Robert E. Spiller and Eric Larrabee, eds., *American Perspectives* (Cambridge: Harvard Univ. Press, 1961), pp. 59-60.

3. David Bidney, *Theoretical Anthropology* (New York: Schocken, 1967), p. xxx.

4. *American Perspectives*, p. 67.

5. Don DeMichael, "1965: The Year in Review," *Downbeat Yearbook: Music '66* (Chicago: Maher Publications, 1966), p. 11.

6. John Tasker Howard, *Our American Music* (3rd ed.; New York: Thomas Y. Crowell, 1946), p. 3.

7. Note the recording, "Mission Music in California," Curé Hispanico de Mallorca (American Recording Society, ARS-32).

8. Howard, p. 12.

9. David Ewen, *Music Comes to America* (New York: Thomas Y. Crowell, 1942), pp. 47-48.

10. Wilfred Mellers, *Music in a New Found Land* (New York: Knopf, 1967), p. 30.

11. For a discussion and survey of the proportionate emphasis given non-European traditions, see the chapter "American Music and the Musical Establishment" in Henry Pleasants, *Serious Music and All That Jazz* (New York: Simon and Schuster, 1971).

12. I am indebted to Professor Marshall Stearns and his *The Story of Jazz*, especially Chapters 2 and 8, for this insight.

13. Marshall Stearns, *The Story of Jazz* (New York: Mentor, 1958), p. 22.

14. Ibid.

15. Ibid., p. 23.

16. Phyl Garland, *The Sound of Soul* (New York: Pocket Books, 1971), p. 4.

17. Ibid., p. 20.

18. Pleasants, p. 90.

19. Ibid., p. 103.

20. Mellers, p. 39.

21. Ibid., p. 84.

22. Ibid., pp. 101-102.

23. Ibid., p. 40.

24. Ibid., p. 101.

25. Victor Borge, as quoted in the *Boston Globe*, Jan. 3, 1972, p. 27.

DISCOGRAPHY*

Art Ensemble of Chicago.	'Les Stances a Sophie'.	Nessa
Armstrong, Louis.	'Louis Armstrong Story'.	Columbia
Bay Psalm Book (excerpts).	Margaret Dodd Singers.	ARS.
Bernstein, Leonard.	'West Side Story'.	Columbia
Berry Chuck.	'Greatest Hits'.	Chess.
Cage, John	'Concert for Piano and Orch'.	Avakian.
Carter Family.	Any early recordings	Folkways
Chavez, Carlos.	'Six Symphonies'.	
Coasters, The	'The Best of the Coasters'.	Atco
Coleman, Ornette.	'Free Jazz'.	Atlantic
Coltrane, John.	'Blue Train'.	Blue Note.
	'Giant Steps'.	Atlantic.
	'Ascension'.	Impulse.
Curtis, King.	'Live at the Filmore'.	
Copland, Aaron.	'Appalachian Spring'. New York Philharmonic; Bernstein.	Columbia.
Davis, Miles.	'Kind of Blue'.	Columbia.
	'Sketches of Spain'.	Columbia
Dolphy, Eric.	'Out to Lunch'.	Blue Note.
Ellington, Duke.	'Solitude'.	Columbia.
	'70th Birthday Concert'.	Columbia.
Farina, Richard and Mimi.	'Celebrations for a Grey Day'.	Verve.
Foss, Lukas	'Good for Orch.'.	Candide.

---

*Compiled expressly for the author by Peter Bloom. —Ed.

Franklin, Aretha.	'Greatest Hits'.	Harmony.
Guthrie, Woodie.	Any recordings.	RCA-Vintage.
Gershwin, George.	'Porgy and Bess'.	Columbia.
Hawkins, Coleman.	'Bean and the Boys'.	Prestige.
Holiday, Billie.	'Golden Years'.	Columbia.
Henderson, Fletcher.	'Study in Frustration'.	Columbia.
Hanson, Howard.	'Symphony No. 2 (Romantic). Eastman-Rochester Symphony; Hanson.	Columbia.
Ives, Charles.	'Concord Sonata'.	Mainstream.
-----	'Symphony No. 4'.	Columbia.
Jazz at the Philharmonic.	Any recording, any label.	
Jackson, Mahalia.	Any Early recordings.	
Jazz Composers Orchestra.	(Album of the same name).	VCOA.
Jelly Roll Morton.	Vintage Recordings.	RCA.
Johnson, Robert.	'King of the Delta Blues'.	Columbia.
King, B.B.	Any early recording, any label.	
Leadbelly.	Any recordings.	Folkways.
MacDowell, Edward.	'Woodland Sketches'.	Columbia.
Mingus, Charles.	'Better Get It In Your Soul'.	Columbia.
Partch, Harry.	'The World of Harry Partch'.	Columbia.
Parker, Charles (Chan).	'Jazz at Massey Hall'.	
Ra, Sun.	'Heliocentric Worlds'	ESP.
Redman, Dewey.	'Tarik'.	Actuel.
Rollins, Sunny.	'Tenor Madness'.	Prestige.
Ruggles, Charles.	'Sun Treader'. Boston Symphony; Thomas.	D.G.G.
Seegers, The	Any early Folkways recording	Folkways.
Shorter, Wayne.	'Juju'.	Blue Note.
Subotnick, Morton.	'The Wild Bull'.	Nonesuch.

Staples Singers.	Any early disk.	
Strayhorn, Billy.	'And His Mother Called Him Bill'.	Victor LSP
Taylor, Cecil.	'Air'	Barnaby.
Waters, Muddy.	Early disks.	
Young, Lester.	Hear the Billie Holiday disk mentioned above.	
Zappa, Frank.	'Chunga's Revenge'	Bizarre.

BIBLIOGRAPHY

Aids to Research

Bibliographies

Ewen, David. *Tin Pan Alley*. New York: Funk & Wagnalls, 1964. (Biblio. at end)

Hayward, Charles A. *A Bibliography of North American Folklore and Folksong*. New York: Greenberg, 1951. Rev. ed., 2 vols; New York: Dover, 1961.

Henry, M.E. *American Folk Songs: A Bibliography for the Study of*. London: Mitre Press, 1937.

Howard, John Tasker. *Our American Music*. 4th ed. New York: Crowell, 1965. (Extensive bibliography covering all areas at end)

Lawless, Ray M. *Folksingers and Folksongs in America: A Handbook of Biography, Bibliography, and Discography*. New York: Duell, Sloan and Pearce, 1960.

Laws, G. Malcolm. *Native American Balladry: A Descriptive Study and a Bibliographic Syllabus*. Philadelphia: American Folklore Society, 1964. (Biblio. at end)

Lomax, John A., and Alan Lomax. *American Ballads and Folk Songs*. New York: Macmillan, 1934. (Extensive biblio. at end)

Mattfield, Julius. *Folk Music of the Western Hemisphere*. New York: New York Public Library, 1925.

Merriam, Alan P. *A Bibliography of Jazz*. Philadelphia: American Folklore Society, 1954.

Reisner, Robert George. *The Literature of Jazz: A Preliminary Bibliography*. New York: New York Public Library, 1954.

Sonneck, Oscar G. *Bibliography of Early Secular American Music*. Washington, D.C.: Library of Congress, 1945.

Stearns, Marshall W. *The Story of Jazz*. Rev. ed. New York: Oxford
Univ. Press, 1971. (Biblio. at end quite extensive)

Warrington, James. *Short Titles of Books Relating or Illustrating the
History and Practice of Psalmody in the United States*. Philadelphia:
privately printed, 1898.

White, N.I. *American Negro Folk-Songs*. Cambridge: Harvard Univ. Press,
1928. (Biblio. at end)

Biographical Dictionaries and Encyclopaedia

American History and Encyclopaedia of Music. Toledo, O.: Irving Squire,
1908.

*A.S.C.A.P. Biographical Dictionary of Composers, Authors and Pub-
lishers*. New York: A.S.C.A.P., 1966.

*Bio-Bibliographical Index of Musicians in the United States of America
from Colonial Times*. Washington, D.C.: Pan-American Union, Music
Div., 1941.

Feather, Leonard. *The Encyclopaedia of Jazz*. Rev. ed. New York:
Horizon, 1966.

Grove's Dictionary of Music and Musicians. Ed. Eric Blom. 9 Vols. plus
supplements. New York: St. Martin's, 1954.

Handy, W.C. *Negro Authors and Composers of the United States*. New
York: Handy Bros. Music Company, 1938.

Roxon, Lillian. *The Rock Encyclopedia*. New York: Grosset & Dunlap,
1968.

Journals and Magazines

Billboard. New York.

Current Musicology. New York: Columbia Univ. Music Department.

Downbeat. Chicago.

Ethnomuiscology. Middletown, Conn.: Wesleyan Univ. Press.

Journal of the American Musicological Society. Philadelphia.

Music Journal. New York.

Musical Quarterly. New York.

National Music Council Bulletin. New York.

Perspectives of New Music. Princeton, N.J.: Princeton Univ. Press.

Rolling Stone. San Francisco.

Schwann Catalog. Boston.

Sing Out. New York.

General Works
Theory and Criticism

Barzun, Jacques. *Music in American Life.* Garden City, N.Y.: Doubleday, 1956.

Cage, John. *Notations.* New York: Something Else Press, 1969.

-----. *Silence.* Cambridge: M.I.T. Press, 1966.

Keppel, Frederick P. and R.L. Duffus. *The Arts in American Life.* New York: McGraw-Hill, 1933.

Merriam, Alan P. *The Anthropology of Music.* Evanston: Northwestern Univ. Press, 1964.

Partch, Harry. *Genesis of Music.* Madison: Univ. of Wisconsin Press, 1949.

Pleasants, Henry. *Serious Music and All That Jazz.* New York: Simon & Schuster, 1969.

Weber, Max. *The Rational and Social Foundations of Music.* Carbondale: Southern Illinois Univ. Press, 1958.

History

Chase, Gilbert. *America's Music: From the Pilgrims to the Present.* New York: McGraw-Hill, 1955.

Ewen, David. *Music Comes to America.* New York: Crowell, 1942.

Howard, John Tasker. *Our American Music.* 4th ed. New York: Crowell, 1965.

Kaufmann, Helen L. *From Jehovah to Jazz: Music in America from Psalmody to the Present Day.* 1937; rpt. Port Washington, N.Y.: Kennikat Press, 1969.

Mellers, Wilfrid. *Music in a New Found Land.* New York: Knopf, 1965.

Slonimsky, Nicholas. *Music Since 1900.* Rev. ed. New York: W.W. Norton, 1971.

Special Fields
Indian

Burton, Frederic R. *American Primitive Music:* With Special Attention to Songs of the Ojibways. Port Washington, N.Y.: Kennikat Press, 1969.

Densmore, Francis. *The American Indians and Their Music.* New York: Women's Press of the YWCA, 1926.

Fenton, William N. *Songs from the Iroquois Longhouse.* Washington, D.C.: Smithsonian Institute, 1946.

Nettl, Bruno. *North American Indian Musical Styles.* Philadelphia: American Folklore Society, 1954.

Folk

Allen, W.F., C.P. Ware, and L. McK. Garrison. *Slave Songs of the United States.* New York: Peter Smith, 1929.

Brand, Oscar. *The Ballad Mongers: The Rise of the Modern Folk Song.* New York: Funk & Wagnalls, 1962.

Carmer, Carl. *America Sings.* New York: Knopf, 1942.

Charters, Samuel B. *The Poetry of the Blues.* New York: Oak Pub., 1963.

Courlander, Harold. *Negro Folk Music, USA.* New York: Columbia Univ. Press, 1963.

Greenway, John. *American Folk Songs of Protest.* New York: Octagon, 1970.

Guthrie, Woodie. *American Folksong.* New York: Oak Pub., 1961.

Jackson, George P. *White and Negro Spirituals.* New York: J.J. Augustin, 1943.

Johnson, James Weldon, and J. Rosamond. *The Book of American Negro Spirituals.* New York: Viking Press, 1940.

-----. *Religious Folk Songs of the Negro as Sung on the Plantation.* Hampton Institute, Va.: Institute Press, 1909. Rev. and enl. ed.; G. Schirmer, 1926.

Krehbiel, H.E. *Afro-American Folk Songs.* New York: G. Schirmer, 1914.

Locke, Alain. *The Negro and his Music.* New York: Arno Press, 1969.

Lomax, Alan. *Folk Song Style and Culture.* Washington, D.C.: American Assoc. for the Advancement of Science, 1968.

Lomax, John A. *The Adventures of a Ballad Hunter.* New York: Macmillan, 1947.

-----, and Alan Lomax. *American Ballads and Folk Songs.* New York: Macmillan, 1934.

-----. *Cowboy Songs and Other Frontier Ballads.* New York: Macmillan, 1916. Rev. and enl. ed.; New York: Macmillan, 1948.

Newell, W.W. *Games and Songs of American Children.* New York: Harper Bros., 1883.

Shelton, Robert. *The Country Music Story: A Pictorial History of Country and Western Music.* New York: Bobbs-Merrill, 1966.

Wells, Evelyn K. *The Ballad Tree: A Study of British and American Ballads, Their Folklore, Verse, and Music.* New York: Ronald Press, 1950.

White, Newman I. *American Negro Folk-Songs.* 1928; rpt. Hatboro, Pa.: Folklore Associates, 1965.

Work, John W. *American Negro Songs and Spirituals.* New York: Crown, 1940.

-----. *Folk Songs of the American Negro.* Nashville, Tenn.: Fisk Univ. Press, 1915.

Popular

Browne, C.A. *The Story of Our National Ballads.* New York: Crown, 1919.

Dolph, Edward A. *Sound Off! Soldier Songs from the Revolution to World War II.* New York: Farrar & Rinehart, 1942.

Ewen, David. *A Journey to Greatness: The Life and Music of George Gershwin.* New York: Holt, 1956.

-----. *American Popular Songs from the Revolutionary War to the Present.* New York: Random House, 1966.

----. *The New Complete Book of the American Musical Theatre.* New York: Holt, Rinehart & Winston, 1970.

----. *Panorama of American Popular Music.* Englewood Cliffs, N.J.: Prentice-Hall, 1957.

----. *Tin Pan Alley.* New York: Funk & Wagnalls, 1964.

Goldberg, Isaac. *Tin Pan Alley: A Chronicle of the American Popular Music Racket.* New York: John Day, 1930.

Green, Abel, and Joe Lowie. *Show Biz, from Vaude to Video.* New York: Holt, 1951.

Kobbe, Gustav. *Famous American Songs.* New York: Crowell, 1900.

Mates, Julian. *The American Musical Stage before 1800.* New Brunswick, N.J.: Rutgers Univ. Press, 1962.

Paskman, Dailey, and Sigmund Spaeth. *Gentlemen, Be Seated: A Parade of the Old-Time Minstrels.* New York: Doubleday, Doran, 1928.

Shay, Frank. *Drawn from the Wood: Consolations in Words and Music for Pious Friends and Drunken Companions.* New York: Macmillan, 1929.

Spaeth, Sigmund. *The Facts of Life in Popular Song.* New York: Whittlesey House, 1934.

----. *A History of Popular Music in America.* New York: Random House, 1948.

----. *Read 'Em and Weep.* New rev. ed. New York: Arco Pub., 1945.

Vallance, Tom. *The American Musical.* New York: A.S. Barnes, 1970.

Wilder, Alec. *American Popular Song: The Great Innovaters.* New York: Oxford Univ. Press, 1972.

Jazz

Armstrong, Louis. *Satchmo.* New York: Prentice-Hall, 1954.

Dexter, Dave. *The Jazz Story.* New York: Prentice-Hall, 1964.

Ellington, Edward Kennedy. *Music is My Mistress.* Garden City: Doubleday, 1973.

Feather, Leonard. *Inside Be-Bop.* New York: J.J. Robbins, 1949.

Garland, Phyl. *The Sound of Soul*. New York: Henry Regnery, 1969.

Gitler, Ira. *Jazz Masters of the Forties*. New York: MacMillan, 1966.

Handy, W.C. *Father of the Blues: An Autobiography*. New York: Macmillan, 1941.

-----, and Abbe Niles. *A Treasury of the Blues*. New York: Boni, 1949. (Orig., *Blues: An Anthology of Jazz Music from the Early Negro Folk Blues to Modern Music*, 1929)

Hentoff, Nat. *The Jazz Life*. New York: Apollo, 1961.

Hughes, Langston. *The First Book of Jazz*. New York: F. Watts, 1955.

Jones, Leroi. *Black Music*. New York: William Morrow, 1968.

-----. *Blues People*. New York: William Morrow, 1963.

Keepnews, Orrin, and Bill Grauer. *A Pictorial History of Jazz*. New York: Crown, 1955.

Keil, Charles. *Urban Blues*. Chicago: Univ. of Chicago Press, 1966.

Kofsky, Frank. *Black Nationalism and the Revolution in Music*. New York: Pathfinder, 1970.

Lomax, Alan. *Mr. Jelly Roll*. New York: Duell, Sloan & Pearce, 1950.

Mezzrow, Milton, and Bernard Wolfe. *Really the Blues*. New York: Random House, 1946.

Mingus, Charles. *Beneath the Underdog: His World as Composed by Charles Mingus*. New York: Knopf, 1971.

Oliver, Paul. *Blues Fell This Morning. The Meaning of the Blues*. London: Cassell, 1960.

Ramsey, Frederic, and Charles E. Smith. *Jazzmen*. New York: Harcourt, Brace, 1939.

Russell, Ross. *Bird Lives*. New York: Charter House, 1973.

Schuller, Gunther. *Early Jazz*. New York: Oxford Univ. Press, 1968.

Shapiro, Nat, and Nat Hentoff. *Hear Me Talkin' to Ya*. 1955; rpt. New York: Dover, 1966.

Simon, George T. *The Big Bands*. New York: Macmillan, 1967.

Southern, Eileen. *The Music of Black Americans: A History.* New York: W.W. Norton, 1971.

Stearns, Marshall. *The Story of Jazz.* Rev. ed. New York: Oxford Univ. Press, 1971. (This work is the essential book on jazz.)

Ulanov, Barry. *A History of Jazz in America.* New York: Viking, 1952.

Wells, Dickie, and Stanley Dance. *The Night Life.* Boston: Crescendo, 1971.

Williams, Martin. *The Jazz Tradition.* New York: Oxford Univ. Press, 1970.

Wilmer, Valerie. *Jazz People.* New York: Pathfinder Press, 1971.

Rock

Belz, Carl. *The Story of Rock,* 2nd ed. New York: Harper, 1972.

Eisen, Jonathan. *The Age of Rock.* 2 vols. New York: Vintage, 1970.

Gabree, John. *The World of Rock.* New York: Fawcett, 1968.

Meltzer, R. *The Aesthetics of Rock.* New York: Something Else Press, 1970.

Williams, Paul. *Outlaw Blues: A Book of Rock Music.* New York: Dutton, 1969.

"Serious"

Chase, Gilbert. *The American Composer Speaks: An Historical Anthology 1770-1965.* Baton Rouge, La.: Louisiana State Univ. Press, 1966.

Cowell, Henry, ed. *American Composers on American Music: A Symposium.* New York: F. Ungar, 1962.

-----, and Sidney Cowell. *Charles Ives and His Music.* New York: Oxford Univ. Press, 1955.

Damrosch, Walter. *My Musical Life.* New York: Scribner's, 1923.

Grant, Margaret, and Herman S. Hettinger. *America's Symphony Orchestras.* New York: W.W. Norton, 1940.

Hart, Philip. *Orpheus in the New World.* New York: Norton, 1973.

Hipsher, Edward E. *American Opera and Its Composers.* Philadelphia: Theodore Presser, 1927.

Howard, John T. *Our Contemporary Composers: American Music in the Twentieth Century.* New York: Crowell, 1941.

----, and George K. Bellows. *A Short History of Music in America.* New York: Crowell, 1957.

Ives, Charles. *Essays Before a Sonata.* New York: Norton, 1962.

Kinscella, Hazel G. *History Sings: Backgrounds of American Music.* Lincoln, Neb.: Univ. Pub. Co., 1940.

Krehbiel, Henry E. *Chapters of Opera.* New York: Holt, 1909.

Mueller, John H. *The American Symphony Orchestra: A Social History of Musical Taste.* Bloomington, Ind.: Indiana Univ. Press, 1951.

Russell, Charles E. *The American Orchestra and Theodore Thomas.* Garden City: Doubleday, Paget, 1927.

Sablosky, Irving. *American Music.* Chicago: Univ. of Chicago Press, 1969.

Simpson, Eugene. *America's Position on Music.* Boston: Four Seas Co., 1920.

Sonneck, Oscar G. *Early Concert Life in America.* Leipzig: Breitkopf & Haertel, 1907.

----. *Miscellaneous Studies in the History of Music.* New York: Macmillan, 1921.

Stringfield, Lamar. *America and Her Music.* Chapel Hill: Univ. of North Carolina Press, 1931.

Upton, William T. *Art-Song in America.* Boston: O. Ditson, 1930.

Church Music

Barbour, James M. *Church Music of William Billings.* East Lansing: Michigan State Univ. Press, 1960.

Ellinwood, Leonard. *History of American Church Music.* New York: Morehouse-Gorham, 1953.

Foote, Henry W. *Three Centuries of American Hymnody.* Cambridge, Mass.: Harvard Univ. Press, 1940.

Ives, E., and D. Dutton. *American Psalmody.* Hartford, Ct.: Huntington, 1830.

Lowens, Irving. *Music and Musicians in Early America.* New York: Norton, 1964.

Metcalf, Frank J. *American Psalmody: 1721-1820.* New York: C.F. Heartmann, 1917.

Scholes, Percy. *The Puritans and Music in England and New England.* New York: Oxford Univ. Press, 1934.

Miscellaneous Titles of Interest

Berk, Lee Eliot. *Legal Protection for the Creative Musician.* Boston: Berklee Press, 1970.

Career Opportunities in Music. Chicago: American Music Conference, 1966.

Emerson, Luthor O. *The American School Music Reader: A Systematically Graded Course for the Instruction of Music for Public Schools.* Boston: O. Ditson, 1873.

Fisher, William A. *One Hundred and Fifty Years of Music Publishing in the United States.* Boston: O. Ditson, 1933.

Hopkins, Edward J. *Music and Snobs; or, a Few Funny Facts Regarding the Disabilities of Music in America.* New York: R.A. Saalfield, 1888.

Kostelanetz, Richard, ed. *The New American Art.* New York: Collier Books, 1965.

National Bureau for the Advance of Music. *American Music that Americans Should Know.* New York, 1928.

Niles, John Jacob, and Douglas Moore. *Songs My Mother Never Taught Me.* New York: Macaulay Co., 1929.

Shelton, Robert. *The Country Music Story.* New York: Bobbs-Merrill, 1966.

Shemel, Sidney, and M. William Krasilovsky. *This Business of Music.* New York: Billborard Pub. Co., 1964.

Spaeth, Sigmund. *Opportunities in Music Careers*. New York: Vocational Guidance Manuals, 1966.

----, and Robert H. Schauffler. *Music as a Social Force in America*. New York: Caxton Institute, 1927.

Who Uses Music and Why. New York: A.S.C.A.P., 1935.

THE CONTRIBUTORS

RESEARCH ON THE POLITICS
OF AMERICAN CIVILIZATION

Paul J. Piccard

Born in Lausanne, Switzerland, PAUL J. PICCARD did his undergraduate and M.A. work at the University of Minnesota. He earned the Ph.D. in political science at the University of Texas. He is a professor of government at Florida State University where he has been since 1953. Professor Piccard's primary teaching areas are American national government, local government, and the relationship between government and science. He is editor of *Science and Policy Issues: Lectures in Government and Science* (1969) and he was book review editor for *The Journal of Politics,* 1968-1971.

AMERICAN HISTORY

Eric Brunger

Born in Kent, England, ERIC BRUNGER received his master's degree and Ph.D. in history from Syracuse University. He has taught at Harpur College, Cornell University, and State University College at Buffalo, where he is currently professor of history, and also serves as Director of the Program in American Studies. Professor Brunger has been secretary-treasurer, vice-president, and president of the American Studies Association of New York State; and he is the co-author of *Outposts of Empire* (1961) and *Historical Land Valuation of the Big Tree Cession* (1970). He has for some time served as a consultant, author, and reviewer for publications of the Buffalo Historical Society.

PHILOSOPHY IN AMERICA

Paul Collins Hayner

Chairman of the philosophy department at California State University, Fullerton, California, until his death PAUL COLLINS HAYNER had previously taught at Hamilton College and at Washington and Lee University. He earned his A.B. degree from Union College, the B.D. *magna cum laude* from Union Theological Seminary, and the Ph.D. at Columbia University. A member of Phi Beta Kappa, he served as president of the Virginia Philosophical Association, a member of the Executive Council of the Southern Society for Philosophy of Religion, and the chairman of the Committee on Information Services of the American Philosophical Association. He was the author of numerous articles on philosophy and religion, including the entry on Friedrich Schelling in the 1963 edition of the *Encyclopedia Americana*. His book, *Reason and Existence: Schelling's Philosophy of History*, was published in 1967.

AMERICAN LITERATURE

Rita K. Gollin

RITA K. GOLLIN received the M.A. and Ph.D. degrees from the University of Minnesota, where she wrote her dissertation on "Dream and Reverie in the Writing of Nathaniel Hawthorne." She did her undergraduate work at Queens College, graduating *magna cum laude* with honors in English. She has held a Grace Ellis Ford Fellowship of the A.A.U.W. and a State University of New York Research Foundation Fellowship. Before coming to Geneseo in 1967, Professor Gollin taught at the University of Minnesota and the University of Rochester. She is especially interested in the American novel, and in addition to numerous articles her publications include editions of two novels — Sarah Josepha Hale's *Northwood* and Charles Dudley Warner's *A Little*

Journey in the World. At Geneseo she has served as chairman of the program in American civilization.

AMERICAN FOLKLORE

Mary Washington Clarke

MARY WASHINGTON CLARKE, who earned her Ph.D. at the University of Pennsylvania, has taught American literature, language, and folklore at Marshall University, Chico State College, Indiana State University of Pennsylvania, and currently teaches at Western Kentucky University. She has also held special teaching assignments at the University of Nevada and Indiana University. She was the first person to receive the "Distinguished Service Award for Scholarly Research and Investigation" at Western Kentucky and took second place in the 1969 Chicago Folklore Prize competition. Her range of activities includes chairmanship of the Folklore Section of the South Atlantic Modern Language Association, subject-matter coordinator for grants from the National Endowment for the Humanities for programs on "Kentucky Heritage," and consultant in folklore and language for institutes and special programs in California, Kentucky, and Tennessee. Professor Clarke is co-author of three textbooks in folklore — *Introducing Folklore* (1963), *A Folklore Reader* (1965), and *A Concise Folklore Dictionary* (1971). Her *Jesse Stuart's Kentucky* was published by McGraw-Hill in 1968.

ABORIGINAL CULTURES AND AMERICAN ANTHROPOLOGY

Bruce Raemsch

Professor of anthropology at Hartwick College, BRUCE RAEMSCH earned an A.B. degree from Syracuse University, an M.A. from the University of Oregon, and his Ph.D. from the

University of Pennsylvania. He is assistant curator of the Yager Museum and editor of the *Yager Museum Publications in Anthropology*. He has published principally on New World archeology but he has contributed also to journals in the area of ethnohistory of the Plains Indians. His prime interest is with the antiquity of Early Man in the New World, and he has conducted research at the Adequentaga site near Oneonta, New York; in Wyoming, and in Maine. His investigations into Early Man have resulted in demonstrations of man's occupation of the Northeast of North America as many as 70,000 years ago. Professor Raemsch is a member of the American Anthropological Association and is an Associate in *Current Anthropology*, an international organization for anthropological research sponsored by the Wenner-Gren Foundation.

THE STUDY OF AMERICAN ART

James K. Kettlewell

A member of the art faculty at Skidmore College, JAMES K. KETTLEWELL received his A.B. degree *magna cum laude* from Harvard University, where he also took his A.M. in American architecture and became a Teaching Fellow. His first curatorial position was at the Museum of Art of Ogonquit, Maine, where he gained experience at arranging exhibits of the works of such American artists as Homer and Wyeth. As a Fulbright scholar at the Courtauld Institute of the University of London, Mr. Kettlewell did research work on the relationship of 19th century English and American architecture, and, thereafter, taught courses in Italian, American, and modern art at the University of Toronto. At Skidmore College since 1958, he has arranged many important exhibits of 19th century American paintings for the College and serves also as an assistant curator of the Hyde Collection in Glens Falls, which has been described as one of the great small museums in America. He serves, in addition, as a consultant to the New

York State Council on the Arts and has worked with the Hudson Valley Commission in classifying architecture along the Hudson River.

AMERICAN MUSIC

Mark Sumner Harvey

MARK SUMNER HARVEY has studied jazz composition with George Russell and Jaki Byard at the New England Conservatory, has been a music education consultant for Headstart, and is a member of the music advisory panel of the Massachusetts Council on the Arts and Humanities. In addition, he has worked for three summers with Summerthing, Boston's neighborhood arts festival, as assistant music director of that program and as musical director and arranger for its resident street theatre company. Mr. Harvey holds an A.B. in American Studies from Syracuse University and a Th.M. from Boston University School of Theology. Additional studies include the Institute in Arts, Harvard University and the Berkshire Music Center at Tanglewood. An ordained deacon in the United Methodist Church, Mr. Harvey conducts a ministry with the arts community of Greater Boston. He is also the leader of his own contemporary music ensemble which makes frequent appearances along the Eastern seaboard, as well as in the Boston area.

INDEX

Aarne, Antti, 151-152
Abrahams, Roger, 157
Abstract Expressionism: and U.S. leadership in world art, 217
Adams, Henry, 56, 59-60, 119, 120
Adams, John, 249
Addison Gallery of Art (Andover, Mass.), 224
Agassiz, Jean Louis: attacks evolution 84
Åhnebrink, Lars, 121
Albee, Edward, 124
Alcott, Bronson, 115
American art. *See* Art (American)
American architecture. *See* Art (American)
American folklore. *See* Folk dance; Folklore; Folk music; Folksong; Folktale
American Folklore Society, 153, 162
American government. *See* Democracy; Political science
American Historical Association, 59
American history. *See* History (American)
American literature: and political science, 20; interdisciplinary applications of, 37-38; exploitation as villain in, 106-107; individual's search for fulfillment in, 106-107; its celebration of the frontier, 107-108; myth fashioned from wild Nature, 108; symbolism an attribute of, 108-109; and Transcendentalism, 108-109, 115; and Puritans, 108, 109, 112; and magazines, 109; literary history of, 110; graduate theses in, 110; and phenomenology and structuralism, 110; and the women's movement, 110, 127; recent textual scholarship in, 111; in